Cajun Country

Lynwood Montell, General Editor

FOLKLIFE IN THE SOUTH SERIES

CAJUN COUNTRY

Barry Jean Ancelet, Jay D. Edwards, and Glen Pitre

WITH ADDITIONAL MATERIAL BY

Carl Brasseaux, Fred B. Kniffen, Maida Bergeron, Janet Shoemaker, Mathe Allain

University Press of Mississippi Jackson and London

Copyright © 1991 by University Press of Mississippi

All rights reserved

Manufactured in the United States of America

Print-on-Demand Edition

THIRD PRINTING 1998

The paper in this book meets the guidelines for
permanence and durability of the Committee on
Production Guidelines for Book Longevity of the
Council on Library Resources.

Library of Congress Cataloging-in-Publication Data

Ancelet, Barry Jean.
   Cajun country / Barry Jean Ancelet, Jay D. Edwards,
  and Glen Pitre ; with additional material by Carl
  Brasseaux ... [et al.].
     p.   cm. — (Folklife in the South series)
  Includes bibliographical references and index.
  ISBN 0-87805-466-9 (cloth). — ISBN 0-87805-467-7
  (paper)
   1. Cajuns—Social life and customs. 2. Louisiana—
Social life and customs. I. Edwards, Jay Dearborn.
II. Pitre, Glen, 1955- . III. Title. IV. Series.
F380.A2A53 1991
976.3′00410763—dc20   90-28931
                                 CIP

British Library Cataloging-in-Publication data available

Contents

List of Illustrations

Folklife, a familiar concept in European scholarship for over a century, is the sum of a community's traditional forms of expression and behavior. It has claimed the attention of American folklorists since the 1950s. Each volume in the Folklife in the South Series focuses on the shared traditions that link people with their past and provide meaning and continuity for them in the present, and sets these traditions in the social contexts in which they flourish. Prepared by recognized scholars in various academic disciplines, these volumes are designed to be read separately. Each contains a vivid description of the traditional cultural elements—ethnic and mainstream, rural and urban—of a geographic area that, in concert with other recognizable southern regions, lend a unique interpretation to the complex social structure of the South.

Cajun Country, the first in the Folklife in the South Series, is by far the broadest survey of traditional Cajun culture ever assembled. While other books have treated specific aspects of Louisiana Cajun life, this one examines a variety of the cultural elements alive today, including cooking, music, storytelling, architecture, arts and crafts, and traditional occupations such as fishing, hunting, and trapping. It not only describes the traditions as they are but also explains how they came to be.

William Lynwood Montell
SERIES EDITOR

A c k n o w l e d g m e n t s

The research upon which this book is based was financially supported by the National Park Service's Jean Lafitte National Historic Park of Louisiana. In addition to preserving natural resources such as alluvial swamps and coastal marshes, Jean Lafitte Park is intended to address people and their cultural resources in its designated Mississippi Delta region. We wish particularly to thank the former director, James L. Isenogle, who oversaw the project for Jean Lafitte Park, and who encouraged the scholarly and artistic research required for its successful completion. His successor, Ann Belkov, graciously granted permission for publication of this material.

We also wish to acknowledge the organizational expertise and fatherly influence of Sam W. Hamilton, AIA, of the architectural firm of Hamilton & Associates, who gathered together the team of specialists who conducted the background research. The team members and their areas of specialization were: Barry Jean Ancelet, folklore; Dewey Balfa, Cajun music and programming; David Barry, linguistics; Carl Brasseaux, history; Jay Edwards, cultural anthropology; Ruth Fontenot, foodways and festivals; Fred Kniffen, cultural geography; Randall Labry, film; Elemore Morgan, Jr., visual arts; Glen Pitre, wetlands folklife; Robert Smith, furniture and furnishings; and Jane Vidrine, cultural programming. The project was directed by Barry Jean Ancelet, coordinated by Sam Hamilton, and managed by Jennifer Charnews; the report was edited by Claude Oubre, and Sam Hamilton served as general editor. In the best spirit of such cooperative ventures, the experience of each participant was much wider than his or her slot, so that there was constant overlap and what Elemore Morgan called "cross-lateral re-communication," which encouraged all to view their areas from new perspectives.

This book is based upon the five-volume project report, *The Cajuns, Their History and Culture*, published in 1987. The authorship of the chapters in this book is as follows: Introduction, Barry Jean Ancelet; chapter 1, "Origins," Carl Brasseaux and Jay Edwards; chapter 2, "Settlement and Society," Jay Edwards, Fred Kniffen, and Glen Pitre; chapter 3, "Acadian Folklife," Barry Jean Ancelet, Carl Brasseaux, and Jay Edwards; chapter 4, "Family Organization," Jay Edwards; chapter 5, "Religious Rituals and Festivals," Barry Jean Ancelet; chapter 6, "Folk Medicine," Jay Edwards and Maida Bergeron; chapter 7, "Folk Law and Justice," Jay Edwards, Janet Shoemaker, and Barry Jean Ancelet; chapter 8, "Folk Architecture," Jay Edwards; chapter 9, "Foodways," Barry Jean Ancelet; chapter 10, "Music and Musical Instruments," Barry Jean Ancelet and Mathé Allain; chapter 11, "Games and Gaming," Barry Jean Ancelet; chapter 12, "Oral Traditions," Barry Jean Ancelet; Conclusion, Jay Edwards; Bibliographical Essay, Glen Pitre.

Finally, we wish to thank the many people of French Louisiana who invited us into their homes for interviews and who provided their time and information so generously. Without their enthusiastic support, no such study of Cajun folk culture would have been possible.

The People

The French founded Louisiana in 1682 when Robert Cavelier de La Salle stood on the banks of the Mississippi near the Gulf of Mexico and claimed all the land drained by that great river in the name of King Louis XIV. La Salle probably intended to claim a large territory, but it is doubtful if he understood that he was in fact claiming roughly half of what is now the United States. French settlers first began to arrive in Louisiana in the early eighteenth century, but France's efforts to colonize Louisiana were at best half-hearted. Colonial speculator John Law's financial bubble burst early in the game, making the recruitment of prospective settlers difficult. But even without that, Louisiana could hardly be considered the ideal place for French men and women to relocate. It was hot and humid, with none of the conveniences of continental life, and crawling with reptiles and insects. An early traveler, Père du Poisson, observed that mosquitoes had caused more cussing in the French language since the founding of Louisiana than in the entire history of France up to that time. Nevertheless, a few French settlers succeeded in establishing themselves along the waterways of the colony. They learned about the flora and fauna of the area from local Native American tribes, and managed to adapt to life in this subtropical region. They eventually imported slaves from Africa to work the large farms or plantations they developed here.

The descendants of the first French settlers in Louisiana, those born in the colony, were called Creoles to distinguish them from French immigrants. Originally, *Creole* meant simply "local, home-grown, not imported," and referred to people and things as well as to ways of doing things. Slaves born in Louisiana were called Creoles to distinguish them from the blacks whom slave traders continued to capture in Africa and bring to the colony. In time, the word acquired a more positive connotation. Creole slaves were more valuable because they were already acclimatized and acculturated, so they were less likely to die from new diseases, more likely to speak the language of their masters, and less likely to try to escape since they had been born into the system of slavery. Creole tomatoes were more likely to be fresh and vine-ripened. Creole horses were hardier and already adapted to the heat and humidity. Creole houses were raised above the damp ground and adapted to keep the heat outside instead of inside. The Creole French language reflected the physical and ethnic realities of the Louisiana context.

Essential to this "creolization" process were improvisation and adaptation. Migration, whether voluntary or not, caused a break in ancestral patterns. The New World provided the opportunity to experiment. While individual cultures did preserve some of their old ways in the New World, the frontier environment also provided the opportunity for them to create new ways based on the old. This opportunity was at the heart of the creolization process in Louisiana.

In the mid-eighteenth century, France transferred administrative control of Louisiana to Spain. Spain wanted Louisiana primarily as a buffer zone between its gold and silver mines in the Southwest and Mexico and the Anglo-American settlements on the Atlantic coast. But for the colony to function as a buffer, it had to be populated. Spain sent in some settlers, but the established French Creole population continued to dominate everyday life. In addition, during the Spanish tenure, German-speaking settlers arrived from Alsace and Germany, and English-speaking settlers came from England, Ireland, Scotland, and the new United States. But by far the largest group that came to Louisiana were the Acadians, who arrived in several waves between 1765 and 1785. They had been expelled in 1755 from their homeland, now called Nova Scotia, by the British authorities.

These Acadian exiles were the descendants of the first northern European settlers in the New World. Most of the people who eventually became the Acadians had left, in 1632, an area within a radius of about twenty miles from the town of Loudun near the border between the provinces of Poitou and Vendée in France. In the New World, they settled the colony that Samuel Champlain had founded for France in 1604. It was named La Cadie, after the Micmac word for "land of plenty." Later, perhaps because of the linguistic overlap with Arcadia, the Greek land of milk and honey, the colony came to be called *l'Acadie,* or Acadia. The people who lived there began calling themselves Cadiens or Acadiens. They were among the first European colonists to develop a sense of identity apart from that of the old country. This distinct Acadian identity resulted from several factors: the sense of community the people brought with them from France, the frontier experience, and the unique blending of those first French settlers, Native American tribes such as the Micmac and Souriquois, and a small number of Catholic Irish and Scottish families.

When the Acadians were exiled in 1755, they brought with them a tenacious sense of ethnicity created in Acadia. They struggled to survive as a group. The work of historian Carl Brasseaux has shown clearly that those who eventually resettled in southern Louisiana between 1765 and 1785 fully intended to reestablish their broken society there. Even those who had been repatriated to France volunteered to the king of Spain to help settle his newly acquired colony. In Louisiana, the Acadians encountered the French Creoles who had been in the colony since the Lemoine brothers, Iberville and Bienville, had planted the first permanent settlement there in 1699 and who had also developed a sense of their own identity. The two groups remained distinct for the most part. The French Creoles considered the Acadians to be peasants, while many Acadians considered the Creoles aristocratic snobs. Some Acadians aspired to the affluent French Creole plantation society and climbed up the social ladder toward the gentry. There were even two Acadian governors. Most, however, were content to work their own land to provide for their own families.

In Louisiana, the Acadians interacted and intermarried with their neighbors. They encountered a new set of Native Americans, including the Houmas, the Chitimachas, and the remnants of the Attakapas. They also encountered German/Alsatians, Spanish, Anglo-Americans, Irish, and Scots. This blending process continued and eventually produced the group called Cajuns (as close as Anglo-Americans could come to pronouncing *Cadiens*). This is why one finds people who call themselves Cajuns yet who have last names like Hoffpauir and Schexnayder, Ortego and Romero, Johnson and Reed, and McGee and Melançon. Cajun last names include even French Creole names such as de la Houssaye and du Boisblanc, Fontenot and Vidrine, along with those of Acadian stock, such as Arceneaux and Ardoin, Broussard and Babineaux, Comeaux and Chiasson. Black Creoles also contributed to the Cajun blend in areas such as music, dancing, and cooking, although they remained distinct from the Cajuns, the French Creoles, and even the English-speaking blacks from other parts of the plantation South.

In 1803, Louisiana was sold to the United States by Napoleon, who had reacquired the colony from Spain just in time for the deal. The Louisiana Purchase was soon cut up into several smaller territories, and in 1812 the southernmost piece became the present-day state of Louisiana whose boundaries ignored historical settlement patterns to include the English-speaking northern and eastern parishes (counties) along with the remnants of the original French settlements in the south. At first the various French-speaking populations maintained the hope of remaining distinct, but the end of the Civil War finally made clear that Louisiana was going to become American to be a part of this nation. Upwardly mobile Cajuns, who participated in the social, economic, political, and educational systems, understood this, as did the French Creoles. But the small plot-farming Cajuns, who were marginal to these systems and who had little or no stake in the war, did not take part in the changes until later. An indication of this is the rate of desertion among Cajuns drafted into the Confederate Army—in some units as high as 85 to 100 percent. They simply walked home from the nearby battlefields to resume taking care of their farms and families.

The majority of the Cajuns did not begin to Americanize until the turn of this century, when several factors combined to force the pace. These factors were the nationalistic fervor of the early 1900s followed by World War I; the discovery of oil in 1901 in Jennings, Louisiana, which brought in outsiders and created salaried jobs; the mandatory Education Act of 1916, which made English the only language allowed at school; the improvement of transportation; the development of radio; and the leveling effects of the Great Depression. During the 1930s and 1940s, the Cajuns were educated and acculturated into the American mainstream. Yet, somehow the Cajun culture survived this period of homogenization to emerge from World War II with enough identity to renew itself beginning in the 1950s and 1960s. Traditional Cajun music made a comeback, and politicians and educators became interested in preserving and reviving the language. Institutional support eventually came in the form of educational programs at all levels, media and publicity campaigns, and a state agency called the Council for the

Fight to preserve the French language (Photo by Barry Ancelet)

Development of French in Louisiana. Cajun culture regained its footing, and nowadays it has become not only acceptable, but even fashionable, as Cajuns have learned to negotiate a place for themselves in the contemporary world on their own terms.

To understand today's Cajuns, one must take a long, hard look at their culture and history. Friendly, yet suspicious of strangers; easygoing, yet stubborn; deeply religious, yet anticlerical; proud, yet quick to laugh at their own foibles; unfailingly loyal, yet possessed of a frontier independence—Cajuns are immediately recognizable as a people, yet defy facile definition. As the saying goes, "You can tell a Cajun a mile away, but you can't tell him a damn thing up close."

Non-Cajun visitors to south Louisiana often must reassess their expectations in the light of certain realities. French Canadians, for instance, who expect to find in Cajuns a symbol of dogged linguistic survival in a predominantly Anglo-Saxon North America find virtually no open Anglophone–Francophone confrontation and a confounding absence of animosity in cultural politics. The French who seek quaint vestiges of former colonials find instead French-speaking cowboys (and Indians) in pickup trucks. They are surprised at the Cajuns' love of fried chicken and iced tea, forgetting this is also the American South; at their love of hamburgers and Coke, forgetting this is the United States; at their love of cayenne and cold beer, forgetting this is the northern tip of the West Indies. American visitors usually skim along the surface, too, looking in vain for romantic traces of Longfellow's *Evangeline* and a lost paradise where the noble natives are not yet adrift on a sea of plastic.

The most consistent element in Cajun country may well be an uncanny ability to swim in the mainstream. The Cajuns seem to have an innate understanding that culture is an ongoing process, and appear willing constantly to reinvent and renegotiate their cultural affairs on their own terms. This adaptability has become indeed the principal issue of cultural survival in French Louisiana. Earlier, change was slow, organic, and progressive. Now, it comes at a dizzying pace. The fight to save the French language looms large because many fear that if it is lost, the whole culture will go with it. Can Cajun culture be translated into English without loss of cultural identity? To be sure, Cajuns will eat gumbo and crawfish forever, but is "Jolie Blonde" sung in English still Cajun music? These and other questions will of necessity have to be addressed in the Cajuns' quest for cultural viability.

In the midst of this debate are signs of renewed vigor. Young Cajun parents are deliberately speaking French to their children. Cajun music, once dismissed as "nothing but chanky-chank," has now infiltrated radio, television, and the classroom. With festivals and recording companies watering the roots at the local and national levels, young musicians are not only preserving the music of their tradition but improvising to create new songs for that tradition.

Yet, while the French language struggles to maintain its role in the cultural survival of south Louisiana, there are other changes that reflect the successful incorporation of modern influences. Contemporary musicians would be less than honest if they pretended that they never listened to the radio or watched music videos. Thus, the sounds of rock, country, and jazz are incorporated today as were the blues and the French *contredanses* of old. Sportsmen have found that the waters around offshore oil rigs provide excellent fishing, and cooks have discovered how to make *roux* in microwave ovens. Cajuns are constantly adapting their culture to survive in the modern world. Such change, however, is not necessarily a sign of decay, as was first thought; it may even be a sign of vitality. People have been predicting the demise of Cajun culture for decades. Yet every time someone tries to pronounce a funeral oration, the corpse sits up in the coffin.

Past Studies

The French-speaking cultures of south Louisiana have occupied a prominent place in the study of American folklore. Before sociology had become an academic discipline, a few literary figures provided much information about Louisiana French culture. LePage du Pratz's *Histoire de la Louisiane* (1758) is a vivid description of life in colonial Louisiana. C. C. Robin recorded a wide variety of cultural information in his travelogue, *Voyages à l'intérieure de la Louisiane* (1807). An anonymous manuscript (attributed to Louisiana Justice Joseph A. Breaux) is filled with information on Cajun folklife as early as 1840. Nineteenth-century author George Washington Cable based many of his stories on observations he recorded among the Cajuns and Creoles. Journalist Lafcadio Hearn collected Creole proverbs in his *Gumbo Zhèbes* (1885) and foodways in his *La Cuisine Créole* (1885). Alfred Mercier's *L'Habitation St. Ybars* (1881) includes a vast amount of information on nineteenth-century plantation folklife.

Tulane professor Alcée Fortier was Louisiana's first folklore scholar and one of the founders of the American Folklore Society (AFS). His landmark collection of black Creole animal stories, *Louisiana French Folk-Tales*, was the second publication in the Memoirs of the American Folklore Society series (1895). In the 1890s, Fortier also organized the New Orleans branch of the AFS, which later became the Louisiana Folklore Society.

In the early twentieth century, much collecting was done by graduate students. Corinne Saucier based her M.A. thesis (George Peabody College, 1923) on her collection of Avoyelles Parish folktales. She expanded this preliminary work in her doctoral dissertation, "Histoire et traditions de la paroisse des Avoyelles en Louisiane" (Université Laval, 1949), under the direction of the French Canadian folklorist Luc Lacourcière. Calvin Claudel also worked in his native Avoyelles Parish. He completed his doctoral dissertation on Louisiana French folktales at the University of North Carolina in 1947. Like Saucier, Elizabeth Brandon studied under Lacourcière at Laval. Her study of Vermilion Parish folklore and folklife (1955) included songs and tales as well as social history and folkways. In addition to these major names, a host of M.A. and Ph.D. students (especially at Louisiana State University under professors Broussard, Major, and Guilbeau) collected folklore, especially tales and songs, for their studies of Louisiana French dialects during the 1940s and 1950s. These studies provided a veritable mine of information and transcribed texts. The same is true of the Louisiana Writers Project, material collected during the Depression years under the direction of Lyle Saxon.

While the Louisiana French language was studied for its linguistic interest, it had acquired a social stigma with the Americanization of the Cajuns that began at the turn of this century. Virtually none of this cultural research was recycled in the French classroom. The few who tried, such as Marie Del Norte Theriot, were isolated and even discouraged. A few English professors, such as George Reinecke at the University of New Orleans and Patricia Rickels at the University of Southwestern Louisiana, eventually began including Louisiana French material in their English Department folklore classes.

Outside folk music researchers working in Louisiana tended to have a much more activist approach than folktale scholars and linguistics students. When record companies, such as Columbia, Okeh, Decca, and RCA began recording Cajun music in 1928, they captured the tail end of a formative period in the development of Cajun and Creole music styles. The recordings John and Alan Lomax made in south Louisiana between 1934 and 1937 while documenting the folk music of America for the Library of Congress go even further back. The Lomaxes avoided popular styles already well-documented by the record companies in favor of unaccompanied singing and solo instrumental traditions, often performed by people who were old then and whose memories reached back well into the nineteenth century and earlier. The Lomaxes included Louisiana French material in *Our Singing Country* (1941).

Folk music researchers continued to visit French Louisiana. In the late 1930s, Herbert Halpert recorded Creole songs in New Orleans. In the 1940s, William Owens recorded ballads in the Cajun prairies. In the 1950s, I. Bonstein and Harry Oster recorded some of the newly revived Cajun dance music as well as older styles. From his position as a member of the Newport Folk Festival board, Alan Lomax sent Ralph Rinzler to south Louisiana to search for performers in the 1960s. Rinzler brought a well-received Cajun trio to the Newport Festival in 1964. One of the trio, Dewey Balfa, returned to Louisiana determined to bring home the echo of the standing ovation they had received from the crowds. He worked tirelessly to rehabilitate the tarnished Cajun self-image on the home front. Balfa's eloquent advocacy on behalf of traditional culture earned him a reputation beyond his native state.

Rinzler continued to work with Balfa and members of the Louisiana Folk Foundation to regenerate interest in Cajun and Creole music at the grass-roots level. Rinzler and Balfa worked with the Council for the Development of French in Louisiana, established in 1968, to create the Tribute to Cajun Music festival, first presented in 1974 and now an annual event. That same year, Rinzler and Roger Abrahams, then president of the American Folklore Society, met with University of Southwestern Louisiana president Ray Authement to lay the foundation for the Center for Acadian and Creole Folklore. Since then, this center has provided a focal point for Louisiana French folklore research. Copies of important past field work have been added to more recent research, much of it conducted by center staff and students, to create the largest such collection in existence. The center also organizes festivals, special performances, and television and radio programs, and offers classes and workshops through the University of Southwestern Louisiana's French and Francophone Studies Program. In 1987, Dewey Balfa and Creole fiddler Canray Fontenot were appointed adjunct professors at the University, providing them an institutional base from which to disseminate their rich store of knowledge.

Other state and national programs have also contributed to these efforts. Louisiana State University's School of Cultural Geography, under the direction of Fred Kniffen, has produced a corps of specialists, such as Malcolm Comeaux and Jay Edwards, who have helped to define French Louisiana, primarily through its material culture. Nicholls State University recently established a center for the study of Louisiana boat building. In 1978, with support from the National Endowment for the Arts, Louisiana's Office of Cultural Development established the position of folk arts coordinator, first held by Nicholas Spitzer, who had come to Louisiana to study the Cajuns and black Creoles, and now held by Maida Bergeron, who has conducted her own valuable research on Cajun folk culture and crafts.

Some of the most exciting opportunities for research in Cajun folklife have recently been provided by the National Park Service through its newly created Jean Lafitte National Historical Park,

Rolls Royce and horse-drawn vegetable wagon, Lafayette, 1981 (Photo by Philip Gould)

dedicated to preserving cultural as well as natural resources. This book is based on research commissioned by the Jean Lafitte Park for the development of three Acadian culture centers (to be located in Lafayette, Eunice, and Thibodaux).

The information and recommendations collected in the report of that research, "The Cajuns: Their History and Culture" (1987), are being incorporated into the development of the park's Acadian interpretive centers. This book represents a desire to make that information available to a wider audience. It is built upon the collective knowledge and contributions of the entire research team, covering a wide range of Cajun folklife, from oral traditions and music to foodways and games, viewed from historical and contemporary perspectives. It traces the origins and development of, and changes in, the traditional culture of south Louisiana, distinguishing subregional varieties that have resulted from geographic and demographic differences within the area. These include wetlands Cajuns, prairie Cajuns, and urban Cajuns.

It is important to remember that all Cajuns, especially young people, have a modern, mainstream side in addition to their unique cultural heritage. They are in many ways just like their Anglo-American neighbors. They enjoy organized sports and video games. Some work in banks and investment firms, others in the offshore oil industry or as computer programmers. There is great diversity within the culture. Cajun cane polers in pirogues frequently find themselves fishing alongside Cajuns in fancy fiberglass boats. Yet there is undeniably a distinctive character to the people who call themselves Cajun. This volume attempts to portray their character by presenting the traditional culture of Cajun country and examining the effects of tradition on modern ways, the ways Cajuns today work and worship, play and plant, construct and converse.

Our study begins with a historical presentation. We describe the founding and development of Acadia (now called Nova Scotia) primarily by farmers who left France in the early seventeenth century to settle in the New World. We also trace the settlement patterns and social development of French Louisiana, beginning with the original French settlers who came in 1699 and their Creole descendants. The opening chapters then describe the other groups—Spaniards, Germans, Anglo-Americans, Native Americans, and Africans—that contributed to the blend that eventually transformed the Acadian exiles, who came to Louisiana in the mid-eighteenth century, into today's Cajuns. An overview of traditional Acadian folklife provides a background for the discussions of more specific and contemporary issues that follow. The areas of culture that help to organize everyday life are treated in chapters on family, religion, folk medicine, and folk law. These are followed by chapters on the expression of folklife in material culture, including folk architecture and foodways. Finally, chapters on music, games, and oral traditions cover the more public forms of cultural performance. The conclusion synthesizes the specific discussions in the preceding chapters, and a bibliographical essay lists the main works underlying this study* and points the way to further reading on Cajun culture and Cajun country.

---

*The key works cited in the body of this book are listed in the bibliography following the bibliographical essay.

PART ONE

History

1

Origins

For decades, it was generally believed that most of the Acadian colonists were originally Normans, a misconception created by Henry Wadsworth Longfellow's 1847 epic *Evangeline* and perpetuated by historical literature. This misconception lives on today in Louisiana through the so-called authentic "Evangeline" costume, a seventeenth-century Norman outfit consisting of light blue skirt, white apron and blouse, and black corset.

The popular image of the early Gallic settlers of Nova Scotia (Acadia) has little basis in historical fact. Only one Norman family settled in seventeenth-century Acadia. The predispersal Acadian pioneers, particularly the women who were said to have "a passion for scarlet cloth," generally wore brightly colored costumes often consisting of striped cloth. Yet our stereotype was not entirely without foundation, for the French colonists who settled Acadia were in fact a remarkably homogeneous group—the result of the circumstances under which the Canadian colony was settled.

Acadians in France

Between 1632 and 1654, when most Acadia-bound French colonists crossed the Atlantic, Acadia was a proprietary colony operated by the Company of New France. The company maintained a recruiting office in La Chaussée, Poitou, France. Some 55 percent (and possibly as much as 70 percent) of Acadia's seventeenth-century immigrants were natives of the Centre-Ouest provinces of Poitou, Aunis, Angoumois, and Saintonge or the adjacent province of Anjou, while 47 percent were drawn from the La Chaussée area alone (Map 1).

As peasant immigrants, the Acadians sought to escape the violence that had disrupted their lives in France and destroyed what

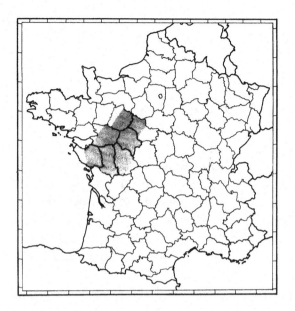

Map 1. France: Principal Zones of Acadian origins

generations of their families had sought to build. Because Poitou and the Centre-Ouest were bastions of Protestantism, these provinces were the scene of some of the most intense fighting during France's religious wars of the late sixteenth and early seventeenth centuries. Fighting between Catholics and Protestants erupted at Poitiers in 1559, and within two years the entire region was consumed by the increasingly bitter civil warfare. Much of the fighting in the 1560s centered in Haut-Poitou, from which most of the Acadian settlers were drawn.

The Protestant occupation of these communities was challenged by Catholic forces, and the resulting confrontations, which continued until the Edict of Nantes (1598), ravaged the entire region. Many of the worst atrocities of the religious wars were committed in Poitou. The population had to be constantly on guard against attacks by marauding bands of religious fanatics, foraging mercenaries, and brigands capitalizing upon the breakdown in local law enforcement machinery. Excesses against the peasantry—which finally precipitated a series of peasant revolts in the Centre-Ouest during the mid-1590s—persisted well into the seventeenth century.

Protestant-Catholic disputes began again at Poitiers in 1614 and persisted until 1616, when an accord was signed at Loudun by the French regent. The realm's Huguenot leaders guaranteed the seignorial rights of France's Protestant princes. As early as 1620, peace was disrupted once again in Poitou and the Centre-Ouest by the opening

Some misconceptions about the origin of the Acadian colonists still exist. (Photo by Barry Ancelet)

shots of the French Counter-Reformation. Poitou once again became a staging and foraging area for the rival forces. The fighting, which ended with the fall of La Rochelle in 1628, brought much misery in its wake.

Years of unseasonable weather brought famine and a series of epidemics. The plague of 1631, the worst epidemic in modern French history, decimated the peasant and urban populations between Poitiers and the ocean.

The years of trauma stemming from decades of civil warfare, heightened by the famines and epidemics of the early 1630s, produced intense emotional stress in Haut-Poitou, which eventually was vented in the highly publicized Loudun witch hunt of 1634. This pervasive sense of despair apparently motivated many Loudunais peasants to begin life anew in North America in 1632. For these pioneers, the hardships they would face in the wilderness were more palatable than the misery they were leaving behind.

The vast majority of the Acadian immigrants shared a common socioeconomic heritage. Fully three-fourths of the settlers in the 1671 census of Acadia were former peasants of the *laboureur* caste. *Laboureurs* constituted the highest of the five peasant classes in France of the *ancien régime*. Industrious, frugal, and tied together by an intricate extended family system, they shared a deep and abiding attachment to the land they farmed. Only the religious wars of late sixteenth- and early seventeenth-century France, which destroyed the meager economic gains of their families, could have uprooted them from their home provinces and driven them across the Atlantic into the Maritime Canadian wilderness. Their peasant heritage would profoundly influence the course of Acadian cultural development.

The Acadians in Nova Scotia

The coasts of the Bay of Fundy had been settled by the French as early as 1603, but farming by Acadians did not begin at Beau Bassin until about 1671, and at Grand Pré in Minas Basin until about 1680 (see Map 2). The reason had to do with the unusual nature of the bay. The Bay of Fundy experiences some of the highest tides in the world. It is shaped like a gigantic funnel through which rising tidewater surges towards the restricted neck. One result of this was vast tidal marshlands surrounding the head of the bay. In the 1680s these were the only areas in the region that were free of almost impenetrable forest. Immense fields of grass were available for exploitation—if only the tidewaters could be controlled.

Port Royal (now Annapolis Royal) is located along the southern coast of the bay's protected interior (Map 2). With its own inlet, it was a natural location for early French settlement. The newly arriving Acadians discovered that three vast salt marshes—at Port Royal, Minas Basin-Cobequid, and Chignecto Bay—could be transformed into enormously fertile fields if the salt could be removed from the soil. It was easier to tap the rich tidal soils by building dikes than to cut down the forests and construct fields out of the rocky uplands. The forests, the home of the Micmac, were exploited for fuel and food. The effort expended by the early Acadians was enormous. Diking is a time-consuming business, requiring about three years after the dikes have been completed until the land has been leached of its salt content. Many square miles of the marshlands at the eastern end of the Bay of Fundy were recovered through the application of primitive tools and strenuous cooperative effort. These rich lands are still farmed today. The impoverished peasants of Poitou were capable of miracles when it was clearly in their best interest to perform them.

As servants bonded to the Company of New France, Acadian peasants were generally indentured to work for five years. In most cases they worked their obligations off as fur trappers with the local Micmac Indians. Between 1632 and 1654 the Company had divided

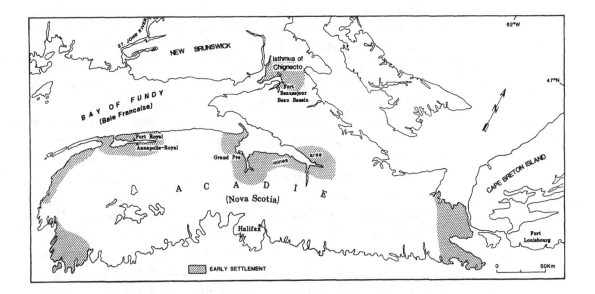

Map 2. Original Acadian
Settlement Areas

the lands of Acadia between fifty-six investors and leading settlers. After the return of French and Company sovereignty from the British in 1670, the *seigneurs* proceeded to reinstate their land claims and attempted to populate their properties with Acadian peasants, now freed of their duties as *engagés;* but, the Acadians had learned to hate and resist the onerous duties and obligations required by the land owners. They did everything possible to avoid the seignorial rents and obligations, which they saw as a persistence of the medieval system from which they had fled. The spread of the Acadian population away from Port Royal may have been the result of the desire to avoid seignorial duties. In addition, Port Royal was subject to attacks by the British. French officials there tried to prevent trade with the New Englanders, but the newly settled Acadians discovered that contraband trade with the merchants of New England was far more lucrative than controlled trade with the French Royal Company.

Throughout the seventeenth and eighteenth centuries, wars strongly colored the relations between the English and the French settlers in North America. Acadia/Nova Scotia changed hands periodically as a result of these wars. It was captured by the British in the Second Dutch War, in 1647. In 1667, the Treaty of Breda returned Acadia to the French (although British control lasted until 1670). On returning, the French took a census. The population around Port Royal was recorded as sixty-seven families. Perhaps another hundred or so *métis* (half-breeds) resided in the area. Three hundred colonists, mostly men, had arrived in 1632. A full generation later the colony had grown only by about 50 souls, but by 1675, 515 Acadians were tallied, despite France's utter neglect of this isolated colony.

Later in the seventeenth century, King William's War (1689–97, the American phase of the larger European War of the League of Augsburg) resulted in a second capture of Acadia by the British. When the Treaty of Ryswick restored all captured territories to the French, the British colonists in New England were outraged. The Acadian population had risen to over 1,450 by the outbreak of Queen Anne's war (1702–1713, the American phase of the War of the Spanish Succession). By 1710 most of Acadia had once again been captured by the British. At the conclusion of hostilities, England adamantly refused to surrender its holdings. Consequently, under the terms of the Treaty of Utrecht in 1713, much of Acadia became a British colony, leaving the French on its eastern tip and in Chignecto. The British now administered a colony of about 2,500 conservative, Catholic, French-speaking Acadians. And the population was growing rapidly, due both to the success of the application of a northern European model of cultivation to the region, and to Acadian industry.

Acadian Settlement Patterns in Acadia/Nova Scotia

The Acadian people settled along the banks of the rivers and along the coast, above the predike high tide line. Their houses overlooked vast fields of grass and wheat; rye, corn, and oats were also cultivated, together with peas, potatoes, cabbages, apples, flax, and hemp. Pigs, sheep, and cattle were left to roam in the forest in the summer and were fed on cabbage in the winter. The original Acadians were carpenters, coopers, blacksmiths, fishermen, shipbuilders, trappers, and sealers, as well as farmers and herders. Acadians in the Chignecto peninsula raised cattle on small ranches.

The notion of a lineal settlement pattern was already well established in Acadia before the Acadians moved to Louisiana. After moving to the bayous of lower Louisiana, the Acadians seem to have perpetuated their familiar settlement pattern, in which houses lined the banks of the watercourses. In Louisiana the strip village is as much an artifact of Acadian history as it is an adaptation to Louisiana's peculiar geography.

Le Grand Dérangement

In 1744, at the beginning of the War of the Austrian Succession (King George's War) the French held the fort at Louisbourg, on Cape Breton Island near the eastern end of Nova Scotia. It was supplied and provisioned by the Acadians. Louisbourg was taken by the British in 1745, but returned to the French in 1748 by the Treaty of Aix-la-Chapelle. Since the Acadians had not helped the British with provisions during this war, they were considered unreliable and undesirable. Their loyalty was only to Acadia. The British imported about twenty-five hundred Protestant colonists to Halifax as a counter to the French presence at Louisbourg.

After this treaty, the British ordered the Acadians to take an oath of allegiance or to be expelled within three months, but relaxed the demand temporarily when they realized that the Acadians were as resistant to French pressure as they were to British demands. Over the next decade matters between the French and the British grew steadily worse, with the Acadians caught in the middle. At the beginning of the French and Indian War, the British struck first, attacking and capturing Fort Beauséjour at the head of the Bay of Fundy in June of 1755. Unfortunately, three hundred Acadian conscripts were discovered together with French military personnel within the walls of Fort Beauséjour when it surrendered. To the British, this implied that the Acadians were combatants and a potential threat to British sovereignty. Fort Louisbourg, the most powerful fort in North America, was still in French hands, and the Acadians and their Indian allies would help to provision and defend it (Map 2). The Acadians, now over twelve thousand strong, were given another chance to swear allegiance to the English king, which they refused to do. In the words of historian Carl Brasseaux, in his study *The Founding of New Acadia* (1987, p. 21):

The rapid expansion of the Acadian population . . . indicated all too clearly that the perceived threat to the Empire would increase geometrically each year if left unchecked. The problem defied easy solution: the occupation by the francophones of the region's choicest farmlands, plus their ability to absorb all rival cultures, discouraged Anglo-Protestant immigration, thereby frustrating English designs to anglicize the French neutrals.

To the new British military governor, Major Charles Lawrence, deportation was the best solution to the problem of the British inability to neutralize the allegiance of the Acadian population to French ways. Instead of returning the Acadians to French soil, however, they would be separated and sent to the English colonies, there to become proper British subjects. The threat of deportation was made in a meeting in July, 1755, but the Acadians assumed that if it were ever carried out, they would be deported into French Canadian territory.

The deportations began almost immediately. The first communities affected were those in Chignecto because of the involvement of Acadians at Fort Beauséjour. All men and boys were told to present themselves at the British fort on August 9, 1755. About four hundred came in and were taken prisoner.

The prisoners were held and then shipped to the Carolinas and Georgia (the distance calculated in proportion to the magnitude of their treason). Since the Chignecto area was one in which small cattle ranches were very common, we can trace the route of migration and diffusion of cattle raising from Chignecto to the southern colonies. Over the next decade, most of the Acadian deportees either returned eventually to Nova Scotia or found their way to the West Indies, before moving on to Louisiana.

Acadian farming settlements along the northeast side of the peninsula of Nova Scotia received the same treatment. Many Acadians did not believe that they would actually be deported, and so they behaved in a docile manner. After the men were interned, the women and children remained in the houses until transports were available. Then families were loaded on board the ships, their houses and crops were burned, and their livestock was confiscated (to "pay for the costs" of deportation).

For the unfortunate Acadians, years of untold hardship and misery began. Much of it was not due to deliberate cruelty on the part of the British, but rather to poor preparation and planning for the care of the Acadians during and after the deportation. Disease took a terrible toll. One ship left Nova Scotia with 417 Acadians on board and arrived in South Carolina with only 210 still alive. In Philadelphia, the Acadians were forced to remain on board their ship for three months in the middle of winter. Over two hundred lost their lives to smallpox and other diseases during this time.

Many Acadians escaped the British roundup. Some joined French forces to fight an effective guerrilla war against the British, forcing them to abandon several forts and capturing or killing many of them. Seventeen British vessels were captured in the Bay of Fundy, but in general the surviving Acadians were forced to move their homes farther and farther to the north and west. Gradually, the French weakened until their military forces collapsed in 1759.

Many of the Acadians eventually returned voluntarily to Nova Scotia, both from French Canada and from the English colonies. Some were permitted to settle once again in the province, but care was taken to ensure that they were widely scattered. In addition, several thousand Acadians who had fled into the woods of New Brunswick now gradually moved back to give themselves up. This was an act of desperation largely in response to British raids and military successes, and because of the threat of imminent starvation. These Acadians were interned near Halifax. Living under miserable conditions, they longed to leave, but were not able to do so until the end of the war, when sea travel for civilians became possible once again.

In terms of Louisiana history, one of the most significant events involved the group of Acadians who had returned to the Halifax area from French Canada. Six hundred agreed to resettle in Saint Domingue (today Haiti). In November of 1764, they departed at their own expense. In all, over two thousand Acadians traveled to the West Indies in 1764 and 1765, but most remained there only for a short time before reembarking for Louisiana. As early as February 1765, 192 Acadians had moved to New Orleans. Others followed in the spring.

The first Acadians to settle in the Bayou Teche (St. Martinville, Louisiana) area were mostly not deportees from the 1755 Grand Dérangement (Map 3). Instead, most were Acadians who had remained in Canada, only then to move temporarily to Saint Domingue before sailing to Louisiana. In 1766, at least one ship departed from Halifax directly for New Orleans. Most of those who settled along Bayou

Teche in 1765 and 1766 had never suffered the rigors of life as deportees in the English colonies.

Acadian Settlement in Louisiana, 1764–1800

The first documented arrival of Acadians occurred in New Orleans in April of 1764. Twenty unidentified exiles reached the colony from Mobile, Alabama. Louisiana was still under a caretaker French administration at this time, before being transferred to Spain, as agreed in the secret Convention of Fontainebleau (November 1762). The immigrants were provided some modest assistance and settled near the Cabannoce Post in present day St. James and St. John the Baptist parishes, above New Orleans on the Mississippi River. This area later became known as the Acadian Coast (Maps 3, 4).

Beginning in February 1765, Acadians began arriving in New Orleans by ship from Saint Domingue. At the time, Louisiana was in the process of being transferred from French to Spanish control. These new settlers were also given some material assistance and transported to the Attakapas Post in western Louisiana. They were given land on Bayou Teche, but the land turned out to be of poor quality (the result of a land swap arranged by a former French military officer to improve his holdings). The Acadians rejected the low-lying parcels and moved downstream to find better quality land. Factionalism troubled the early settlements; many settlers moved yet again, dispersing the population along Bayou Teche and back to the previously established Acadian settlements on the Mississippi River. Gradually, these and other newly arriving Acadian settlers pushed northward and westward into the prairies of south-central Louisiana. They established both farms and *vacheries* (cattle ranches), constructing their homesteads along the banks of the rivers and water courses that laced the open grasslands of the area.

Other groups of Acadians continued to arrive from the English colonies of the eastern seaboard and later directly from France. Perhaps as many as three thousand arrived in all. St. James Parish on the Acadian Coast was the early center of the Acadian settlement on the Mississippi. As more exiles arrived, the settlement spread gradually upriver to the site of the present town of Donaldsonville. This town lies at the head of Bayou Lafourche, a 140-mile-long distributary of the Mississippi River (Map 4). Late in the 1760s, Acadians began moving down Bayou Lafourche as a result of rapid population

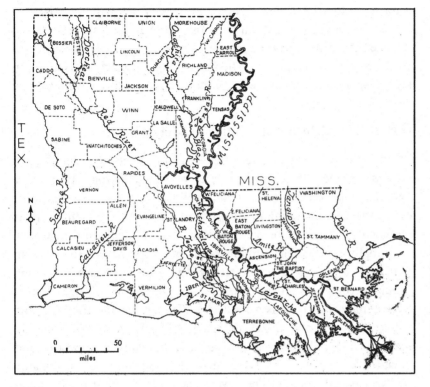

Map 3. Parishes of Louisiana by name (Drafted by Ada Newton)

Map 4. Acadian Settlement Areas ca. 1790 (Based on data from *An Essay on Lower Louisiana* by Stephen Duplantier)

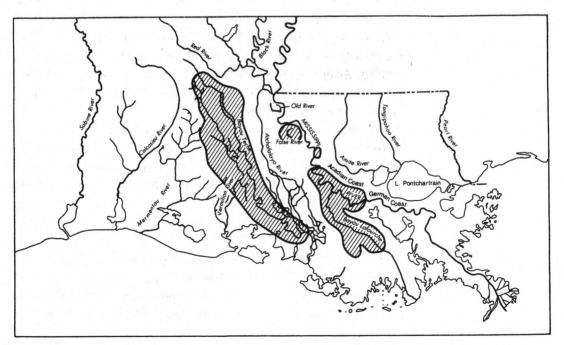

growth, both natural and immigrant, which resulted in a lack of availability of arable lands on the Mississippi River. In 1785, sixteen hundred Acadians arrived directly from France—their passage paid by the Spanish government. The majority of the newly arrived group settled on Bayou Lafourche and other bayous further to the south.

Governmental Support for the Acadians

At the time of their arrival, the Acadians were considered ideal settlers by the Spanish administrators of Louisiana. They were Catholic, small farmers, very poor, apolitical, and were thought to be uninterested in meddling in governmental matters. In addition, their sentiments, like those of the Spanish, were decidedly anti-British.

Initially, the Spanish administrators of Louisiana saw the Acadian settlement as a benefit to the struggling colony. The newly arriving Acadians could be moved towards the peripheries of the zone of settlement to function as a kind of buffer against the English, who represented a strong threat to Spanish Louisiana at this time. In addition to their military usefulness, the Acadians were prolific and provided a much-needed increase in the population of this highly underpopulated colony. They were industrious and hard-working. They cleared and planted land, provided extra food for New Orleans markets, and facilitated communication along the Mississippi. They were clearly worth the initial investment in aid that had to be extended. As one observer commented, "They are so poor that when they arrive in these settlements, they come burdened with a family but have not a shirt to wear."

Land was given in small concessions at specified locations along the Mississippi. Rations of corn were provided to each person. Each family received "an ax, a hoe, a scythe or sickle, a spade, two hens, a cock and a pig of two months, with which they may easily found and establish a household which will provide them a living or even make them a fortune," according to a proclamation of Governor Galvez in February 1778.

Each head of a family also received a shotgun. Sufficient food was delivered from the rations at military posts to enable the Acadians to survive until the first crop was in. The commandant of the local fort also organized hunts on a rotating basis. Meat from these was

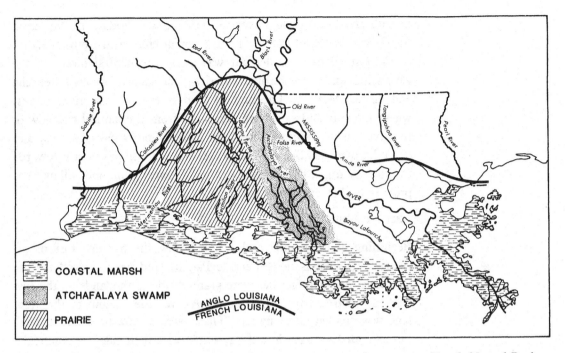

Map 5. Natural Regions of French Louisiana

apparently shared between the soldiers and construction workers and the Acadian settlers.

One of the better documented settlement projects occurred in Iberville Parish. It provides a good example of early Acadian settlement in Louisiana. In July 1767 a group of 210 Acadians arrived from Maryland. They were settled near the small fort at St. Gabriel de Manchac, in Iberville Parish, on the east bank of the Mississippi River (Map 3). A second group soon followed them. This settlement represented Governor Ulloa's policy of defensive settlement.

Fort St. Gabriel was constructed in 1767 as protection against the British who held Baton Rouge at that time. From the Spanish perspective, everyone would benefit by establishing the Acadians near the Spanish fort. Guns and ammunition were available. The commandant of the fort supplied the settlers with medical services. There was better defense in case of an Indian (or British) attack. Young unmarried Acadian men found employment at the fort. Skilled artisans were paid full wages by the Spanish. In addition, a chapel was constructed at the fort and a chaplain was available for services. This small church was soon moved a few miles downstream, enlarged at both ends, and turned over to the Acadians. Today, the church at St. Gabriel is the oldest surviving colonial church in Louisiana.

Almost all early settlement was along the natural levees of the Mississippi and its major distributaries—particularly bayous Lafourche and Teche (Map 5). The highest land is close to the river banks, where the silts and sands are deposited from the natural overflow of the rivers in the spring. The high land supports oaks, pecans, and other hardwoods. Beyond the levee, the land slopes gently towards the back swamps, where cypress, tupelo, sweet gum, and willow trees provide timber and cover for game.

Farm Layout

Beginning about a mile and a half below the Spanish fort of St. Gabriel, in what is now Iberville Parish, land was reserved for the Acadians. Acadian families were granted title to the lands on the east bank downstream from that point. As was the custom of the area, land was divided into long-lots. These were narrow on the river bank but extended far back into the swamps, with their sides perpendicular to the river bank. Plots of land were measured in "arpents of face," using the French measure established in Quebec in the early seventeenth century. Each Acadian family was granted a plot that most typically varied between three and six arpents in width on the river. (One arpent equals about 192 English feet.) Thus, the typical family concession varied between about 576 and 1152 feet in width. These concessions were further subdivided according to the French laws of inheritance, which reserved an equal portion to each child (Fig. 1).

Each house was set next to the road, which paralleled the bank of the river. Other farm buildings were placed behind the main house. Behind the house was a summer kitchen or *cuisine*, and perhaps a *four*, or hemispherical bread oven of clay, which was covered with a shed roof (*fournil*). Gradually other outbuildings were added: chicken coops, a forge, granaries, perhaps a pigeon- or dovecote, *magasins* (storehouses), and, for some, slave cabins. All of this was in contrast to the farms of Acadia, where a single barn served most of these functions.

Fences (*clôtures*) of *pieux* (split planks) divided the farmyard into several parts. The house and *cuisine* were roofed with bark, *merrains*, or shingles. The *merrains* were split planks up to ten feet long, used as shingles. They were pegged to roof lathing.

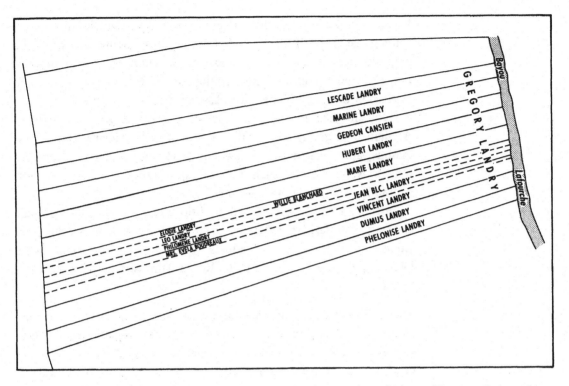

Crops grown by the early Acadians included: rice, maize, fruits (oranges, peaches, figs, apples, plums, and grapes) and vegetables, such as squash and pumpkins, melons, watermelons, peppers, potatoes, and beans. The primary grain after 1710 in Louisiana was corn. The French Creoles preferred wheat and imported it from upper Louisiana and from France, but it was expensive, and most Acadians learned to use corn in its place. Corn was often ground with a wooden mortar and pestle. Mills of stone were occasionally used.

Before the arrival of the Acadians, draft animals were in extremely short supply. The German coast was the area first settled above New Orleans on the Mississippi River. It was almost devoid of draft animals in 1730. After 1735, however, the supply of horses arriving from the Spanish borderlands via Natchitoches improved the situation. By the time the Acadians arrived in 1765, horses were available to those who could afford them. Dairy products, especially milk and butter, were obtained on the Acadian Coast through possession of a family cow. Every surviving inventory at Donaldsonville, for example, mentions either cattle or cows. Creole butter was manufactured by whipping or shaking cream in a jug, rather than by churning.

Figure 1. Gregory Landry concession of Bayou Lafourche (Redrafted from "The Agricultural Settlement Succession on the Prairies of Southwest Louisiana" by James William Taylor)

Farmers in the eighteenth and early nineteenth centuries also raised commercial crops. These included indigo (until about 1790 when the crop was destroyed), tobacco, and cotton. After 1793, sugar production changed the entire configuration of the river settlements. (See discussion on fourth generation Acadian house, p. 129.)

Not all Acadians worked as small farmers. Among the arriving Acadian immigrants were skilled craftsmen, particularly carpenters, masons, and blacksmiths. A few listed their profession as "seaman." Others were artisans such as bakers, armorers, tanners, tailors, shipbuilders and edge-tool makers.

Although the Acadians had traditionally favored wool for their clothing, this fashion gradually gave way to cotton in semitropical Louisiana. Before long, Acadians were weaving cotton in home looms. About 1800, traveler C. C. Robin witnessed the importance of cotton:

The Acadian women and children go into the fields to pick corn and cotton.... They spin the cloth, mosquito nets, and that multi-colored striped cotton cloth so agreeable to the eye, resembling very much our saimoises, out of which they make skirts and blouses, and for the men, pants and jackets.

Pierre-Clément de Laussat described a visit to an Acadian household in 1803:

I wanted to see one of those Acadian families which populated this coast (St. James Parish). So I went to the house of Pierre Michel, a cotton and corn planter. He and his wife are sexagenarians. Both born in Acadia, they were married in Louisiana and had seven or eight children. Everybody in the house was at work—one daughter was ironing; another was spinning; and the mother was distributing the cotton, while a number of little Negroes, all under twelve, were carding it, picking out the seeds and drying it.

As the Acadians gradually spread out across the new country of southern Louisiana, they found themselves almost as isolated from one another by topographical conditions as they had been in Acadia by British internment. Moreover, geographical conditions demanded different ways of life and economic practices. The adaptable Acadians, however, met the challenges doggedly.

2

Settlement and Society

In the nineteenth century and the first half of the twentieth, the social order of Acadians had become fixed firmly in a long-established rural mode of life founded on three main elements. These were the farmstead, the rural community with its local church, and the larger social and political order such as parish and state government. These elements interacted with physiographic variations to shape the patterns of Acadian settlement and communication in the colonial and post-colonial periods. Three principal zones of settlement emerged: the banks of the major rivers and bayous, the swamps and marshes, and the great western prairies (Map 5).

The River Settlements

In the nineteenth century Acadian life fell into two basic patterns of settlement—the rural strip village and the prairie hamlet. Terrain and ecology determined the settlement pattern. Strip villages were, of course, located along the waterways, principally the Mississippi River (the Acadian Coast section), Bayou Lafourche, and Bayou Teche. Along bayous Teche and Lafourche, for instance, strip settlement ran continuously for many miles (Map 6). A great number of smaller bayous and rivers also attracted similar patterns of settlement.

In a study of Bayou Lafourche in 1932, T. Lynn Smith found approximately thirty houses per mile on each side of the bayou in the area south of Thibodaux. The smaller farms averaged approximately 220 feet wide and a mile and a half deep. Settlers constructed their

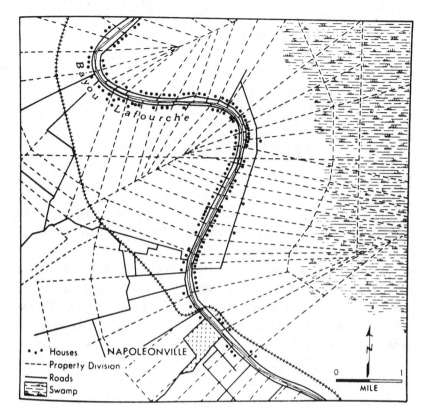

Map 6. French land divisions at Napoleonville, on Bayou LaFourche (Map by Fred Kniffen, from *The Human Mirror*)

• • • Houses   NAPOLEONVILLE
- - - Property Division
——— Roads
Swamp

0   1
MILE

houses along the river road, near the bayou (Map 6), and larger plantations could be found along the eastern side of the bayou.

Cajuns living in the strip settlements communicated mostly by water originally. Each family had one or more *pirogues* (canoe-like craft), *bateaux* (flat-bottomed rowboats) or sailboats (luggers), which made transportation relatively easy, if slow. Later, when roads were built along the crests of the natural levees, Cajuns adopted horse-drawn vehicles. Acadian settlement patterns and transportation networks retained their strongly linear forms. After the colonial period, Cajuns could depend on finding most local services such as churches and stores in their immediate area. (This was not true, however, for the more isolated communities, such as those in lower Lafourche and Terrebonne parishes.) As late as 1932, Saturday night dances were attended by families within a radius of fifty miles, despite the fact that less than a third of the families owned automobiles at that time.

The most common kind of neighbor in the strip community was a close relative: a child, a parent, or a sibling. Inheritance patterns, which required that the land be divided into strips of equal width, resulted in family-owned sections that sometimes ran for a mile or more along the bayou. Often such sections were named after the founding family, for example, *Côte Landry* (Fig. 1). Social life was intense in such a community. The 120 families surveyed by Smith contained 127 children under the age of 12, all of whom were potential playmates. Sixty of these children lived within a mile of each house.

Adults, too, drew most of their friends and help from the immediate vicinity of their home. Cooperative work parties helped friends and neighbors bring in the crops, build structures, and move houses. Such work was traditionally paid for in one of two ways—and often both. First, everyone recognized the power of reciprocity in cooperative work. People participated cheerfully because they knew that the same group would be around to help them at a later time. Second, helping out in the larger undertakings, such as house moving (*trainage*) or house erection (*coup de main*), was compensated by food and drink.

In the early days, the great southern triangle of Louisiana that has become known as Acadiana had few formal social institutions. City officials, police, public schools, markets, and even churches did not exist for most people until the second half of the nineteenth century. These spread outward from the urban centers only gradually. Informal work and social groups were relied upon in the more isolated areas. Several distinctive forms of social units, such as *boucheries*, *coups de main*, the *bals de maison*, and the *veillées*, were common to rural Acadiana.

Most commercial activity revolved around merchants traveling in boats and in wagons who stopped at each house to display their wares. Especially attractive were new things: novelties in fabrics, kitchen utensils, tools, and notions generated much enthusiasm among Cajun housewives and children. Chickens and particularly eggs were universally accepted as payment for goods of all kinds. A secondary function—the transmission of news and gossip—was also a significant part of the success of the traveling merchant, ice-man, and tinsmith. By the end of the 1920s, however, the itinerant peddler had vanished, replaced by truck-borne delivery men who worked for local merchants with stores in Thibodaux, Raceland, Opelousas, St. Martinville, or other local centers.

Even in the nineteenth century, Cajuns loved festivals and fairs. At first, fairs were sponsored by churches. Later, civic organizations began to create larger festivals that centered on local products or events. To a rural family, the festival was the social highlight of the year. Writing about the early 1930s, Lynn Smith noted:

Within the neighborhood, the annual church fair is a time of great celebration. Two days of festivities, Saturday and Sunday, with dances each night constitute the proceedings. Literally every one attends, male and female, young and old, well-to-do and poor, owner, tenant, and laborer, all are there. In addition, the whole-hearted enjoyment arising from the frequent assemblages of friends and relatives, gives recreation within the settlement a tone similar to that of the recreation characteristic of the village community.

The Prairies

Prairie grasslands form a large part of southwestern Louisiana. However, it is not one single prairie but rather a series of them set off by forest growth that bounds the major streams cutting across the grasslands (Map 7). The largest prairies are named Faquetique, Mamou, Calcasieu, Sabine, Vermilion, Mermentau, Plaquemine, Opelousas, and Grand, and there are many other smaller ones (Map 8). A claypan largely impervious to water or roots underlies the topsoil except where the larger streams, such as the Mermentau, Calcasieu, Nezpiqué, and Plaquemine Brulé have breached it and permitted the growth of thae deciduous gallery forest, and left deposits of productive alluvial soils. Between the major streams are smaller ones that do not breach the claypan or carry a boundary forest. Also in the open prairie are shallow, intermittent streams, or *coulées,* in addition to shallow, round ponds, *platins* and *marais,* that may have water seasonally and support a growth of trees. Ponds that fill only seasonally are called baygalls by English-speaking settlers, perhaps due to the bay trees frequently found around them.

On the prairies, as elsewhere, the major streams were the significant early routes for travel and transport. Long before the age of steam, wind-powered schooners ascended the Mermentau and other rivers to collect meat, hides, fruit, and other agricultural products for delivery to ports that ranged from Galveston and New Orleans to Central America. This gave Prairie Cajuns something of a world perspective. Even into the twentieth century with competition from railroads and highways, rivers have been important routes of trans-

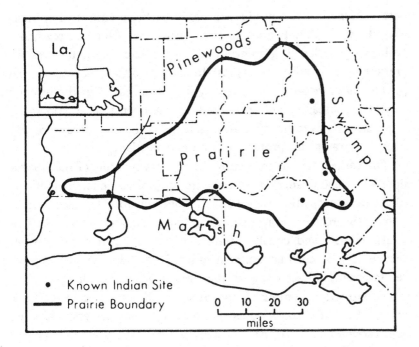

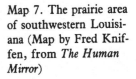

Map 7. The prairie area of southwestern Louisiana (Map by Fred Kniffen, from *The Human Mirror*)

Map 8. The great southwestern prairies (Redrafted from *Atlas of Louisiana* by Miles Newton)

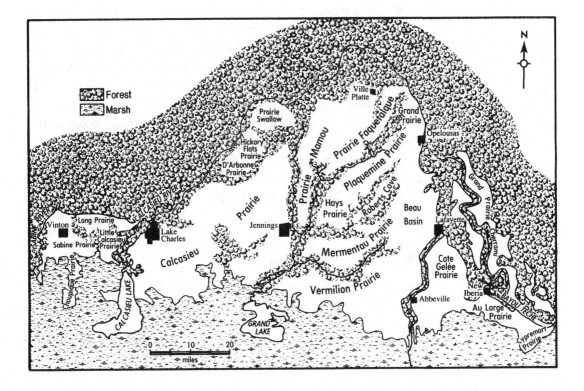

port. Commercial rice production began on the prairies of Louisiana after the Civil War. It grew rapidly during the 1870s and reached a peak in the 1880s. Beginning in the east in the 1770s, the western prairies were invaded by Cajuns. In the age before the commercial production of rice on a large scale, the Cajuns lived in the wooded areas along streams, and only rarely on the open prairie. Along the major streams were transportation and the best soils; there were also wood and water and protection from bad weather.

The earliest Cajuns to occupy the western margins of the Mississippi River floodplain and the easternmost prairies generally cultivated the same crops that were familiar from life along the Mississippi: cotton, sugarcane, okra, rice, corn, potatoes, and fruits. With a similar climate and equally productive soils, their harvests saw no decline. The Spanish government to which they were subject continued to grant land according to the French practice of dividing river fronts into strips fronting on the streams and extending to the back swamp. But the Spanish added the *sitio*, a rectangular grant of large (and variable) size that was normally not oriented to a stream or to the cardinal directions.

As years passed and Cajun settlement edged ever more into the open prairie, a newer pattern emerged that more resembled the French long-lots found along the Mississippi River. The American government to which the Cajuns became subject after 1803 continued to divide the land into strips (the American long-lot), but the strips were of equal width instead of tapered to fit the curvature of the stream like the French long-lot. The Cajuns lived in the wooded areas along the streams, cultivating the productive alluvial soils (Map 8). If there were *marais* and *platins* in the adjacent open prairie, settlers grew what they called crops of "providence rice" when the ponds carried water. In some years they got nothing, hence the reliance on Providence.

The Prairie Settlements

Life on the Louisiana prairies in the nineteenth century was considerably different from that of eastern Acadiana. North and west of New Iberia and Lafayette and extending across the prairies as far as Avoyelles and Evangeline parishes, isolated local settlements were the rule (Map 8). Settlement density was low, with people often grouped

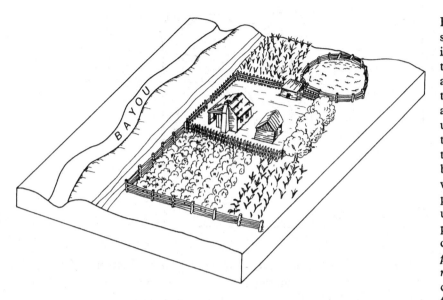

Figure 2. An idealized sketch of an early Acadian farmstead, showing the location of the house and crops in relation to the natural levee. Corn and sweet potatoes were usually grown nearer to the crest of the levee in the coarser textured and better drained land, while sugarcane was placed lower on the natural levee in the more poorly drained land. The circular enclosure is a *pieux* fence around a *marais* planted in Providence rice. (Redrafted from "The Agricultural Settlement Succession, on the Prairies of Southwest Louisiana" by James William Taylor)

into *anses* or "coves." Prairie settlers were far more self-sufficient than those on the rivers. A high proportion of items needed for daily life were produced on the farmstead, rather than being purchased, and while fabrics were bought from merchants in eastern Acadiana, most cloth was hand-woven on upright looms in the west. Isolation and self-sufficiency encouraged settlers to develop strong in-group loyalties and even in-breeding. Cooperative labor such as *coup de main* work flourished in this environment.

Prairie Cajun settlement might best be described as a compromise between the typical European agricultural village, with its advantages of high social density and better services (school, church, stores), and the isolated American farmstead with its close proximity to the fields and livestock.

For all the social differences, however, the individual houses looked much like those of the river parishes, as pointed out by Fred Kniffen in 1987 (Fig. 2):

The houses were commonly of the Creole type; the fences were a yard paling (*pieux*) fence, and field post-and-rail type. In every front yard there was a chinaball, or chinaberry, tree, its branches clipped back to provide firewood and to thicken the crown for better shade.

Many such communities also were adjacent to waterways so water transportation was often available, particularly along the tributaries of

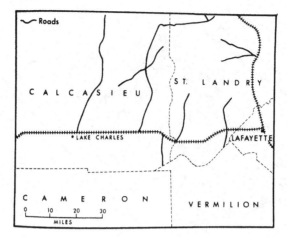

Map 9. The prairie road pattern in 1884 (Map by Fred Kniffen, from *The Human Mirror*)

upper Bayou Teche, the Vermilion, and Mermentau Rivers. However, for many prairie communities land transportation was the only available method. Generally, buggies and farm wagons were used whenever a family traveled together. Roads were bad, particularly before the era of Governor Huey P. Long in the 1930s, so long-distance travel was difficult and isolation was severe (Map 9).

Diaries and letters tell of Cajun farm families on the prairies making only two or three long trips per year. One of these was generally to the parish seat, where legal business was conducted and annual taxes paid. If the trip was made in October, the family brought farm produce to market to be sold and reaped the profit from a year of difficult toil. Family reunions, particularly at weddings, first communions, and funerals, also required extended trips. Aside from these brief periods of excitement, though, the world of the Cajun farmer, his wife, and children, was circumscribed by the unchanging monotony of the distant horizon surrounding the farm house.

At about the same time substantial agriculture developed in the Opelousas and Attakapas Post districts, came growth in cattle rearing. Between 1860 and 1920 the open grasslands invited Cajuns to establish *vacheries* or ranches. Increasingly, both horses and cattle were of Spanish or Spanish-American origin, and a relationship developed with Texas as a source for stock as well as methods and equipment to handle it. The westward movement of the Cajuns began as early as

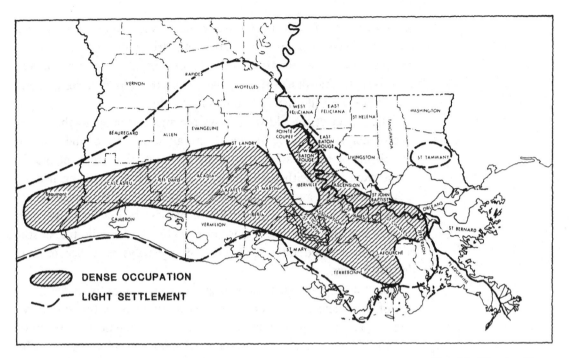

DENSE OCCUPATION

LIGHT SETTLEMENT

Map 10. The Acadian population in 1981 (Redrafted from *An Atlas of Louisiana Surnames of French and Spanish Origin* by Robert C. West)

1780 and continued until the present. Cajun settlements had reached the Louisiana-Texas border region by ca. 1890 (Map 10).

There were annual round-ups and brandings and even drives to posts, originally government seats on the frontier of French Louisiana, or as far as markets on the Mississippi. In the east, cattle might graze during times of stress in the plantation fringe. But on the western prairie expanses, the stock was totally dependent on prairie grasses, even through the harshest winters. Also, cattle roamed more freely in the west because it was more difficult to fence them out of the crops than in the east where agriculture predominated and where French attitudes put the responsibility for control on the stock owners. This was a reversal of the American practice under which it was the farmer's responsibility to protect his crop from livestock. Prairie fences were built and used, but were often of little avail where ranching occurred on a large scale.

Cattle rearing remains part of Prairie Cajun life today, but the spread of agriculture, especially rice, has reduced both its economic importance and much of its flamboyant ways. In the nonagricultural coastal marshes, however, much of the old-style of cattle rearing remains. Only a few years ago, one rancher was reputed to own forty thousand head. Up until recently, long drives through the marsh brought the cattle to areas where the summer insects were less abundant. But nowadays trucks have replaced the long drives and one corner of Cajun life has lost some of its color.

One aspect of the old range days remains unchanged—the Cajun love of horses and horse racing. Long after the rest of the country had abandoned horses in favor of automobiles, the streets of prairie towns were lined with horse-drawn buggies. Harness racing had an ardent following, and half-mile oval tracks could be discerned on air photos into the 1960s. The heyday of harness racing seems to have passed, but quarter-horse racing on straight quarter-mile tracks still commands devoted interest. Many Cajun jockeys have become nationally known.

The Cajun prairie landscape began to change rapidly in the latter part of the nineteenth century with the coming of an east-west railroad (Map 9), an invasion of midwestern farmers from the north, a boom in the oil industry, and agricultural mechanization. Nevertheless, the solidest bastions of Cajun life in prairie Louisiana are the clusters of small farms that still dot the landscape along the major streams.

Continuity with the past remains in foods, games, music, and the church—many of the same categories as in other American rural societies. Crops of corn, cotton and vegetables are grown according to improved traditional methods, and cattle are fenced. French may be the prevailing tongue, but the importance of speaking unaccented English is realized by those Cajuns who want to make their mark in the world at large. While Cajuns are solidly Roman Catholic, that confers no great distinction nor can it instill a cohesiveness such as that which holds together the Amish and Mennonites. But regardless of the fate of Cajun French, there will remain many other distinctive Cajun ways, and the heritage of how to live on the prairie will not vanish.

The Coastal Wetlands

The most distinctive—and to the early settlers, alien—portion of Louisiana lies in its coastal plain. Here, the unusual topography, climate, vegetation and fauna combined to produce an environment dramatically unlike anything in the experience of settlers from Europe or Canada. Yet so completely did the Acadian immigrants adapt to this somewhat mysterious world that today many identify it as being distinctly Cajun.

Louisiana lacks a typical American recreational coastal zone composed of broad sand beaches, dunes, and clear ocean waters. The problem is that the Mississippi River has been dropping its heavy load of sediment along the Louisiana coasts for many millennia. The river has changed its course countless times, melding many overlapping deltas into a broad, low plain composed of silts and clays. The plain's elevation lowers steadily and gradually until it simply disappears under the murky waters of the Gulf of Mexico.

Several factors complicate this picture of uniformity. The coastal zone is actually subsiding slowly and the sea is moving landward. Saltwater bays encroach upon the land and former freshwater zones. In addition, the Mississippi, the Atchafalaya, and other rivers have cut channels through the deltaic plain. The smaller watercourses that meander slowly are generally called bayous. The annual overflow of the silt-laden water produces natural levees—ridges of higher land along the banks. Some levees run for as much as 150 miles through the plain before they enter the gulf. The levees are crowned with species of trees that thrive in somewhat elevated soil: live oak, gums, elms, pecans, and the ancient magnolia. It is a place made more impenetrable because the trees wear mantles—the oaks, particularly, are draped with Spanish moss. It was on these levees that the newly arrived Acadian hunters, trappers, and fishermen constructed their first houses and camps.

Cajuns learned to exploit the natural resources of the swamps and the marshes as well as the tidal estuaries and freshwater bayous. Swamps occur throughout most of the coastal plain. The swamps are freshwater and support trees, particularly cypress, tupelo gum, red maple, willow, and ash. There are both freshwater and saltwater marshes, with the latter lying closer to the coast. Marshes are covered exclusively with grasses.

The swamps and marshes support an abundance of animal and aquatic life, which the early settlers quickly learned to identify and capture. Fur-bearing animals, such as beaver, mink, otter, muskrat, raccoon, bear, and, later, nutria, were trapped and skinned. Oysters, shrimp, crabs, and an abundance of fish supplied a rich and varied source of seafood for the developing Creole cuisine. Seafood was shipped daily to New Orleans beginning early in the nineteenth century. Waterfowl, too, were hunted, as were alligators, turtles, frogs, and crawfish. According to an old saying, "If it walks, crawls, swims or flies, it ends up in the Cajun's pot."

Cajuns invented or adapted many cultural traits to live better in the wetlands environment. Some of these traits are found only in this region even today. Boats adapted to the shallow waters of the swamps have been in continuous development since the colonial period. Some, such as the *pirogue*, appear based on Native American models (dugouts), while the sailing lugger and skiff are clearly of European design. Yet others—the popular flat-bottomed and flat-ended *bateau* or flatboat—may have been invented on the spot. One early nineteenth-century observer noted that

people of this country are so accustomed to travel by water that the generic term, '*voiture*' (standard French for "carriage") is always applied to a boat. If a Louisianian says to you, 'I brought my voiture'; 'Can I give you a lift in my voiture;' he is referring to his pirogue or skiff as a Parisian using the same word would mean his coach.

Many of the boats developed in the coastal area of Louisiana are so changed from their predecessors that they amount to local inventions. The *joug* is a skiff rowed in a standing position. The Lafitte skiff is characterized by an extended shelf behind the transom upon which the fisherman stands to manipulate gear. The *bateau* is often built with such a wide beam that the fisherman may stand on one gunwale while lifting a heavy load without fear of capsizing. This is required in certain fishing operations, such as hauling in the large handmade hoopnets used in fishing the rivers and lakes. All of these craft were originally poled, paddled, rowed, or sailed. In the twentieth century, most have been fitted with internal combustion engines. The art of building boats without plans or modern tools has not entirely disappeared, however, despite the changes wrought by mechanization. Even quite large boats are still occasionally made by hand according to traditional folk methods.

Many other cultural traits, and indeed, entire industries, also characterize the coastal zone. The *tarabi* (var. *taravia*) is a tool unique to Louisiana's coastal zone. It is a two-piece spinner used to manufacture rope or twine from heavy fibers such as those of Spanish moss or horsehair. The gathering and curing of Spanish moss, which was widely employed for stuffing of mattresses and automobile seats until after World War II, was an industry found only in the area. Cajun fishermen, in the pursuit of their quarry, invented or modified numerous devices: nets and seines, crab traps, shrimp boxes, bait boxes, trotlines, and frog grabs.

In the twentieth century, heavy industry somewhat changed the character of the coastal zone. Lumbering cut most of the excellent cypress between 1890 and 1920. Oil was discovered in southern Louisiana, leading to widespread drilling both on- and off-shore. With the development of a cash economy, roads, railroads, communications, and commercial and tourist facilities have pushed further and further into the area, bringing a more cosmopolitan appearance to a once wild and somewhat lawless country.

Throughout their history, however, Cajuns have shown themselves amazingly adroit at adjusting to change when it was forced upon them. They have also eagerly embraced progress when it filtered into their community. The spurts of growth in Louisiana's agriculture and fisheries can usually be traced to technological advances or new markets. And today's generation of Cajun oilfield entrepreneurs shows that such adaptability is not limited to traditional occupations.

Camps

The camp is a Louisiana institution. It began with humble origins, as trappers' and oystermen's shacks in the marsh. It was a place to live only when there was money to be made. All temporary housing in the marsh, swamp, or woods came to be called a camp, even long after it had developed a permanency that was limited only by the Gulf Coast's violent tropical storms. A variant was the camp boat, hauled home in the summer. This had the advantage that seasonal creature comforts were not tied to the same trapping grounds year after year. Moreover, inland berths were safer from hurricanes.

Long before improved transportation reduced the need for working and living for extended periods in remote camps, Cajuns came to appreciate camps for their recreational value. The need to get far away from civilization for both hunting and fishing has increased their popularity. Many Cajun families now own a camp for recreation and sports. Also, groups of friends, usually men, enjoy banding together from time to time to take advantage of the isolation of camp life. Some camps are located in the Atchafalaya Basin or along the numerous bayous that meander through south Louisiana. Others are in the saltwater marshes along the coast. Still more are in the pine and oak forests that abound in the region. Some camps are elaborate cooperative efforts, while others are modest family affairs. Some are usually reserved for men only, while others welcome entire families.

The need to improvise entertainment far from civilization generates abundant camp folklore. Because of its isolation, the camp has become a means of reactivating and preserving oral lore. Hunters and fishermen play cards, tell stories, and sing songs to while away the evenings. Before the season begins, work crews are formed to prepare the camps. Members of a camp gain privileges according to their efforts in preparing and maintaining the camp; certain members are appointed to clean game and fish, to cook, and to clean up.

In recent times, summer vacation for many a southeast Louisiana family was a week spent out on a shrimp-drying platform or other form of camp. Modern camps can range from elegant summerhouses to corrugated steel shacks hardly more sturdy than the palmetto huts of old. Some front on the beach, others are actually built over the water. Near the coast, camps are built on tall pilings, their stilts protecting them from hurricane water, if not from wind. Perhaps the oddest sight is a mobile home used for a camp. Raised ten feet in the air, it will often get a porch, then a roof to keep it cool, then an addition, then a bigger porch, and so on, until the original mobile home has completely disappeared.

The geographical diversity of southern Louisiana demanded different responses from the relatively isolated groups of settlers in the eighteenth and early nineteenth centuries. It also created a varied environmental backdrop against which the cultural adaptability of the Acadian—now well on the way to becoming a Cajun—showed its strengths.

Acadian Folklife

The development of Acadian society in the nineteenth century has been almost completely neglected by historians. What little is known about the era is based primarily upon travelogues, written by outsiders who were generally interested only in the more exotic aspects of local life. Almost without exception, commentators failed to comprehend the complexity of Acadian society and totally ignored all but the most impoverished strata of the community.

Despite the emergence of distinctive socioeconomic groups within the antebellum Cajun community, members of the lower social strata of Acadian society, particularly yeoman farmers and *petits habitants* (subsistence farmers), shared a similar life style, language, and values little different from those of their forebears. The survival—indeed the domination— of Acadian culture was a direct result of the strength of traditional social institutions and agricultural practices that promoted economic self-sufficiency and group solidarity.

French settlers first began to arrive in Louisiana in 1699, sixty-six years before the arrival of the first settlers from Acadia. As they gradually settled along the waterways, primarily the Mississippi River, the immigrants from France interacted frequently with the Native American tribes. Many individuals were incorporated into the fledgling Creole society in various capacities, particularly as servants, laborers, and mistresses. Native American traders and trappers played an important role in the early years of the colony, supplying the settlers with basic foodstuffs and trade goods. Native Americans knew the country and how to exploit its resources. A knowledge of how to do things "in the Indian manner" was considered essential knowledge by the early *coureurs de bois* or "woods runners." Techniques of hunting, trapping, gathering (herbs and medicinal plants), cooking, agriculture, and house construction were incorporated into the Creole repertoire.

As early as 1724 the French had begun to import slaves directly
from Africa to work the plantation fields, something the independent-
minded Native Americans generally refused to do. The Africans came
with a well-established knowledge of tropical environments and tropical agriculture. Despite their inferior social standing, the Africans
contributed substantially to the cultural melange. Many africanisms
persist today in Creole culture: music, dance, agriculture, social
organization, religion, cuisine, language, oral literature, personal
decoration, art, and technology. Creole slaves from Saint Domingue
(Haiti) and other Caribbean islands also brought the hard-won knowledge of how to survive under the plantation system, with its peculiar
institutions and etiquette.

Even under Spanish sovereignty, the previously established French
Creole population continued to dominate the cultural life of everyday
Louisiana. It was into this curious cultural amalgam that the Acadians
entered between 1765 and 1785. Some German-speaking settlers also
continued to arrive from Alsace and the Rhineland. After 1790,
English-speaking settlers arrived from the eastern states and occasionally from England, Ireland, and Scotland. These varied peoples
found themselves in a regional melting pot that blended these various
ingredients into a gumbo called Creole culture.

Creoles and Creolization

Louisiana is sometimes called the Creole State, and Louisiana French
folklife, like most aspects of French Louisiana, is the result of the
process of *creolization*. In a technical (anthropological) sense, creolization
may be viewed as a process in which cultural traits derived from
markedly dissimilar cultures (African, Franco-German, Native American) were brought together and amalgamated under conditions of
tropical plantation agriculture in the West Indies and Louisiana.

In the typical pattern of American colonial creolization, institutions from each contributing culture were selected for adaptability to
the rigors of the pioneering environment. As with a pidgin language,
they were reduced to their simplest functional level and then blended
together with traits of other cultures with which they bore a general
similarity. African pagan deities, for example, became associated with
Christian saints with which they shared apparent associations such as
water or curative powers. Nonfunctional practices, and those without

cross-cultural associations, were more often discarded. The result was a honed-down pioneering culture composed of "lean and mean" reconstructed patterns that had been shaped and blended into new systems suited to the polyethnic population and the subsistence economy of the struggling new colony. The surviving patterns all shared a certain familiarity to members of each of the ethnic groups. The new patterns were less alien and more acceptable to everyone, regardless of their individual cultural background, because each individual's culture had made significant contributions to the whole.

To pick a single example, Louisiana gumbo (a soupy stew with seafood or game) was based on a foundation of French domestic cooking technology (heavy black iron pots, a brown roux stock), but it incorporated local Louisiana game and seafood, alien to any French cook. In addition, it was carefully thickened (both Africans and Native Americans liked their stews heavily thickened) and flavored with African okra and with Native American *filé* (powdered sassafras). Rice, another local non-European crop, also became an important ingredient of this archetypal Creole culinary composition.

As the Louisiana colony survived and thrived, the newly established Creole cultural traits grew and diversified. Under conditions of economic development, technical specialization, social stratification, and urbanization, simple folk behavior once again developed variants appropriate to a complex society. On the Cajun prairies, for example, one can find basic gumbo spiced only with salt and cayenne pepper, served with squirrel, duck, or alligator and eaten with tin or even plastic spoons. But gumbo is also served in fancy New Orleans restaurants, flavored with exotic spices, loaded with expensive shrimp and oysters and eaten with silver spoons.

In its popular Louisiana sense, *créole* meant simply "local, homegrown, not imported" (but largely derived from Old World sources). It referred to people and objects as well as ways of doing things. Thus there were French Creoles and Creole slaves, Creole horses and tomatoes, Creole language and architecture. The descendants of French immigrants born in the New World were called Creoles to distinguish them from the immigrants who continued to arrive from France.

Slaves born in Louisiana were called Creoles to distinguish them from blacks captured in Africa and brought to the colony by slave traders. Creole slaves were more valuable because they were acclimatized and acculturated and therefore less likely to die from new diseases. They were more likely to speak the language of their masters, and less likely to try to escape, since they had been born into slavery.

Creole agricultural products were home-grown and more likely to be fresh. Creole animals, bred and raised locally, were better adapted to the subtropical conditions. Cultural features like language, material culture and architecture, cuisine, music, dance, oral tradition, and religion were also creolized—blended in the Louisiana melting pot and adapted to the environment.

Improvisation and adaptation were essential to this process. The New World provided opportunities to experiment. While individual cultures did preserve some old ways in the New World, the frontier environment also opened up the possibilities of creating new ways from the old. Innovation lay close to the heart of creolization in Louisiana.

In American colonial history, the term *créole* implies a tropical or subtropical cultural adaptation. The word was originally a Portuguese term. Early in the sixteenth century it was applied to the distinctly American ways of life emerging in the Iberian colonies, particularly in Brazil and Hispaniola. By historical accident, the Creole cultural hearth of the Americas was established in the Spanish West Indies and in South America. On the North American continent, only the culture of southern Louisiana is popularly termed Creole. This recognizes the special historical connection between Louisiana and the French (formerly Spanish) West Indies in the earliest days of Louisiana settlement.

The process of building Creole culture, as outlined above, had resulted in a distinctive form of French culture by the end of French sovereignty in 1763. Instead of "pure" French ways of life, these now well-established Creole patterns were quickly adopted by the Acadians upon their arrival in Louisiana.

Today, creolization has become associated primarily with one of its most important expressions—the descendants of the rural Acadians who intermarried and interacted with most of the other ethnic groups in the area and eventually came to dominate the Louisiana French melting pot by sheer numbers. This cultural and ethnic hybrid is what has come to be called *Cajun*.

The Origins of Acadian Ethnic Identity

An important factor in developing a sense of cultural identity among the Louisiana French was the close-knit nature of the Acadian community during the century before they settled in Louisiana. Like the Caribbean Creoles, the Acadian ancestors were one of the first groups of New World settlers to develop an American identity, entirely separable from that of the old country. For Acadians, a common origin in France, the common frontier experience, common sufferings at the hands of would-be aristocratic French governors, and the common struggle against the English invaders—all resulted in a powerful sense of unity and group loyalty, the emotional core of Acadian identity.

When the Acadians were exiled from Nova Scotia in 1755, they brought into exile with them a strong and tenacious sense of themselves. Those who resettled in Louisiana between 1765 and 1785 had the clear intention of reestablishing their shattered society in south Louisiana. Even those who had been repatriated to France volunteered to the king of Spain to help settle his newly acquired colony.

The descendants of slaves brought from Africa to work on the plantations, primarily along the Mississippi River and bayous like the Teche and the Vermilion, were also creolized and affected by the Louisiana melting pot. They learned to speak the French language of their masters, overseers, and neighbors and eventually blended this new language with their own native languages to produce a grammatically distinct language called Creole. They, in turn, interacted with their neighbors and contributed new ways of cooking, dancing, and singing to the Louisiana cultural mix. They adopted the Christian religion of the Europeans but adapted it to fit their own sense of spirituality.

The Institutions of Nineteenth-Century Cajun Society

Acadians were not hostile to strangers; early nineteenth-century travelers who visited Cajun homes consistently praised Acadian hospitality. But though the outsider was welcome, materialistic values, strange customs, competitiveness, and a preoccupation with business, were not, at least among the poorer classes. Indeed, most Acadian yeomen and *petits habitants* flatly rejected American ideals, preferring instead their ancestors' precapitalistic values and folkways. This value system is vividly reflected in all aspects of traditional Acadian life. In agriculture, for example, Alcée Fortier, prominent turn-of-the-century Louisiana historian, noted that postbellum Cajuns were "laborious, but they appear to be satisfied, if by cultivating their patch of ground with their sons, they manage to live with a little comfort." The 1850 agricultural census indicates that although the typical *petit habitant* was capable of tilling fifteen acres of land, most farmers cultivated between four and twelve acres, depending upon the needs of their families and the number of sons in the family. Of the ninety Cajun farms listed in the 1850 agricultural census of Terrebonne Parish, only twenty-three boasted more than fifteen cultivated acres.

Occupations

Such small-scale farming obligated the Acadian farmer to engage in seasonal occupations to support his family. Plowing, planting, hoeing, mending of fences, branding of calves, and seasonal relocation of his herd (which usually grazed on public lands throughout the cooler portion of the year) to summer pasturage, filled the farmer's spring and early summer days. The comparatively inactive summer and early fall growing season provided the *petit habitant* with the opportunity to undertake extended hunting and fishing expeditions. These forays, which occasionally ranged as far as the central Atchafalaya Basin and the Gulf Coast and could last as long as two weeks, furnished Cajun families with quantities of fresh meat. This minimized the need to slaughter domestic livestock, which in the prairie parishes ranged without supervision on unclaimed prairie lands during the sultry summer months when fresh and even salted meat spoiled quickly.

Cool weather signaled the herd's return to winter pasturage, usually in wooded areas, as well as the beginning of the harvest season. The harvest on the Acadian frontier was a communal undertaking in which all members of the household, as well as large numbers of male and female *ramasseurs* (gatherers) participated. The fruits of each field were gathered in turn, and workers frequently labored by moonlight to pick every boll of cotton. Despite the long hours, the *ramasserie,* or communal harvest, took on a festive atmosphere. One observer noted that the workers, who were provided large quantities of *gateaux de sirop,* coffee, and whiskey by the host family, punctuated the monotony of cotton-picking with shouts of joy, songs, and animated talk.

The *ramasserie* was a serious undertaking calling for long work days, for the corn, Irish potatoes, sweet potatoes, peas, beans, pumpkins, okra, and rice produced on the small farms constituted the farmers' main source of sustenance in the upcoming year. Products of the family farm were supplemented by home-grown fruit, wild game, and domestic livestock. Hogs in the bayou and river parishes, as well as beef cattle in the prairie parishes, served as the *petits habitants'* principal source of meat. Travelers' accounts, however, indicate that fresh beef and pork, as well as old and unproductive hens and roosters, appeared on the dinner table far less frequently than did eggs, salt pork, and wild game.

Clothing

Acadian adaptability and reliance upon locally produced materials were also exemplified in their clothing. In Acadian households on both sides of the Atchafalaya, women and children went into the fields to gather yellow cotton, produced in small quantities on the family farm. Following the harvest, cotton seeds were removed from the lint either by hand cards or with primitive, pre-Whitney cotton gins that closely resembled the wringer mechanisms on early washing machines. Assisted by their daughters, women then spun cotton fibers into thread which was ultimately woven into the coarse cloth called cottonade on the family loom. In some areas, particularly the prairie region, small quantities of cotton fiber were carded and combined with wool to make a heavyweight winter cloth called *jeture de laine.* Summer and winter fabrics were then bleached white or dyed indigo blue, cochineal red, walnut brown, or black with natural dyes, either produced on the family *habitation* or gathered in the neighboring woods. The fabrics were then fashioned into clothing. This tradition is now practiced as an avocation by very few. Woven cotton is no longer the principal source for clothing material. Cajuns, like most Americans, have ready access to department stores.

Clothing styles remained remarkably constant among *petits habitants* throughout the nineteenth century. At the start of the century, the typical man's outfit consisted of knee-length pants, called *braguettes,*

Spinning and Weaving,
Meaux, 1978 (Photo by
Philip Gould)

cottonade shirts and jackets, and *capots,* heavy outer coats with long
tails worn on formal occasions. Headgear consisted of hand-woven
palmetto hats. With the exception of men's pants, which became
ankle-length garments by the 1860s, this outfit served as the basic
male costume throughout the antebellum and Civil War years. Only
with the coming of the railroad in the 1880s and the simultaneous
introduction of large, affordable quantities of manufactured cloth, did

The Miller sisters sewing
a quilt, Arnaudville, 1979
(Photo by Ginette Vachon)

cottonade garments gradually cease to be worn, at least in the portion of Acadiana west of the Atchafalaya.

Like its male counterpart, female costume changed little during the early nineteenth century. This distinctive mode of dress is described in great detail by the so-called Anonymous Breaux Manuscript (attributed to Chief Justice Joseph A. Breaux):

The women used to be dressed in very bright materials, with varied and often clashing hues. The skirts were made of woolen cloth with red, yellow, violet, and green stripes; woolen or cotton stockings were grey or white. A corset [the upper portion of the dress] was made with material different from that of the skirt. This garment allowed the real corset, which was usually dyed red, to be seen above the belt. This outfit was complemented by either wide-striped, and brilliantly colored kerchiefs, or, more commonly, *garde-soleil*, cotton sun bonnets with a *barbe*, or shoulder-length sunshade.

In addition to their own clothes, Acadian women made clothing for their children. Before the Civil War, children of both sexes wore a dress with a catch at the back. Boys younger than six or seven wore neither breeches nor trousers. Children were also not permitted to wear moccasins or *cantiers* until the age of ten or twelve.

All the materials used in the domestic manufacture of clothing, except for small quantities of calico, were the product of home industries. Acadian home manufactures, however, were not confined to clothing. Acadian women also produced fine mosquito netting, cotton sheets, cotton blankets, cotton and wool quilts, and cotton bed shirts.

Footwear was also produced at home with domestically grown materials. Along Bayou Lafourche, Acadians wore *sabots* (wooden shoes) until the Civil War. Acadian women of the river and prairie wore cowhide and deerskin moccasins, while men wore *cantiers*, moccasins with knee-length leather leggings. This footwear persisted in use among poorer Cajuns until the late nineteenth century. In more affluent circles, Acadian women used cash from the sale of eggs and other barnyard products to buy shoes brought from the East or imported from England and France. Shoes were considered a luxury and, except for church and formal occasions, such as weddings and funerals, Acadians went barefoot. According to one observer, Acadian girls going to church, or to a ball, would often carry their shoes in hand, to be worn only when they reached their destination. At home the shoes were carefully hung from the ceiling.

The reverence with which Cajun women cared for their shoes also extended to their best dress. According to Alexandre Barde, a mid-nineteenth-century writer, Acadian women kept in the family armoire a special handmade dress, mantilla, gloves, and whatever jewelry they might own for social gatherings, particularly *bals de maison*.

Tools and Implements

Though the fabrication and care of clothing and shoes fell clearly within the female sphere of activities, construction of implements, wagons, furniture, and homes lay decidedly within the male domain. Throughout the antebellum period, Cajun farmers relied exclusively upon homemade agricultural implements, particularly ox-drawn wooden plows and harrows. Also made by *petits habitants* were ox-carts for transporting hay, corn, and cotton. Though the men traveled on horseback, Acadian women used horse-drawn *calèches*, gigs whose frames, body, wheels, axles, leather harness, tracings, and shock absorbers, even the feather cushions, were all produced by hand on Cajun *habitations*. Home-grown products also figured large in the construction of Acadian homes, barns, furniture, and fences. Houses were put up in a day or two by groups of neighbors who received no compensation other than food, drink, and good cheer.

Social Gatherings

The group cohesiveness seen in Acadian house raisings also typified other Cajun social institutions, such as *boucheries* and *bals de maison*. By regularly bringing together isolated frontier families for practical purposes or for entertainment, social events served to reinforce the social and cultural bonds made tenuous by distance and lack of communication. Such reinforcement offset the tendency towards factionalization, often manifested in arguments and fist-fights, particularly on Election Day and Mardi Gras.

Meals

Not all socializing related to work. Meals, for example, have long been pivotal in Cajun and Creole society, achieving an importance far beyond simple nutrition. Cooking is a highly cultivated art. It is often said of the Louisiana French that they do not eat to live, but live to eat. Weather and season are two of the factors that determine what kind of social event meals will be. There are outdoor crawfish, crab, and shrimp boils in the spring and summer, and indoor gumbos in winter. Generally, women cook in the kitchen and men cook outdoors. There are cases when men invade the kitchen, but only rarely do women cook outdoors.

Blessed with such a broad variety of foods, the Acadian cook historically had little need for store-bought products. Excepting small quantities of flour, which could not be produced locally, *cuisinières* relied exclusively upon home-grown vegetables. The dishes they prepared were remarkably similar to those eaten by poor whites throughout the Deep South. In his travelogues, Frederick Law Olmsted, the famous New York landscape architect who toured Louisiana twice in the 1850s, recalled meals served to him by an Acadian family in St. Landry Parish:

Upon the supper-table we found two washbowls, one filled with milk, the other for molasses. We asked for water, which was given us in a battered tin cup. The dishes, besides the bacon and bread, were fried eggs and sweet potatoes. The bowl of molasses stood in the center of the table, and we were pressed to partake of it, as the family did, by dipping in it bits of bread. But how it was expected to be used at breakfast, when we had bacon and potatoes, with spoons, but no bread, I cannot imagine.

Though milk and bread were delicacies reserved for celebrations and special guests, meals were often rather mundane gastronomical experiences, noteworthy only for their monotonous lack of variety. Cornbread, boiled Irish potatoes, baked sweet potatoes, fresh peas or beans, and meat (fresh in winter and salted during summer) or wild game were the mainstays of the nineteenth-century Acadian diet. The meat of semi-wild, grass-fed longhorn cattle, wild game, and old chickens was invariably tough and thus required lengthy cooking to become palatably tender. Salted meat required extended boiling, usually with Irish potatoes, to reduce the high levels of salt.

An extensive use of boiling in the preparation of food, a legacy of colonial Acadian cuisine, reflects an adaptation of traditional French and Acadian dishes to Louisiana products—hence the appearance of roux-based stews, gumbos, and gravies. Boiling water was also used to prepare small quantities of home-grown providence rice for jambalaya, corn soup (a dish quite similar to traditional Acadian *fricot*), and for crawfish, which were harvested in the *marais*, low lying wetlands, for use on meatless Lenten days. Also boiled, usually in gumbos, were saltwater shellfish caught on coastal hunting and fishing forays by Acadian farmers from the lower prairies and the Lafourche area. Finally, although not mentioned in antebellum travel accounts, *boudin* (a type of homemade sausage) and hogshead cheese undoubtedly played minor roles in traditional Cajun cuisine and were probably produced only during winter *boucheries* (see below). Like other products of the early Cajun kitchen, these delicacies were cooked in boiling water. Boiling techniques were dictated not only by the toughness of locally produced meats, agricultural produce, and game, but also by the available cooking technology. Lacking the cash to buy Dutch ovens, the overwhelming majority of Cajun cooks prepared meals in kettles suspended above the hearth. Even frying pans were scarce in mid-nineteenth-century Acadian homes and appear to have been used primarily to cook *couche-couche* (fried corn meal) and to bake cornbread.

In addition to the meal, cooking itself has become a social event. Cooking is considered a performance, and invited guests often gather around the kitchen stove or around the barbecue pit (more recently, the butane grill burner) to observe the cooking and comment on it. Participants can also be pressed into service by the head cook to cut onions, wash crawfish and so on. All the while, the cooperative and performance aspects of cooking provide an opportunity for exchanging news, discussing issues of mutual interest, telling jokes, and singing songs. Large indoor or outdoor affairs are frequently accompanied by informal performances of music and stories.

Meals, like *coups de main* and other cooperative social functions, often involve a circle of participants who exchange invitations. Sometimes these circles are large enough to require eating in shifts. In this case, tables are sometimes grouped by sex. Women eat together and men eat together, giving each group a chance to engage in conversation that may be uninteresting to the opposite sex or outright inappropriate to a mixed group.

Boucheries

Like the *cuisine*, the *boucherie*, or rural butchery, served a dual role within Acadian society. Sponsorship of butchery was on a rotating basis and all members of the Acadian community within a small geographic area participated. In addition to providing an efficient way of distributing fresh meat to participating families, *boucheries* also were an important part of the social life of many regions, providing a chance for friends and relatives to get together on a regular basis. While the people worked together, they also visited and talked. They found out who was doing what, who was seeing whom, who was hosting a house dance that weekend, who was ill and who had recovered, who needed help and who could give it, who was born and who had died. Laughing and gossiping, they also reinforced their sense of community as they slaughtered the animal, and cut, cleaned, and divided the meat. They also made sausages and other by-products. Nothing was wasted. *Gratons* or cracklings were made of the skin. The internal organs were used in the sausages and *boudin* or cooked in a *sauce piquante de débris* or entrail stew. The intestines were cleaned and used for sausage casings. Meat was carefully removed from the head and congealed for *fromage de tête de cochon* (hogshead cheese). Brains were cooked in a pungent brown sauce. As in other frugal societies, it was said that the only thing lost in a pig was the squeal.

Boucheries also nurtured a sense of community in the sense that the reciprocal system on which they were based created an interdependence between members of a community that paralleled and underscored their other social ties. *Boucheries* depended on members of the cooperative taking turns providing a pig, calf, or cow, according to the nature of the agreement. Sometimes animals were slaughtered collectively, with at least one representative of each family present to help. Other times, one family's share in the cooperative was the work of slaughtering and preparing the meat for members of the other families to pick up on a regular basis. Since fresh meat usually could be preserved only a few days, many *boucheries* operated on a weekly basis. The size of the cooperative was limited to the number that could be adequately served by the animals involved. *Boucheries de grosses bêtes* (beef cooperatives) had more available meat than *boucheries de petites bêtes* (usually pork and sheep cooperatives) and thus involved more families.

In any case, the society depended on faithful participation in the system for a break in the chain could sow mistrust throughout the entire system. In times of trouble, of course, the cooperative covered for the ailing or the distressed. But able members were expected to carry their full load. This interdependence underscored the sense of common identity in many communities.

Today *boucheries* are rare, but they have not entirely disappeared from Cajun folklife. The advent of refrigeration and supermarkets has eliminated the need, but not the desire to gather. A few families still hold *boucheries* for the fun of it, and a few local festivals feature *boucheries* as a folk craft.

Bals de Maison and Salles de danse

Rural settlers regularly held neighborhood folk dances, with neighbors taking turns sponsoring the gatherings. The importance of these dances in the social life of the average Acadian can hardly be underestimated. Invitations were often issued on an individual basis. According to custom, a youth on his pony would take a small wand and tie to its top end a red or white flag. He then rode two or three miles up and down the bayou or road from the house where the ball was intended. On returning, he tied the wand above the gate to inform one and all that "this was the place." All neighboring settlers were welcome and the turnout was inevitably heavy. The participants, clad in their finest attire, usually maintained their best behavior.

The main purpose of the *bals de maison* was, of course, entertainment, but dances also gave opportunities for regularly using (and thus preserving) traditional Acadian music, cuisine, dances, and language. Something of the importance of the *bal* in the life of a typical Acadian girl can be found in a description drawn from the diary of a young Acadian lady in the 1890s by Lauren Post:

Marie Schexnaidre lived in Martin Duralde vacherie in Acadia Parish, just north of Rayne. She lived at a time when the old features of Acadian life were still in vogue, but when new features were coming in. . . . She wrote, "I attended a ball." Then she proceeded to list 122 of them, giving dates, places (by the name of the owner of home or hall), and the occasion for the special dances. Most of them were week-end dances, but there were the usual holiday dances for Mardi Gras, Easter, and other such occasions. Special dances were the wedding balls which usually came in the fall of the year. For some of these she was maid of honor. Further along—"I danced with"—and she listed 187 men and boys. Apparently she names a man only when she danced with him for the first time.

For a *bal* families cleared the furniture from the largest room in the house. Even after public dance halls sprang up, some families continued to host *bals de maison*. Because attendance at house dances was usually by invitation, these tended to be somewhat safer than dances at the public halls, but occasionally house dances were also broken up by invading hoodlums and competing suitors as well. Musicians and dancers who were not ready for public performance first honed their skills at these *bals de maison*.

Alcée Fortier described an Acadian *bal* of the 1880s. A planter friend took Fortier to the country. They arrived at 8 p.m. at a large house with galleries all around. People were already dancing to the music of three fiddlers when the two arrived. No admission fee was charged them, and this amazed Fortier. He was informed that only decently dressed, white people could get in free, but those admitted were expected to buy drinks from the proprietor: beer, lemonade, or coffee. At midnight, a free supper was served in traditional Creole fashion. It was a chicken gumbo with rice, the popular Creole dish. To Fortier, the men seemed ill at ease but the women caught his eye. They were elegant, well dressed, and exceedingly handsome with large, soft black eyes and black hair. French was spoken by all but occasional English was heard.

"La cage aux chiens," the young men's section of a traditional dance hall, near Crowley, 1938 (Photo by Russell Lee, Farm Securities Administration collection, Library of Congress)

Fortier got to see the *parc aux petits*, where a number of children were sleeping in a bed. This was a space set aside in the house where children were "put down" for the evening. A gambling room also attracted his attention, where a dozen men—for token amounts of money—were playing cards. Out in the back by a barn, six men were gambling seriously by candlelight. These were the black sheep of the group.

By 1 a.m., the two gentlemen visitors had had enough, but the dance went on until 4 or 5 in the morning. The musicians played until the end, or at least stayed on, since they announced the end of the dance by firing a pistol in the air several times and crying out, "Le bal est fini!"

The importance of the *bal* to Acadians may be appreciated by noting that even as they were suffering the pain of exile and abject poverty, the Acadians who arrived in Saint Domingue in 1764 organized a dance immediately after a communal wedding and baptism blessing ceremony. An early nineteenth-century travelogue describes the Cajuns similarly: "They all danced to a fast step, old and young alike."

Late in the nineteenth century, the traditional *bal* began to move from the house into the public dance hall. In addition to being a place for the community to meet, dance halls provided a somewhat more open site for courtship. Young girls and boys began to view one another as young adults when they began attending dances, usually under the supervision of their parents, grandparents, or older siblings. In some public dance halls, young boys were not allowed to roam freely. They were sometimes required to remain in a separate place, called *la cage aux chiens* (the dog cage), unless they were actually dancing or arranging for a later dance. As often in places where courtship is at stake, dance halls tended to become the scene of fights and cruel practical jokes. Many dance hall owners were forced to hire constables or special watchmen to keep the peace.

Veillées

On a smaller scale than the *bal*, another important social gathering was the traditional *veillée*, where families and friends got together for a visit in the evening. These visits usually occurred after supper and often included coffee, dessert, and lots of talk. Storytelling was a popular form of entertainment at these *veillées*. Radio and later television transformed the pattern of family hospitality, but did not entirely eliminate the *veillées*, replacing the storytelling and singers, but not the visits.

Traditionally, *veillées* were held in the idle winter months. Hosts and visitors divided into groups by sex and age. While men carved wooden utensils, repaired their farm tools, and made baskets, women spun thread, mended clothing, and cared for the children who clustered around them. Though the conversation was inevitably dominated by males, the usual topic of conversation was not politics or agriculture, but folktales. As the fireplace cast flickering shadows across the one-room *cabane*, fathers recounted miraculous cures by local *traiteurs* (folk faith healers), or personal encounters with *sabbats* and *feu-follets* (witches and will-o'-the-wisps). After a few fairy tales or animal tales, the children were sent to bed and conversation continued in a more adult vein with jokes and tall tales.

"Coup de main," cooperative haybailing, near Scott, 1977 (Photo by Ginette Vachon)

Veillées mainly relieved the monotony of frontier life during the idle and dreary winter months, which were punctuated only by Christmas, New Year's Day, and Mardi Gras celebrations. But *veillées* also served as a means of preserving Acadian folkways. Folk beliefs and superstitions were more than just a conspicuous part of Cajun oral tradition; they were integral to everyday Acadian life. Most *petits habitants* firmly believed in faith healing. Poor crops or livestock epidemics, for instance, were typically attributed to a bad spell. Omens foretold good or ill fortune, while phases of the moon dictated the proper time for cutting hair and planting.

Coups de Main

A cooperative working effort called the *coup de main* existed to aid those in need of help. It was something like assistance insurance. If someone was too ill to pick his cotton or corn one year, neighbors and family gathered at the house for a *ramasserie*, usually harvesting the entire field in a single day. If someone needed a new well or a new wing on the barn, folks gathered and pitched in. The beneficiary would later do the same for someone else. These *coups de main* (literally, "strokes of the hand") helped strengthen the social fabric by creating and perpetuating mutual interdependence. Today, social security, health insurance, worker's compensation, and the general trappings of a money-based economy have rendered *coups de main* increasingly obsolete, although they survive in diminished form as an important element of rural social structure. Someone who is adding a wing onto the house can expect help from a circle of friends and family. When someone else in the circle needs to build a boat shed, he too can expect the favor will be reciprocated. A strong code of honor is involved in these cooperative efforts. Someone who is asked to participate in a *coup de main* will usually arrange to go, even at great inconvenience, in order to preserve his or her place in the social fabric.

Weddings

Many of the marriage customs of the Cajuns are shared with other peasant peoples of European origin. The earliest Cajun weddings sometimes took place without benefit of clergy. A ceremony in which the newlyweds jumped over a broomstick is said to have cemented the alliance.

By the late nineteenth century, however, the traditional Cajun wedding was often a large affair that drew two extended families together in a religious ritual that was usually accompanied by music. Though honeymoon trips are a relatively recent development, wedding receptions and dances are well rooted in Cajun cultural history. Wedding receptions were usually stocked with homemade cakes and other food. Traditional wedding dances are still popular and surrounded by a variety of traditions. Prominent among these is the wedding march in which the bride and groom walk around the dance floor to the tune of the traditional *marche des mariés*, with their parents, grandparents, godparents, brothers and sisters, and aunts and uncles following in a train of pairs. Afterwards, the newlyweds dance a waltz and invite the party to join them, which officially launches the wedding dance.

Other traditions associated with weddings include requiring older unmarried siblings to dance barefoot, often in a tub, at the reception or wedding dance. This may be to remind them of the poverty awaiting them in old age if they do not begin families of their own.

Guests contribute to the new household by pinning money to the bride's veil in exchange for a dance with her or a kiss. Before the wedding dance is over, the bride will often be wearing a headdress of money. Today, wedding guests have extended this practice to the groom as well, covering his suit jacket with bills.

Funerals

Burial customs often involved elaborate rituals. The coffin was shrouded in black if the deceased had been old, but white was used for the young. Two candles illuminated the body, which was always placed with its feet towards the door. Clocks were stopped at the time of death and no work would be done in the house during the wake, which was traditionally held in the home of the deceased. The body was dressed and laid out in one room of the house. Friends paid their respects to the family and then met in the other rooms to talk about the affairs of life. Joke-telling sessions invariably occurred in one of the back rooms during these otherwise somber wakes. The family of the deceased was expected to feed the mourners, but it was customary for visitors to bring a little something to contribute to the pot.

When the wake ended and people left the house for the funeral, someone was always left behind, for custom demanded that the house be occupied until the body was safely buried. Along the route to the cemetery, people would close doors, gates, and shutters, allowing no entry to wandering spirits. Vehicles stopped as the body passed, out of respect mainly, but perhaps also in fear of wandering spirits.

Even when funeral homes began to displace private homes as the setting for a wake, many folk practices endured. A kitchen is a basic requirement in south Louisiana funeral homes, and storytelling sessions continue to thrive in the corners of the lounges and waiting rooms. Funeral processions still stop traffic, even in urban settings such as Lafayette and Lake Charles. Burials are still followed by communal meals at the home of the family.

Occupational Folklife

Occupational activities and the supporting crafts that were practiced by earlier generations are now often called ethnic or occupational folklife. Among nineteenth-century Cajuns, the most important occupations were farming, ranching, fishing, hunting, and trapping.

Examples of support crafts included boat building, blacksmithing, and basket making.

Farming

The French settlers who arrived in Acadia were above all farmers, so they set about doing the kind of work they knew. Very quickly they realized that they would need help to discover what would grow best in the unfamiliar land and climate. Native American tribes like the Micmac and Souriquois showed the Acadians how to grow corn and potatoes and other indigenous crops. They also learned what native wild foods, like mushrooms and berries, were edible. Before long the Acadians developed prosperous farms. Within a few generations, when there began to be a shortage of cleared farm land, they developed a remarkable system of dikes to reclaim low lands along the coast. After the exile, they discovered that many of the agricultural techniques and products they had developed in Acadia would not work in subtropical Louisiana. Wheat, for example, rotted soon after sprouting in the hot, humid Louisiana climate. Once again they learned from their neighbors. Local tribes like the Chitimacha and Houma taught them about native edible foods and how to cultivate yams, melons, squash, and pumpkins. They learned from the French and black Creoles to grow cotton, sugarcane, and okra. From Anglo-Americans they eventually learned to grow rice and soybeans. Most Cajuns cultivated small self-sufficient farms growing a wide variety of vegetables and livestock. They ate what they produced, yet established and maintained family and neighborhood cooperatives to assure a safety net in case of a bad season. Bartering was the common way to redistribute surplus food produced by a family. An overabundance of potatoes might be traded for cane syrup or some other commodity. Nothing went to waste. Corn, for example, was cooked fresh, ground into corn meal, and dried as grain for the cows, horses, and mules. Corn shucks were fed to the cows and the corncobs were burned to increase the heat of fires under cooking kettles. Cash crops, such as cotton, were also cultivated to produce the money necessary to buy commodities such as coffee, flour, salt, and tobacco, as well as fabrics and farm implements.

Many Cajuns and Creoles still make their living on the farm. There are also many who have turned to more commercial or industrial occupations, but who preserve an attachment to the land by growing a garden in their backyards or on family land where they spend their weekends and free afternoons. Many of these Cajuns cultivate extended plots that are more than mere gardens and produce much more than their families can consume. They distribute the overflow to their extended families and friends, reducing their dependence on store-bought foods.

Many farmers once believed in the ability to predict the weather by observing natural signs. Some of these signs, however, have no obvious connection with the predicted weather. For example, when the tips of a crescent moon point upward, it is supposed to be dry for a week. A halo of light around a full moon supposedly means clear weather for as many days as there are stars visible inside the ring. Other signs have relatively plausible connections to the weather. The flocking of blackbirds, for example, is considered a sign of a coming cold snap. If cows lie down under a threatening sky, this is a sign that it will rain heavily. Conversely, if they remain standing, this is a sign of no rain, or only a light shower.

Ranching

Cajuns and black Creoles were among the first cowboys in America, participating in some of the earliest cattle drives in this country. Those who settled the southwestern prairies of Louisiana had many things in common with the great American West. They became excellent riders and ropers, doggers and drivers. Towns on the southwestern prairies show the traces of their cattle-town origins. Older store fronts look like the facades on a western movie set. In some towns, concrete sidewalks have only recently replaced the wooden plank ones called *banquettes*. Hitching posts can still be seen along the main streets in the older parts of many of these towns. Horses and horsemanship still command great respect, and there are still craftsmen like Boo LeDoux and Noah Comeaux who make saddles, *cabresses* (horsehair ropes), and other western tack. Younger artisans are now making a point of learning these skills from older masters. Whipmaker Blue Andrus has passed on his craft to several apprentices such as Linda Stelly.

Neighborhood horse shows provide an outlet for demonstrating skills once essential to make a living out on the range. Times change, and traditions adapt to them. Trail rides still traverse the prairies. Now trail riders must first secure a permit from the local sheriff. The

Driving herds to new pasture, near Forked Island, 1978 (Photo by Philip Gould)

sheriff and state police, on the other hand, still maintain an active mounted posse and can arrange to escort such events on horseback as well as pursue suspects into the deep woods. There are even still a few ranchers who let their cattle graze freely, especially in the marshlands along the coast, and round them up annually to count, brand, and sell them.

Fishing

Many settlers supplemented their food supply by fishing. Eventually some came to choose this as their principal occupation. A few sailors and fishermen came to Acadia from Brittany, Normandy, and the area around La Rochelle in France. It was likely they who led the way. Soon, a number of the Acadians developed "sea legs" of their own and fished for cod, haddock, lobster, clams, and scallops in the cold Atlantic along the coast of Canada. When they resettled in Louisiana, however, the Acadians had to learn new fishing techniques appropriate for catching the speckled trout, redfish, shrimp, crab,

Patrick Mire handfishing
in Bayou Mallet, 1988
(Photo by Jerry Devillier)

and oysters in the warm coastal waters of the Gulf of Mexico. Freshwater seafood also abounded in Louisiana: bass, perch, catfish, and crawfish. What began as a way to supplement farming developed for many into an occupation or at least an important avocation.

It has been said that the symbol of the successful Cajun is the two-trailer family—one for the horse and the other for the boat. Commercial fishermen catching nongame fish share the Atchafalaya Basin and the lakes and bayous of south Louisiana with sports anglers, fishing for *patassa* (bream or sunperch), *sacalait* (crappie or white perch), *perche* (bass), and other game fish. Some fish with wire loops for *poisson armé* (alligator gar). Some run trot lines to catch *barbue* (channel catfish), *machouaron* (yellow catfish), and *goujon* (spotted catfish). In the brackish lakes along the coast and in the bays and the Gulf, commercial and sports fishermen catch fish like red-fish, speckled trout, catfish, snapper, and flounder.

The French names of most saltwater fish are generally less used than those of the freshwater and coastal fish, which may indicate that deep sea fishing in the Gulf is a relatively recent development. Commercial trawlers are regularly joined in the bays and inland

Crawfishing in Atchafalya Basin, near Bayou Benoit, 1978 (Photo by Ginette Vachon)

waters by smaller private boats catching shrimp and crabs for family, friends, and freezer. Individuals gather oysters in public beds along with oystermen working to supply restaurants and stores. In the bayous and rice canals, some fishermen preserve an ancient art, catching large catfish and turtles by hand in underwater holes along the banks. At night froggers work the banks of bayous, ponds, and drainage ditches, catching bullfrogs by hand and with mechanical gigs. In the spring, entire families may often be seen crawfishing in borrow pits (large ditches along levees and elevated highways), in flooded rice ponds, and in swampy areas everywhere in south Louisiana.

Hunting

In their Canadian homeland, Acadians hunted to supplement their supply of fresh meat. They had learned from Native Americans to hunt a variety of game, including turkey, pheasant, moose, deer, and elk. In Louisiana, the Cajuns had to learn new hunting techniques for the subtropics. Because of present-day laws banning commercial hunting, this activity has remained a recreation, but an intensely popular one. Louisiana is located at the southern end of one of the world's major flyways providing an abundance of migratory birds like dove, woodcock, and a wide variety of ducks and geese. There is also an ample supply of native small game like quail, rabbit, and squirrel. For those interested in larger game, there is primarily deer. Bears, once abundant, still survive in diminished numbers in the woods and the basin.

A wide range of folk practice is associated with hunting—how to build blinds, how to call game, how to handle, call and drive packs of hunting dogs, and how to make decoys. People who hunt together over a long period of time develop a language all their own, with colorful references to game and activities, as well as an active stock of stories about great hunts and poor hunts, narrow escapes, and techniques for escaping from town, wife, or boss. For example, there is the tall tale about the hunter who finds that he has gone to the woods with only one bullet. By using it carefully and with more than a little luck, he is able to bring home a deer, a pot of honey, a rabbit, six quail and a dozen fish.

Trapping

America's most extensive wetlands lie in coastal *Louisiane*. Back-water swamps and thousands of miles of treeless marshes provide habitat for waterfowl. After 1918, commercial duck hunting was banned, but widespread local fur trapping began. In the 1910s extensive alligator hunting allowed huge increases in *rat musqué* populations. Muskrat "eatouts" (overgrazing) promoted marsh erosion. At first trapped mainly to reduce their numbers, cheap Louisiana muskrat pelts hastened New York's capture of America's fur industry away from St. Louis, and spurred the rage for muskrat and raccoon coats that typified the Roaring Twenties. By the mid-twenties one thousand dealers bought furs from twenty thousand trappers. Thousands of miles of *tranasses* (ditches) dug by hand gave access to trapping grounds. Quick fortunes led to armed clashes, as in the St. Bernard-Plaquemines Trappers' War of 1926. Louisiana began its long reign as America's number one fur producer. A pest until techniques developed to treat its fur was the nutria, introduced from

Trapper with nutria pelts
(Photo by Brad Bigley)

South America in the 1930s. By the 1960s the nutria had replaced the smaller muskrat as Louisiana's most valuable fur resource.

Boat Building

Boats are a necessary part of travel in the swamps and bayous. Consequently, boat building has been a part of life for the wetlands Cajuns. They adapted boat styles from their native France and Acadia, and learned new techniques for making a wide variety of boats. These ranged from the *pirogues* and *bateaux* needed to travel in the shallow waters of the swamps, to the larger skiffs used to navigate the sometimes turbulent coastal waters along the Gulf of Mexico, to the still-larger shrimp boats needed to go out into the Gulf. Special boats were developed for certain occupations. Moss-picking boats, oystering boats, and Lafitte shrimping and fishing skiffs were adapted to their respective duties. Some families maintained boats for travel as well as work boats. Some boats were poled, others were paddled. Still

Moss picker (Photo by
Barry Ancelet)

others were propelled by sail or pulled by haulers on the banks of the
interior waterways. Later, motorized one-cylinder "joe boats" or
luggers were designed to withstand the strain of thrashing through
the hyacinths that began to clog the freshwater swamps and the
grasses of the saltwater marshes. With the development of shipping
and especially the offshore oil industry, boatbuilding became big
business. Companies began manufacturing tugboats and tankers, as
well as oil-drilling platforms.

Cypress was once plentiful and made excellent boat-building
material because it retains its natural oils and resists rotting and
termites. As logging diminished the virgin cypress forests, many boat
builders turned to recently developed materials like marine plywood
and later aluminum, steel, and fiberglass. Often, modern materials
are used in designs based on earlier styles; thus one sees the aluminum flat-bottom *bateau* and the fiberglass *pirogue*. Some of these
styles were adapted to accommodate new needs for speed and style
among sports fishermen, like the contemporary Cajun bass boats.

Instrument Making

Just as Cajun and Creole music are the result of the unique blend
of cultural ingredients found in south Louisiana, the instruments
used to produce this music are also the result of an eclectic collection

of influences. Traditional instrumentation in Cajun and Creole bands includes French fiddles, German accordions, Spanish guitars, and a rich array of percussion instruments—triangles, washboards, and spoons—which share European and Afro-Caribbean origins. Although most of these instruments were originally imported from manufactured sources, some were eventually made in Louisiana by craftsmen who acquired these skills from immigrants. This was often the case with fiddle makers. Some skilled craftsmen, particularly accordion makers, were entirely self-taught, simply studying the imported models and learning from their mistakes. Percussion instruments were originally improvised from household materials, like spoons or washboards, and later refined into a form that could be used only as an instrument. When electrical amplification became available, many Cajun bands improvised their own sound systems from radio parts hooked up to a speaker on one end and a crystal microphone on the other, the whole operation being powered, often as not, by the generator of an idling automobile parked outside the building. Perhaps the most popular instrument to come out of this new age was the electric steel guitar, an electrically amplified version of the acoustic dobro guitar.

Fiber Crafts

One of the most important and visible crafts in the Cajun repertoire has been weaving. In the days before manufactured fabrics were generally available, families produced their own. Cajuns learned to grow, harvest, card, spin, and weave cotton in Louisiana, and made their own clothing and other household items like tablecloths, washcloths, rugs, sheets, and blankets. One of the distinctive elements of Acadian weaving tradition involved the use of naturally brown cotton and wool dyed for decorative purposes with natural substances like indigo and berries. In the 1930s, while working for the Louisiana State University extension services, Louise Olivier organized groups of Acadian women to revive traditional skills and market them. This effort developed a group of weavers, some of whom (for example, Gladys Clark of Judice) are still alive and active today. Several other weaver groups remain active in various corners of Acadiana.

The weaving of dried leaves and grasses is also found in Louisiana French tradition. Cajuns learned from their Native American neighbors to make fine hats, fans, and other accessories using dried leaves,

Ferriar Wilbert Lagrange, Grand Coteau, 1977 (Photo by Ginette Vachon)

but this tradition has rapidly eroded in recent years. Elvina Kidder of Arnaudville is one of the last of the Cajun palmetto weavers. Louisiana tribes, such as the Houma and Chitimacha, and later arrivals such as the Coushatta (Koasati), make beautiful baskets, often in the shapes of animals, from dried straw and grasses or pine needles. Ada Thomas, of the Chitimacha tribe, has received a National Heritage Award for her role in preserving her heritage and in inspiring young members of her community to learn this traditional skill.

From Blacksmiths and Farriers to Metalworkers and Mechanics

Although some specialized skills have faded into disuse, there are still a good number of active blacksmiths and farriers. Shoeing horses, for example, remains an active skill, while banding wagon wheels has become extremely rare. Many blacksmiths have expanded their skills and knowledge of metalworking by learning welding. Others, like the Guidrys of Lafayette, produce ornamental and functional metalwork like wrought-iron chairs and barbecue pits. Some who might have been smiths in another time have opened tool shops or sheet metal shops instead. Others have followed the changes in transportation from horse to automobile and have become mechanics. Pierre Montoucet, for example, was a well-known nineteenth-century blacksmith who provided some of the delicate ironwork for the church at Grand Coteau. Pierre's son Jacques was a blacksmith and farrier until he found a set of mechanic's tools in a drainage ditch along Highway 90 (the Old Spanish Trail). Jacques's son Don now owns and operates a successful garage and body shop near that same highway in Scott. Don has also translated his family smithing skills into contemporary terms. He is a skilled welder and iron worker who has fabricated in metal a wide range of things from boats to barns and triangles to trailers. One of Don's sons, Virgil, is also an automobile mechanic trained to service the computerized versions of contemporary vehicles. Another son, Terry, is a machinist, producing precision tools and equipment with metal lathes.

The Transformation of Tradition

Some purists tend to view change as a problem. Yet left to their own, traditional cultures are constantly changing. This is not necessarily a sign of decay, as antiquarians contend. In order to survive and grow in a contemporary context, tradition must shed its dead branches and grow new ones. If tradition is viewed as a process instead of a product, then this necessary change can also be traditional if it conforms to its own rules. Trying to restrict the natural, organic growth of a traditional culture as if real people were forced to inhabit a museum display would only contribute to its demise.

An excellent example is to be found in Louisiana French music and dance. While it is undeniable that some of the traditional dance steps, like reels and quadrilles, contredanses and mazurkas, have been lost in this century, it is also true that new steps have developed within the tradition. These include more individually expressive styles like the Cajun version of the jitterbug and the new Cajun shuffle. Musicians have also adapted to changes, electrifying their music and experimenting with new instrumentation (saxophones and pianos) and new styles (rock and country). In addition to the traditional dance hall and house dance settings, Cajun musicians now also play in the numerous popular festivals of southern Louisiana, in the schools, and on radio and television.

Folklorists who have studied Louisiana French oral tradition lament the loss of long magic tales and animal tales. Yet there is a remarkable persistence of oral tradition among the Cajuns and Creoles despite repeated grim predictions of its imminent disappearance. Storytelling has been described as a dying art in south Louisiana for decades. Yet there is still a tremendous love of talking and storytelling. Stories have not faded from the scene. Instead, oral tradition has transformed to accommodate shorter forms, like jokes and tall tales, which easily fit into the fast pace of modern times.

There is a parallel development in the adaptation of traditional folklife to the contemporary world, including the combination of traditional occupations with modern salaried employment. The schedules of most roughnecks and deck hands (on duty for one or two weeks, then off duty for the same time) make it possible for them to pursue traditional occupations like trapping and fishing. These occupations also have adapted to accommodate modern conveniences.

Moss picking, once an important part–time occupation for many wetlands Cajuns, faded with the loss of the natural resource and changes in technology. Dried moss was replaced by synthetic materials used in stuffing car seats and furniture. Now there is a mild

Recently invented wheel-driven boat designed to gather soft-shelled crawfish, near Krotz Springs, 1984 (Photo by Philip Gould)

resurgence in the tradition as moss is making a comeback from the virus that once threatened it and as catfish and crawfish farmers have found that it makes a perfect breeding nest.

Many crawfishermen now run their traps in boats equipped with special plated wheels mounted on hydraulic lifts which have been designed to operate in the very shallow water of flooded rice ponds. The demand for large crawfish for boiling has resulted in the development of motorized sorting machines. The crawfishing season has also been stretched to begin in November and run until May by the development of ponds based on highly sophisticated scientific research.

Superficial expressions may change but core traditions have a way of enduring.

PART TWO

Social Institutions

CHAPTER 4

Family Organization

Three principal factors combined to shape the traditional Cajun family: cultural history, religion, and adaptation to rural life. The Acadian family is not unique in its basic organization, being much like the families of many other rural ethnic groups in the United States. It *is* distinctive, however, in the quality of its life and its psychological flavor. One must always keep in mind also that Cajun families may be as diverse as those of any other ethnic group. Although basic elements are characteristic, individual families vary greatly in values and organization. The feelings and values that unite Cajun families are subtle and hard to pinpoint objectively, and no attempt to summarize the shared quality of emotional experience will emerge in purely scientific form. Time, too, is a dimension because the traditional Cajun family that existed in the latter part of the eighteenth and in the nineteenth centuries is not identical to the Cajun family of today.

The Central Role of the Wife/Mother

The Acadian mother was the principal means of transmitting and conserving Acadian values and culture. Considering the tiny size of the original Acadian population (fewer than four thousand), the fragmented nature of the immigration, and the enormous number of outsiders who have been assimilated into the Acadian way of life, the ability of the Acadian woman and mother to maintain and preserve the culture must be considered nothing short of miraculous. No sooner had the Acadians arrived in Louisiana, than they were joined by relatively large numbers from other ethnic groups. Creoles, Germans, and Indians were previously established in and around the lands the Acadians colonized. Even before they had settled into their new pattern of life, Anglos, Irish, more Germans, French, West Indian refugees, and other Europeans began to immigrate and settle among them. Wave upon wave of outsiders descended on the Acadian bayous and prairies. Yet, within only a generation or two, most of these outsiders and their descendants had been fully acculturated to Acadian ways. The number of Acadians added to the population through incorporation more than equaled the natural increase of the original exiled population.

The feat of the Acadian woman, supported by her circle of relatives, seems even more miraculous when we consider the fact that the Acadians were generally poorer than the outsiders they assimilated and that rather strong ethnic antagonisms existed.

The Extended Family and the *Joie de Vivre*

How could Acadian women so easily subdue and dominate the culture of so many outsiders? One contributing factor is certainly the intense social interaction that characterizes the extended Acadian family. Whatever else may be said of them, Acadians love large families. They also encouraged much socializing between members of closely related families. Hospitality was raised to a central theme of Acadian life. One could hardly pass the door of an Acadian house without an exchange of greetings and news; the more normal pattern was to be invited inside to chat for a while. Food and drink and repartee played a large role in these informal visits and still do so today. An ambience of vibrant good cheer characterizes Acadian social life. This creates an atmosphere that may be unfamiliar but is highly attractive to many outsiders, particularly those of Anglo-Saxon and Germanic background, where family life may be comparatively rigid and formal, sometimes even austere.

The extended family provides the principal setting for Acadian social life. Large numbers of grandparents, cousins, aunts, and uncles gather regularly. The continual comings and goings within and between extended families exert a profound influence on the individual and on visiting outsiders as well. Whether a suitor for the hand of a daughter or merely a passing stranger, the visitor is impressed—

occasionally overwhelmed—by the amount of talk and informal group pressure that accompanies the day-to-day activity of the traditional Cajun family. Even permission to wed a daughter often depended on the approval of all the adults in the entire extended family. Anyone who attends the *boucherie*, the afternoon *veillée*, the evening *soirée*, the *fais do-do* (the dancehall), the cock fight, the card game, the house raising, or the horse race can sense the widespread social pressure— and the psychological support that accompanies it.

The social atmosphere at such gatherings—a lack of repressive attitudes, the free-wheeling gregariousness, enjoyment of life for its own sake, excited wagering on games, wildly funny stories, social and sexual attractions of dancing, and the continual festive atmosphere— all these contribute to the enjoyment of family life and its fundamental dominance of the lives of individual members. The events at which *joie de vivre* rules provide opportunities for acting out uniquely Acadian performances. Whether a particular activity is overtly oriented towards foods such as the famous *café noir* (drip coffee), gumbo with homemade bread, or crawfish, or whether it centers on an activity such as dancing, horse racing, or even worshiping, Acadian life is invariably family- or kin-oriented.

A principal rule of Acadian life is that no one is left out. This is why small babies are brought to the *fais do-do* rather than being left at home with a baby sitter. Young children dance with elderly adults on the dance floor of bars and restaurants. Every child plays his or her role in the *boucherie* or in the harvesting of crops. This spirit of gregariousness extends to Cajun adults as well, of course, and also to fortunate strangers. So strong is this ethic that Acadian culture assimilates the unwary outsider with considerable ease, almost deliberation, into almost every field of activity and sphere of social interaction. In this lies one of the strengths of Acadian culture. It is a kind of adaptation for survival that has permitted the Acadians to prevail through many a threat to their lives and identities.

The Role of the Male

As in most families of European descent, the male is head of the Acadian household and principal director of its economic and social destiny. This, of course, is the traditional pattern long encouraged by the Catholic church. Among Cajuns, however, the man plays his role in a very special way. Unlike the domineering and rather remote authoritarian father of teutonic culture, the Cajun father interacts intensively with his wife and children. Typically, he shows great compassion for children of all ages. From their earliest years, children are encouraged to participate in all family activities and to play an important role in each. No matter how trivial the actual contributions may be, children are given the impression that their efforts are essential and that they are central to the core of family life.

This is not to suggest, however, that children were kept ignorant of daily reality. For families living at the subsistence level, as most Acadians did in the eighteenth and early nineteenth centuries, children learned early that every hand was important and the skill with which each task was accomplished was critical to the collective well-being. Thus, each of the children of the family was carefully instructed in necessary duties. For most, the work load was heavy, occasionally onerous. It was the father's role to see that work was completed on time. His love for his children did not override his responsibility for enforcing the rules and directing each child's proper behavior. The difficulty of the tasks and the strictness of the father's guidelines were always balanced, however, by the regular return to the *joie de vivre* of the family get-together. Work was hard, but when it was done, everyone could relax and "pass a good time."

Courtship

In Acadian life courtship and marriage were usually a matter for teenagers. Sexual mores were strictly governed by the church law and by mothers. Young girls were almost always escorted to places of courtship, like dance halls, by their parents or at least by an older brother or uncle, who diligently chaperoned the maiden's honor. A young boy with serious intentions had to make official visits to the family home, usually on Sunday afternoon, to negotiate with the young girl's father. Couples were almost never left alone until well into their courtship, and even then only in a quasi-public place like the front porch swing. Marriages were performed according to the rules of the Catholic church. For example, wedding banns, or announcements, had to be published three times before a ceremony was allowed. Much of this has changed, however, and young Cajuns now date just like couples do in most parts of America.

Because kinfolk often lived close together, Acadian families were characterized by frequent marriages between cousins and other relatives. Most early Cajun communities were composed of groups of relatives living on adjacent pieces of property. The density of close relatives grew with the natural increase in population. As a result, it was sometimes difficult for nonrelatives to arrange for appropriate courtships. Marriages were frequently made between cousins of varying degrees. First-cousin marriages were technically forbidden in Louisiana but were sometimes performed anyway; more distant cousins married with no difficulty. Cousin marriage also had the advantage of keeping property within family groupings and sometimes was preferred by parents for this reason. Because there has been a great deal of residential continuity over the generations in most Cajun communities, in small towns a high proportion of residents are related to one another.

The closeness of rural life led to interesting patterns of marriage. For example, it was not uncommon for pairs of siblings from one family to marry those of another family; two brothers often married sisters from the same family. Eligible mates were frequently difficult to find, and it was natural to look first among the members of large families living nearby. Another result of this pattern is the localization of surnames. In any single district of Acadiana, specific surnames (presumably those of the earliest or most prolific settlers) tend to predominate. It is not uncommon for a town to be dominated by fewer than half a dozen family names.

In the rural community, children also tended to marry young. Long ago, a girl who reached the age of twenty without marrying was considered *une vieille fille*—an old maid. Ideally, the newly married couple would set up a household within walking distance of one or both of their parents' houses. All relatives living nearby became part of a support group upon which the young couple could depend for financial help, for labor (as in the *coup de main*), for advice, and for the exchange of tools or food (as with the *boucherie*).

The Role of Religion

The Catholic religion exerted considerable influence on the quality of life within the Acadian family (see also the next chapter). The values of the church shaped and supported the family organization. Church provided another setting for family affairs and gatherings. The yearly round of feast days, fasting days, holy days, and festivals was largely established by the calendar of the church. Many families attended church together and most planned festivals and other church-sponsored events as group projects.

Weddings, christenings, funerals, and feast days all had powerful religious overtones. The parish priest assumed the role of father-figure and adviser in time of need. Work and religion were united through the blessing of the fields, tools, animals, and boats. The spirit of the church entered each home and was apparent in attitudes and interactions between family members. Duties and privileges of husband and wife were sanctioned by the church, and the respect of children for their parents and the responsibility of parents for children were advocated by church doctrine. Of course the church encouraged large families through its restrictions on contraception. This encouragement, which often resulted in many children to help out with the chores, was adaptive in an environment of subsistence farming and hunting. To have as many as a dozen children was not considered unusual in a rural Cajun family. It is, in fact, difficult to find any element of Cajun family life, from the strength of the wife and mother to the lust for the "good life," which was not touched by the church.

The Modern Cajun Household

What aspects of the traditional Acadian family have survived into the 1990s? This is difficult to answer because of the rapid and uneven levels of social change occurring in Acadiana in the past four decades. While some Cajuns, particularly in the more isolated rural communities, retain the traditional family pattern, most Cajuns today have moved towards the standard American model for suburban and rural families.

The principal cause of change in the Acadian family has been acculturation to the dominant American pattern of culture, brought about through a combination of factors. These include the participation of many young Acadian men in the military in two world wars, dramatically improved roads and public transportation, the increased availability and standardization of Louisiana's English-language public education, scholarships and other opportunities for higher education, and the powerful motivation of better economic opportunities available to those who can "defend themselves" in the Anglo-American world. Acadians live under basically the same economic and social pressures as other Americans. In the period between the 1930s, when jobs in the oil industry became available on a large scale, and the 1960s, when the mass media became the dominant force in supplying a unified standard for American culture to Acadian youth, profound changes occurred in Acadian culture and the Cajun family. Nevertheless, the Acadian family still retains much of its distinctive flavor. Traditional values and practices have been modified but have not disappeared.

According to the 1980 census, the typical Acadian household is now only slightly larger than its Louisiana Anglo counterpart. The average household in Anglo-Louisiana has 2.14 people, as compared to 2.94 for the Louisiana French (including urban families). The average Anglo family has 3.28 people, as compared with 3.40 for the French. The percentage of households with six or more persons is 5.35 for the Anglos and 6.67 for the French.

Modern Cajun women have accommodated their lives to modern American culture. While the traditional rural farmwife is still to be found, she is no longer the most common type of Cajun wife. She is rapidly being replaced by the modern working housewife. In 1980, 39.4 percent of Anglo wives were employed (not including farm-employed wives), and 36.2 percent of French wives.

Neither does the Cajun woman speak French for the most part. Informal surveys show that women, far more than their men, now speak English on most if not all occasions. It appears that the Cajun mother has been willing to give up her traditional language in order to provide a better education and life opportunities for her children. Many Cajun men do not live by the same linguistic values. They retain French for communication, particularly in the male-dominated work place and for male amusements as well. This produces the rather ironic situation in which young Cajun men of today learn English at home. Later, when they leave their families and enter the work force, many pick up a French language that they have never before spoken on a regular basis, despite their cultural identity.

Nicknames

When strangers look at the telephone directory for a small town in south Louisiana, they usually notice the preponderance of a handful of last names. What next catches their eye are the nicknames in the listings. Usually given in quotes between first and last names, the nicknames sometimes replace the first name altogether.

The flowery names bestowed on most Cajun children a generation or two ago were invariably shortened in common usage. Elenora became NoNor. Alida or Florida became Da or DaDa. Nor were the boys spared. No Joseph, Jr., for them: you were 'Tit Joe (from *petit*, or little). Justilien becomes 'Tit Yien. And you remain Little Yien, even when you are six feet tall and in your late seventies. Then there are the colors. We have personally known four 'Tit Blacks, three 'Tit Blues, and at least one 'Tit Brown.

Cajun nicknames can follow their owners to other places and into other pursuits. A 1970 *Newsweek* story profiled the leader of New York's "most militant feminist faction," Ti-Grace Atkinson. Ti-Grace, the magazine told us, "is Cajun for 'Little Grace'."

Akin to nicknaming was the custom of like-named siblings, often a mean trick in large Cajun families. An example describes it best: a few years ago the Lafourche *Daily Comet* ran an obituary for eighty-two-year-old Winnie Grabert Breaux. The article listed Winnie's brothers and sisters, living and dead: Wiltz, Wilda, Wenise, Witnese, William, Willie, Wilfred, Wilson, Weldon, Ernest, Norris, Darris, Dave, Inez, and Lena.

CHAPTER 5

Religious Rituals and Festivals

As we have noted, religion has played a powerful role in shaping institutions such as the family. But what *is* religion in a folk society? It is even legitimate to ask which kind of religion exerts more influence on the lives of the average Cajun—the formal church with its clergy and teachers, or the complex system of extra-ecclesiastical and informally transmitted religious beliefs that have remained a basic ingredient of the life of rural people such as the Cajuns?

Folklore is knowledge passed along from one person to another, or from one generation to another, through traditional, nonofficial channels. In this respect, folk religion includes beliefs and practices that are not sanctioned by a church but have become an integral part of the religious lives of a people by custom. This includes such practices as giving gifts on Christmas and New Year's Day, as well as events like the immensely popular Mardi Gras, which occurs on the day before Lent begins. However, less well-known practices are also popular in Acadiana: the making and giving of king's cakes between the beginning of Epiphany and Mardi Gras, the special commemoration celebration of certain saints' feast days, like the making of bread altars for St. Joseph's Day (influenced by the Italian community of New Orleans), or the whitening and decorating of tombs for *La Toussaint,* or All Saints' Day.

Often there is considerable overlap between nature beliefs and folk religion. Even within the Catholic Church, Christmas day was originally determined by the time of the winter solstice, and Easter is still defined as the first Sunday after the first full moon after the spring equinox. It is perhaps a consequence of the ritual importance

Whitewashing the family tombs for La Toussaint, Scott, 1978 (Photo by Philip Gould)

of spring as a period of rebirth that a number of traditional activities take place during this time of year. The huge bonfires that are lighted on the levees of the Mississippi River between New Orleans and Baton Rouge on Christmas Eve are descendants of the bonfires lit by ancient European civilizations, particularly along the Rhine and Seine rivers, to encourage and reinforce the sun at the winter solstice, its "weakest" moment.

Epiphany is announced by the making of king's cakes in which a bean, a symbol of growth and fertility, is hidden. The one who gets the piece with the bean is chosen king for the day. The fertility symbolism is even more overt as a tiny plastic baby is now substituted for the bean in the thousands of commercially baked king cakes consumed before Mardi Gras in the cities of southern Louisiana. Getting the baby in your piece of king cake is now said to obligate you to buy the next king cake from the bakery. (Mardi Gras itself, a complex series of rituals with origins in both classical and medieval societies, is discussed in the next section.)

The relative lack of traditional religious activity during the late spring, summer and fall may reflect the effort needed to plant, maintain and harvest crops. There are, however, a few folk religious practices directly associated with farming and fishing. Each year, priests go out into the fields in places like New Iberia and Jeanerette to bless the sugar cane. In many coastal towns, such as Lafitte, Delcambre, and Morgan City, priests formally bless the shrimping

Blessing the sugar cane crop, 1978 (Photo by Philip Gould)

fleets by saying prayers over them and sprinkling them with holy water. Participants devote considerable effort to decorating the shrimp boats for these occasions.

Also included in folk religion are personal or family rituals, such as the building and maintenance of home altars in Cajun and Creole households. Home altars serve not only as places for prayer but also as shrines to commemorate deceased family members. They are illustrated with holy cards and death announcements, and contain tokens like watches, rings, scapulars, rosaries, and prayer books. These home shrines are often lovingly kept with fresh flowers and other decorations.

Another popular kind of folk religious observance among Cajuns and Creoles alike is lawn statuary. Many Cajun families pay their respects to their patron saint, usually Our Lady of the Assumption, with homemade grottoes or shrines that house statues of the Virgin. Other popular statues include the Sacred Heart of Jesus and Saint Theresa (who is often confused with the Blessed Virgin). Some of

Makeshift grotto (Photo
by Barry Ancelet)

these shrines simply present the statue all alone. In others the statues
nestle in havens such as porches, carports, or under trees. Still other
shrines can be quite remarkable, consisting of complex brick or
cement grottoes and elaborate landscaping, with small ponds and
flowering bushes. Makeshift grottoes are also fashioned from such
things as used bathtubs or oil drums.

Because of the predominance of the Roman Catholic faith among
Cajuns and Creoles, religious rituals surround the major steps in a
person's life, including birth, courtship and marriage, and death.
Children are almost invariably baptized as Catholics within the first
few months of their lives. The business of godfathering and
godmothering is still very important in Cajun country. Almost always
referred to by their French names, even by non-French-speaking
youth, *parrains* and *marraines* are not just spiritual guides and insurance in case of the loss of both parents. They become family. They
enlarge the circle of people who like you "just because." They give

gifts at Christmas and on birthdays. They are also among the ones
children can run to in case of trouble at home. A typical statement
concerning godparents can go something like this: "Well, my dad
can't go fishing this weekend, so my *parrain* is taking me." Consequently, there has long been a great deal of importance given to
choosing these representatives. One commonly held tradition is that
one cannot ask to be made a child's godparent. There may, however,
be a great deal of lobbying and jockeying for position behind the
scenes as soon as a woman becomes pregnant—and sometimes even
before.

Death involves another set of religious rituals. Long ago, most
families held wakes for their dead in the home. Nowadays, most use
funeral homes. Yet there are a few durable traditions no matter where
the body is exposed. Traditionally, wakes can last nonstop through
the night for several days, which requires special arrangements so
that the body is never alone, even in the middle of the night.
Recently, funeral homes have begun closing at 10 p.m. or midnight,
easing the strain on survivors, but upsetting many who are disturbed
that their loved ones are left alone. At intervals during the wake, the
rosary may be recited for the departed. Certain members of the
community, in addition to the priests and members of the lay clergy,
become known as leaders of rosary, primarily for their ability to recite
unwritten prayers that occur between decades and at the beginning
and end of the rosary. Those who are able to perform this ritual in
French are in especially high demand today.

Another aspect of folk religion includes the relationship between
religion and everyday life. This ranges from the belief that the Virgin
will slap children who whistle at the dinner table to doubts concerning the celibacy of the clergy. It includes the belief that it is forbidden
to break ground on Good Friday, and that if one does, one will see
the blood of Jesus Christ. Paradoxically it is also holds that Good
Friday is the best day for planting parsley. This combination of
beliefs has caused many a gardener to come up with a clever plan for
the preparing and planting of a parsley patch. Many Cajun families
still go to church on Palm Sunday to receive blessed palm leaves and
holy water, which they keep in their houses to sprinkle during storms.

Praying is considered an important part of life, and prayer is
thought of as a means of intercession with which one can change the
course of fate. Some persons, not necessarily appointed by the

Mardi Gras participants, Church Point, 1978 (Photo by Ginette Vachon)

church, are thought to have a particularly good relationship with the Deity and/or the saints and are frequently asked by others to help in obtaining favors. These individuals thus become mediators between the Deity and people, in much the same way as the prophets and high priests of their ancestors.

Traditional observances like the eating of seafood on Fridays and during Lent provide another example of the relationship between religion and everyday life. Fish markets gear up for a heavier demand on days historically set aside for fasting, despite the fact that the Catholic Church has officially eased its rules in this matter. In south Louisiana even public school cafeterias continue to provide alternatives to meat for the predominantly Catholic student body on Ash Wednesday and Fridays during Lent. Waitresses in restaurants will often gently remind regular patrons what day it is if they choose a meat entrée on days like Ash Wednesday and Good Friday—just in case they may have forgotten.

While Mardi Gras signals the beginning of Lent, Good Friday signals its approaching end. It is celebrated with a ceremonial Way of the Cross procession on the road between Catahoula and St. Martinville. The stations of a Way of the Cross are usually mounted on the walls of a church, but the stations of this one are hung on the largest oak trees between the two towns. Members of the faithful gather in St. Martinville and walk or drive the length of the road to Catahoula (about eight miles), stopping at each station to pray.

Easter has traditionally been a time of family gatherings. Many Cajun families have now adopted most of the features of the general American celebration from the media and from personal contacts outside of Acadiana. Rituals now incorporated into the Cajun repertoire include the giving of baskets of dyed eggs and chocolate bunnies, and Easter egg hunts. Historically, however, eggs were not given but prepared for a contest called *pâcquer*, after the French name for Easter, *Pâcques*. Participants still boil and dye their eggs and bring them along on visits to friends and relatives where they will strike them against other eggs to see which is the strongest. Formerly, the winner was allowed to take the loser's broken egg as a prize. This meant that the winners had more to eat than the losers, and there was much competition in these quests for the strongest eggs. This, along with a natural love of practical joking, still leads some to dye smallish goose eggs or largish guinea hen eggs (both renowned for their tough shells) or even rocks in an attempt to stack the odds. Others distribute dyed *uncooked* eggs to grateful but unsuspecting friends— just for the fun of watching their faces when the inevitable occurs.

Perhaps the most important element of this tradition is the visiting and socializing it makes possible, which explains why the tradition is still very popular among many Cajun families today. Extended families and friends take advantage of the spring holiday to get together, not only for a little egg *pâcquing*, but also for a crawfish boil or a barbecue as well. Many of the usual rites of spring are also observed: baseball, volleyball, kite flying, fishing, and napping outside. Easter is, in many ways, a day on which to stake a claim on summer.

Christmas is the other major religious holiday celebrated by the Cajuns. These days, Cajuns buy Christmas trees and exchange battery-operated playthings just as in most of the western world. Cajun children now eagerly await the arrival of Santa Claus, whereas traditionally they once awaited the arrival of *le Père Noël*, or Father Christmas, and received small, often handmade presents. In fact, in the nineteenth century Christmas was more important as a time for family gatherings, family meals, and going together to church for mass (often at midnight) than for exchanging gifts. Although some gifts were given on Christmas Day, the major gift holiday for most Cajun families was New Year's Day, when families and friends gathered and exchanged gifts called *étrennes*.

Mardi Gras

Almost synonymous with Cajun Louisiana itself, Mardi Gras (also called Carnival) occurs on the day before Ash Wednesday, which marks the beginning of the Lenten season. This popular traditional festival has roots in ancient springtime fertility rituals and rites of passage. These often involve such obvious sexual symbols as mock abduction and seduction, real or symbolic nudity, and whips—these last being part fertility symbols, part instruments of intimidation. Mardi Gras is based on medieval European adaptations of even older rituals, particularly those that included reversals of the social order with the lower classes parodying the elite. Men dress as women, women as men; the poor dress as rich, the rich as poor; the old as young, the young as old; black as white, white as black. Survivals of these earlier versions are still evident in contemporary Cajun celebrations of Mardi Gras. Yet even ritualized chaos still has its own system of rules to act as a framework for the ritualistic play. Mardi Gras is usually a processional celebration. Groups of revelers move through towns and countryside alike, taking the celebration to the places they visit and invading public spaces such as roads, making them impassable, and commercial districts, rendering them inoperable. Masks provide anonymity and an opportunity to shed inhibitions and to act out roles for the day. The ritual altering of consciousness, in this case through the consumption of alcohol, enhances the ability of participants to play beyond themselves.

The country Mardi Gras celebration of south Louisiana is also a processional festivity, but unlike its urban counterpart, it stems from the medieval *fête de la quémande*, a ceremonial begging ritual, modified by frontier influences. The *fête de la quémande* was celebrated by a procession of revelers who traveled through the countryside offering some sort of performance in exchange for gifts. Costumed children on Halloween, Christmas carolers, and Irish mummers are all modern vestiges of this ancient rite. In the _course de Mardi Gras,_ masked riders visit farmhouses, singing and dancing to the traditional Mardi Gras song. The goal of these performances is to obtain a contribution to the communal gumbo, to be shared later that day. The ideal gift is a live chicken, which is released by the homeowner and must be captured by the celebrants who are hampered by masks, costumes, and their various states of inebriation. This entails considerable buffoonery and generates great merriment and entertainment for the members of the visited household.

The traditional costumes for _la course_ have roots in medieval dress. In addition to the inevitable modern clowns, monsters, movie heroes, and villains, one sees conical hats (in parody of noblewomen and also long associated with dunces or fools), miters (to ridicule the clergy), and more rarely, mortarboards (mocking scholars and clerics). The medieval atmosphere is enhanced by the processional nature of the celebration, which moves through the countryside. Like medieval jesters who remained marginal to the festivities for which they provided entertainment, the Mardi Gras musicians accompany the ride in a closed wagon or truck and never participate in the activities of the riders.

In some towns such as Kinder, Basile, and Iota, participants are flogged with whips of burlap sacking rolled or braided, reminiscent of the medieval processions of flagellants who whipped themselves and each other to purge their past sins and escape the horrors of Hell. This practice also has roots in the ancient Roman _lupercalia_ when masked and costumed men ritually beat women with animal pelts to insure fertility. Brief spontaneous skits are also sometimes performed, including _The Dead Man Revived,_ a modern version of the pre-Arthurian fisher-king legend. One participant feigns death and his companions "revive" him by dripping wine or beer into his mouth. In _The Animal Burial,_ revelers bury a chicken that has succumbed to the rigors of the day in a ceremony that parodies the Catholic funeral liturgy, replacing Latin sounds with obscene or irreverent Cajun French.

Ancient and medieval elements of the _course de Mardi Gras_ have been modified by the Louisiana frontier experience. In many communities there is a mystique of toughness reminiscent of the American

Above left: Celebration of Mardi Gras in south Louisiana is a processional festivity stemming from the medieval *fete de la quemande*, a ceremonial begging ritual.

Above right: The medieval atmosphere of the procession is heightened by costumes. Conical hats, in parody of noblewomen, is a common sight.

Right: Performance is offered for exchange of a contribution to the communal gumbo served at the end of the day—usually a chicken. (Photos by Barry Ancelet)

Left: In some towns, participants are flogged with whips made of burlap sacking—reminiscent of the medieval floggings for punishment of sins. (Photo by Barry Ancelet)

Below: Not only are masks festive but they also provide anonymity. (Photo by Mary Howell)

The riders charge through the countryside entertaining and intimidating different households. (Photo by Barry Ancelet)

Wild West. The anonymity of the masks once provided an ideal way to settle scores with some impunity. At times the riders mildly terrorized the visited households, forcing women to dance, vandalizing property, or stealing from the kitchen. With Americanization and the civilizing effect of schools and churches, the often rowdy *course* was banned from many communities. The World War II draft further weakened the celebration's social support, and it eventually disappeared from the annual cycle in most communities. In the early 1950s, a group of cultural activists in the Mamou area, under the leadership of Paul Tate and Revon Reed, undertook to revive the traditional Mardi Gras *course*, with guidance from older members of the community.

In reviving the tradition, Tate and Reed took pains to render the celebration respectable and relatively safe for both riders and hosts, while maintaining its traditional aspect. This effort, anchored in the absolute control of the *capitaine*, encouraged the continuation of the *course* by virtually eliminating fights and the element of real danger. The whip now became an element of the *capitaine's* control. The ritual tension between supplication and chaos persists even today. Riders await permission to approach a house, then charge it as though taking it by storm. They sing and dance for an offering, then chase the chicken through the barnyard as though stealing it. Riders play at changing roles from beggar to outlaw to clown, singing and dancing while intimidating and fooling nonparticipants.

Other towns have since revived the *course* as well, and sexuality continues to be an important element in these revivals. Most towns, including Mamou, Church Point, L'Anse Meg, and Kinder, limit participation to men only. Petit Mamou (where the celebration never lapsed) and Basile have separate versions for men and women, while Eunice and Scott allow both sexes to run together, as was the custom there long ago. The "males only" restriction is said to have originated among the women of Mamou to hamper anonymous carousing among their men. Among the riders, there exists the same sort of freedoms that one encounters in other sexually exclusive groups. For example, male riders dance together, walk arm in arm, and embrace each other. In fact, a popular costume on male rides involves the reversal of sexual identity as men wear wigs, dresses, and even false bosoms. The principle is that only the toughest men can afford to play at being feminine without arousing any suspicions concerning their sexuality.

A certain aura of outlawry has not entirely vanished from the modern versions of the Prairie Cajun Mardi Gras, which effectively resists reduction to a simple tourist attraction by virtue of its sheer toughness. In fact, the celebration continues to function as a rite of passage for the young men and women in many communities. Reminiscent of similar rites in primitive societies, the social initiation on the morning of the ride is accentuated by the anonymity and the removal of inhibitions through alcohol. But the essential part of the initiation lies in the ritual play of the day: being all that one dares to be. Except for the list of rules designed to contain the game, there is virtually no limit to the personal freedom of expression available to each participant.

Participation in the Mardi Gras *course* can begin several weeks in advance with a series of informal meetings to discuss administrative and support roles, such as beer truck personnel, tractor drivers, and musicians. The *capitaine*, named for life by his predecessor in most cases, chooses his co-*capitaines*, often the toughest riders and the

Independent of the men, women in the town of Iota participate in their own festival, creating needlepoint masks. (Photo by Barry Ancelet)

hardest to control, thereby channeling their energies in a positive direction. Business is settled quickly, and these meetings become rallies building excitement for the coming ride.

In the days before the celebration, riders make final preparations for the *course*, completing their costumes, preparing tack, and locating horses, often in great secrecy. To avoid being recognized by their mounts, many riders exchange horses several times before Mardi Gras day. In fact, under these circumstances, it is said that one can effectively avoid recognition by riding one's own horse.

At dawn on Mardi Gras next morning, riders don their costumes and masks, saddle their horses, and start down country roads and back streets to join their fellows at an appointed gathering place, usually near the center of town. When enough have gathered, the *capitaine* brings the riders to order and takes charge of them for the day. In some cases, there is a formal reading of the rules. The *capitaine* and his co-*capitaines* are unmasked so that they may represent the band of revelers to each household they visit. In most communities they are further identified by their cowboy hats and long multi-colored caps, usually a two-color combination of the traditional Mardi Gras colors: purple, red, yellow and green.

From the time he takes command of the celebration at the initial gathering to the re-entry into town later in the day, the *capitaine's* reign is absolute. This is the result of a tacit, and necessary, agreement among all riders who play the game. For an entire day, a considerable number of adults willingly suspend reality for the sake of the celebration, the very nature of which demands unquestioning submission to the authority of a chosen leader who acts as intermediary between the ritual madness of the procession and the people they will visit.

The rules of most celebrations are also designed to provide a framework for the festivities. Some are preventative: no Mardi Gras rider shall advance beyond the *capitaine* on the route. No rider shall enter private property without the explicit permission of the *capitaine*. No rider shall consume any liquor except that which is distributed by the *capitaine* or his assistants. No rider shall bear arms or weapons of any kind, including knives, guns, or sticks. Other rules are meant to keep the tradition intact: no rider shall throw beads, doubloons, or trinkets of any sort anywhere along the route. All riders are expected to dismount from horses and wagons to sing and dance at the homes that agree to give an offering for the gumbo. The rules are more than symbolic; riders are actually frisked to enforce the "no weapons" rule. And *capitaines* of male-only rides diligently supervise their bands to prevent women from infiltrating the ranks.

After the rules are read, riders mount their steeds, unmounted participants enter the wagons, and the procession leaves town to the incessant strains of the Mardi Gras song. As the procession approaches the first house, the *capitaine* halts the band of riders on the road and rides ahead alone with raised white flag to ask the residents' permission to enter. According to custom, if permission is refused, he simply turns and leads his troupe to the next house. Many homeowners avoid an outright refusal by arranging to be absent during the visit. If permission is granted, the *capitaine* drops his flag to signal the invitation to approach the house. Mounted participants usually take advantage of this opportunity to charge the homestead as if taking it by assault.

The *captaine* of the charge maintains order throughout the day of celebration. (Photo by Barry Ancelet)

Surrounding the front yard, the riders dismount and begin singing and dancing, often in ritual supplication poses, to the Mardi Gras song, played by the musicians who accompany the ride in their own wagon or truck. Some riders openly express a certain machismo, along with excellent horsemanship, by dancing on their mounts. Some of the more daring riders might playfully snatch up the lady of the house and her daughters and dance with them in the crowd. Children are often the object of a little mock terrorism, being whisked away from their parents for a brief moment. (This teaches them a short and relatively harmless lesson in the risks of being away from the safety of home and family.) Gardens and kitchens are sometimes raided. Riders sometimes play at stealing livestock, such as pigs and calves, but this behavior is carefully controlled by the *capitaine* who is ultimately responsible for any real damage. This ritual play functions best when the home owners know the masked visitors but cannot recognize them. Participants speak in falsetto and wear gloves to avoid being recognized despite their masks. All this is intended to produce a few uneasy but playful moments for the families that are visited.

After an appropriate amount of revelry, the man of the house brings out an offering for the Mardi Gras, a contribution to the communal gumbo to be shared later that day. This may be flour, rice,

Riders surround the household often singing and dancing on their mounts. (Photo by Barry Ancelet)

onions, oil, or even money. The favorite gift, however, is a live chicken which is thrown high in the air. Those closest to it chase it down, and the captor jubilantly holds up his prize for all to see before surrendering it to one of the co-*capitaines* who will place it in a cage until it can be transported back to town to find its way into the gumbo. After a bit more dancing and socializing, the *capitaine* blows his cow horn to call the riders back to order, and the procession moves on to the next house.

At regular (and frequent) intervals between houses, the *capitaine* calls a halt to the procession for a beer stop. A loaded pickup truck parks in the middle of the road and the riders file by to receive their ration of beer under the scrutiny of the co-*capitaines*. On especially cold days, wine and whiskey are also available. Consumption is controlled but liberal, and many riders easily work themselves into a state of ritual inebriation.

The entire scene is repeated as many as twenty or thirty times during the day. Ironically, the smaller rides usually succeed in collecting more chickens than the larger ones. The processions in Mamou, Church Point, and Eunice have a certain amount of inertia due to sheer numbers. The countless photographers, journalists, ethnographers, and other "foreign" observers who accompany huge processions further impede their progress through the countryside. Today the larger rides are often forced to augment their catch with chickens from the market, while smaller bands, usually more mobile and less affected by outside visitors and the media, can visit more houses. Some rides have adapted custom to physical realities. In communities such as Iota, the large distances between farmsteads have made visiting them on horseback impractical, so riders now hitch a wagon to a truck or tractor to cover a larger area during the day.

By mid-afternoon the riders, now weary and ragged from a day on the road, approach the edge of town. The *capitaine* often orders a stop to regroup and repair tack and costumes, and to regain a certain composure for the re-entry parade. Riders present themselves as "survivors" to those who did not participate in the ordeal. With a strong sense of brotherhood based on shared experiences, they parade down the length of the crowded main street, waving to spectators along the way. In towns where organizers have street dances (to keep as many visitors as possible in town) the band yields the stage to the Mardi Gras musicians for a final performance of the Mardi Gras song and other Cajun music. This can last up to half an hour, while riders dance in the crowd. Most riders then retire to a quiet spot to await their hard-earned supper, the ceremonial gumbo. Riders eat first. Some go home to rest or take their horses back to the barn before returning later for the masked ball, which marks the final hours of this revelry before the beginning of Lent the next day. All festivities stop abruptly at midnight, and many of Tuesday's rowdiest riders can be found on their knees receiving the penitential ashes on their foreheads on Wednesday.

6

Folk Medicine

Folk medicine consists of a body of lore and practice for identifying and treating illness and injury. It also deals with the definition of illness and the recognition of culturally defined syndromes. Like the people of most cultures, Cajuns have maintained a well-defined body of folk medicine. Its practices occur at two different levels of Cajun society. On one hand there is a large body of lore that is generally shared among most older Cajuns, particularly those of rural background. Knowledge of how to cure warts or lessen pain during childbirth falls into this category. Another body of lore is the special preserve of the folk curer, the *traiteur*. The aid of this specialist is invoked to treat many particular ailments.

Many of the examples of folk treatments mentioned in this chapter were collected in 1975 by Maida Bergeron. A total of 157 curing practices and beliefs were provided by the women of the Lake Verret area of Assumption Parish. Culturally, the people of this area are fairly typical of rural Acadiana, though they were somewhat less well-to-do and more isolated than the average. Like the descendants of the original Acadian population, they exhibit a high degree of independence and self-reliance. The families were of relatively "pure" Acadian stock.

The Functions of Cajun Folk Medicine

The folk beliefs and practices of the Cajuns are a response to a number of specific problems, many of them not unique to Acadians. The particular practices result in part from the relative isolation and cultural homogeneity of the Acadians in Louisiana, especially those who settled west of the Atchafalaya River. During the eighteenth and nineteenth centuries, professional medical help was generally unavailable to the common people of the swamps and prairies. Even when professional doctors were available, they were often considered too expensive and too impersonal. To rural Cajuns, folk cures were considered superior to those of the professional physician, and folk medical practitioners met special needs not treated by the professional doctor. They dealt with the spiritual and emotional requirements of the affected individual in a perhaps more satisfying manner than with a purely physiological approach.

Until quite recently, only the most serious injuries and illnesses were treated by professionals. In contrast to the extreme sparsity of professional doctors in the nineteenth century, *traiteurs* were found in every community. In many, they still practice actively. Their treatments combine elements of the mystical and the spiritual with the practical and well-proven wisdom of the ages. Powerful agents, such as Catholic prayers, candles, prayer beads, and the full moon, were employed in order to effect a cure. The significance of such objects and symbols was that they drew upon the common beliefs of the Acadian people. Everyone knew that if they were used in the correct manner they worked. It was the *traiteur's* job to specialize in the knowledge of curing performance.

The Classes of Cajun Folk Medicine

Cajun folk medicine can be divided into four general categories. These are: faith healing, religio-magic treatments, magic, and herbal or purely materialistic medicine.

The first, faith healing, is both the simplest and the most spiritual. It is most often practiced by *traiteurs* who believe they have a special charisma—a divine gift for healing. *Traiteurs* who work through faith alone are usually devout Christians, most often Catholics, and look upon their healing power as an integral part of their religion.

Typically, an individual *traiteur* specializes in only one or a few specific kinds of treatment. The *traiteur* may treat sunstroke, bleeding, or other conditions such as thrush, a kind of fungus disease of the mouth common to young children. Curing performances are very individualistic. A typical cure may be accomplished through the laying-on of hands, the sign of the cross, and mumbling of secret prayers drawn from passages of the Bible. As one Cajun put it:

For sunstroke, go to a *traiteur*. They give you some flowers of the chinaball or lilac tree. They tie the leaves all around your head to get the fever out. She never charges you but you may give her a donation. You know prayers never hurt anyone.

Each *traiteur* has a personal repertoire of prayers employed for highly specific cures. Sometimes it is not considered necessary even for the patient to be in the presence of the *traiteur* for the cure to be effective.

Traiteurs learn their trade from other *traiteurs,* usually close relatives in the previous generation. The "gift" is passed on from one person to a single trusted younger individual, usually a member of the same family. The gift is then lost to the one who passed it on. *Traiteurs* were always considered particularly good persons in their communities. The title *doctor* was often given to them. They were never associated with voodoo doctors, however. It is clear that *traiteurs* were once considered to have the same status as professional doctors, and they generally did not request payment for their services. Some even preferred not to be thanked at all, as this would lessen the charitable nature of their deeds. Informants report that *traiteurs* sometimes did accept remuneration for their services, but always in kind rather than in money. The gift of a chicken, some game, or some potatoes would suffice.

In the past, the most popular form of folk medicine in Acadiana was what has been called religio-magic treatment. It relies on some physical agent that has been blessed or charmed through a religious act. The agent may be officially blessed, as in the case of holy water from the church, or it may be blessed on the spot as a part of the treatment itself. Infants and children are often "cured" by placing a string about a portion of their body. The string has a specified number of knots ("balls") tied in it, often nine. The same number of prayers are said at the time the string is tied on. The string is then left in place until it falls off. By the time the string falls off the harmful condition should have disappeared. So strongly did some people feel about the efficacy of this method of curing that professional doctors treating sick children often left the curing strings in place.

Another example of a popular religio-magic treatment is the Litany of the Holy Sepulcher. A prayer is written on a sheet of paper cut in the form of a cross. Such sheets are believed to hold certain miraculous powers, including the prevention of epileptic seizures and bodily injuries, and the reduction of pain in childbirth. Religio-magic healing is often carried out without the aid of a *traiteur*. In the case of a child with a nosebleed, a cross is marked out on the ground with two sticks. The child's blood is allowed to drip onto the cross, and the nose stops bleeding.

Some Cajuns practiced curing with pure magic. Catholic or other religious practices played no role in this form of treatment. Acadian magic was similar to other forms of magic practiced widely in the world. Much of its symbolism relied on the twin principles of contagion and visual similarity (sympathy). Evils such as illness may be removed through a ritual in which contact with some agent permits the illness to be drained away from the body of the victim. This kind of transfer can work both for and against well-being. In Acadiana, for example, there has been a belief that warts may be cured by pricking them with a sharp object, allowing the blood to drop onto some grains of corn, and then getting a chicken to eat the grains of corn. The chicken will develop the warts and the victim will lose them. The scapegoat theory of ancient magic still lives in such folk practices, and they are not unique to Acadian Americans. Most such beliefs have close parallels in the folk medicine of Anglo-America and other areas settled by Europeans. For example, certain *traiteurs* of Lake Verret treated warts by rubbing a nickel on the wart and then allowing the patient to spend the nickel. The person who took it was supposed to acquire the wart, while the spender lost it. This is known as "selling a wart" in Anglo-Saxon folklore.

Homeopathic magic is also practiced. Herbal medicine has been popular in Acadiana since the earliest days of settlement. It involves collecting wild or domesticated plants for curative purposes. The derivatives of these plants are believed to work empirically, rather than through spiritual force. Different substances, not only plants but other common substances as well, are ingested or applied to various portions of the body. They may be made into salves, greases, teas, or poultices. For example, egg whites and spider webs are used in poultices to draw out splinters and to stop bleeding, respectively. For fever, *l'herbe à malot* (swamp lily root) soaked in water was used, with camphor or alcohol rubs and aspirin. Together with Black Draught (a patent medicine), the same herb eased constipation. The smoke of burned sugar was inhaled to relieve sinus congestion, and infected cuts were treated with mashed *la mauve* (a curly, crawling grass).

Various commercially available products find use in folk cures, for example, Octagon soap, Black Salve (Ichthanmol), kerosene, and various liquors. Patent medicines of the late nineteenth and early twentieth centuries are also still relied upon, despite being long out of favor with modern medicine. Turpentine or kerosene is used on bandages to help heal cuts. Paregoric is used for colic, and a poultice of chewing tobacco is applied to bee stings.

Certain remedies apparently evolved because they brought comfort or pleasure to the patient. For colds, hot pepper, whiskey, and sugar was taken as a hot drink. Croup was treated with sweetened hot coffee flavored with melted butter. Lemonade was believed to help purify the blood. On the other hand, certain cures were guaranteed to bring discomfort to the patient. For blood poisoning, a cockroach was put in whisky and placed on the wound for several days. Castor oil was used to treat stomach ache.

Interpretation of Acadian Folk Cures

Acadian folk medicine, like so many other aspects of this culture, is a blend of elements from numerous and far-flung sources. The oldest identifiable source is clearly ancient Greek herbal and homeopathic medicine. The use of sulfur in water to purify the blood, for example, dates back to Greek times at least. Indeed, the near-obsession of many Cajuns with blood purity may derive ultimately from Greece. Like the ancient Greeks, the French and modern Cajuns use alum to cure cold sores, fats to "warm and mollify the body," egg white as a cure for eye troubles, and bags of salt to ease the pain of toothache.

Perhaps the most common source for Acadian folk medicine is post-medieval French homeopathic medicine. The French used rose-water to wash out the eyes, just as Cajuns do today. Many French-derived cures are still found in French Canada as well as Louisiana. The plant *la mauve*, for example, is unknown in English folk medicine. In traditional French medicine it is one of four *ramolitives* or relaxer plants, being used for constipation. The emphasis on herbal preventatives also appears to derive from eighteenth-century French medicine. The Acadian use of a tea made from peach-tree leaves may derive from the peach-flower syrup brought to Louisiana by French colonial doctors in 1730. These doctors believed that lemons had preventative powers and introduced turpentine as a cure for colds, infections and as a purgative for worms in 1731. Other cures with direct parallels in France include placing a warm plate on the stomach for stomachache or cramps, putting vinegar on ringworm, and treating headache with prayers by a *traiteur*.

Certain plant cures, such as tobacco (for infections) and sassafras (for blood purification), are derived from Native American traditions. Cajuns use tobacco poultices for bee stings, headaches, snakebites, boils, and other problems. The popularity of tobacco amounts to a repetition of this plant's original uses, for it was believed to be a general panacea after it was introduced into Europe in the sixteenth century. Other practices, such as tying bags of garlic about the ankles to prevent snakebite, are almost certainly not aboriginal, although they are attributed to Native Americans by Acadians.

Many traditional Acadian cures derive from the best medical thought of the late eighteenth and early nineteenth centuries. A medical handbook of 1812 recommends wearing garlic around the neck as a cure for worms, for example. Camphor was a popular element in the control of fevers in the early nineteenth century. Epsom salt was recommended as a laxative in medical manuals as late as the early twentieth century. Gargling with salt for a sore throat, taking lemon and honey for a cough, and administering paregoric for colic—all these fall into the category of survivals from earlier medical practice. As such, they are not unique to Cajun culture, of course.

However, some of the cures found around Lake Verret do seem to be unique to Louisiana Cajuns. The herbs, *la mauve* and *l'herbe à malot,* are used in several cures. Burning a cane reed under an infection and putting garlic around a baby's neck to cure worms are cures not recorded in other areas of the state or nation.

Although much of this early medicine has been replaced and long forgotten by modern medical science, it persists in varying degrees among the isolated rural folk of North America such as in Acadiana.

Folk Law and Justice

When the Acadians first arrived in Louisiana, they carried with them a well-defined set of assumptions about appropriate behavior and the role of civil authority. Their norms were grounded in a century of common experience in Acadia and shaped by the twin themes of self-reliance and passive resistance to the imposition of external authority. In Louisiana, the Acadians encountered from the beginning conditions similar to those that had prevailed in Acadia, where the goals of the French seignorial authorities, and later those of the British, were in many respects at odds with their own.

As they had in the past, Acadians adapted to Spanish regulations by establishing a clandestine system of Acadian counter-norms. Where the Spanish authorities forbade trading with the British, Acadians traveled at night on the Mississippi River to barter goods in Baton Rouge. Where required to settle on unsuitable land, Acadians simply disappeared and moved to more appropriate locations. Isolation in the swamps and prairies furthered both Acadian independence and the strength of folk norms. Nor did conflicts between the civil authorities and Acadian values disappear or even diminish after the Louisiana Purchase. Although the Napoleonic Code has prevailed in many ways in Louisiana law even to the present, Anglo-American civil, political, and economic power became increasingly dominant. The consequence was that many points of contention existed between Acadian folk norms and those established by the legal codes of the authorities.

One common result was that the civil authorities refused to enforce certain behavior that Acadians felt should fall into the realm of law. Vestiges of these differences still exist, particularly in the more rural areas of Acadiana and may be recognized wherever Acadians initiate extralegal counteractions in response to a perceived breach of a norm. Two examples will suffice, one religious, the other secular.

Courting

A topic often addressed in the literature on Acadians is the norms which regulated courtship and marriage. Reinecke (1966) reports that a Cajun father would whitewash his gate and chimney top to announce that he had a marriageable daughter. For girls, courtships often began at dances, and at a comparatively young age.

In the eighteenth and nineteenth centuries, courting was strictly regulated. The institution of the chaperon was important. Young men could not court a girl without the presence of an adult. At her house, courting began indirectly. The young man paid a visit to the house and was asked to stay for coffee. As he discussed business with her mother or father, the eligible daughter continued her household duties without interruption, seemingly paying no mind. A series of increasingly less coincidental meetings followed: at the dance hall on Saturday night, at church on Sunday morning, or at her house on Sunday afternoon—a time set aside for social visits. Before long the young man was alone in the kitchen with the girl, while her parents sat in an adjoining room. At no time before he asked her parents for her hand, however, did he see her alone. While young men could leave a *fais do-do* to get some air or to drink, the girls were strictly forbidden to leave a dance hall unescorted by their mothers or other relatives. To do so resulted in severe ostracism. Premarital pregnancy is said to have resulted in banishment until marriage.

For the young man, courtship was complex, but not lengthy. A few months to a year was adequate. This was serious business. An unmarried girl of twenty was an old maid—*une vieille fille*. If it seemed that a courtship was being dragged out indefinitely, the young man might receive a coat in an envelope sent by his intended—the sign that it was over.

Proposals were presented formally, on Thursday nights, and were delivered to the father and mother, rather than to the fiancée herself. If accepted by parents, close relatives, and the young woman herself, the license was secured the following Saturday and the banns were read in church the following three Sunday mornings. The wedding took place the Saturday after the last reading. Young men often escorted their brides to the church to be married, with the father following. Mothers are said to have stayed at home, "as the occasion was too sad." A formal reception and dance was held after the wedding. Although modern Cajun weddings are similar to those of other North Americans, certain customs from those times survive today in rural areas—pinning money to the bride's dress during the wedding dances is one. Cajuns sometimes still bring cakes and gifts, including chickens, to the reception. In rural areas, receptions are still sometimes held in a commercial dance hall with the entrance fee going to the newlyweds.

Another norm which still prevails is the feeling that persons of markedly different ages should not marry. While the marriage itself is not proscribed, the wedding night of unmatched couples can still be celebrated publicly by a particularly rowdy *charivari*. Friends and relatives congregate outside the couple's bedroom window on the wedding night, banging pots and pans to make a terrible racket. They refuse to leave until they have been invited in for cake and coffee, or even a full meal. In some communities the custom is extended to any widow or widower who remarries, or to an estranged couple that decides to reconcile and reunite.

Hunting, Fishing, and Trapping Rights

Folk law on boundary disputes among the fishermen and hunters of the bayous is pretty clearcut. Through traditional use, a fisherman comes to consider a portion of a particular river or bayou his personal zone of exploitation. Neighbors recognize the claim and don't question the person's right to use the property provided theirs is not infringed upon. Consequently, anyone who consistently maintains a certain area is recognized to have a claim on that area through usufruct; others can travel through, but they must not exploit its resources. Occasionally parish officers are called in to settle a dispute over such a claim. For example, one who moves a houseboat to different locations where fish are biting is very likely to cause a stir among the more settled neighbors.

When disputes arise, there are recognized methods for dealing with trespassers, summed up under the term "trapper's justice." In the marsh areas, for example, a land user is thought to be justified in shooting anyone caught trespassing on his trapping land. Likewise, Cajun fishermen think it perfectly acceptable to use whatever force is necessary to remove someone from "their" fishing grounds.

In one trespassing account, an old trapper was running his traps one day when he spotted the sheriff hunting ducks on his "property." After informing the sheriff that he was trespassing, at which the sheriff made no move to leave, the old man punched him in the face. Naturally, the case was taken to court, but the trapper was let off, and the sheriff was never seen around the property again.

An increasing cause of antagonism is the presence of large numbers of sportsmen in the marshes. On the whole, the activities of sportsmen and commercial fishermen need not conflict, but some sport fishermen will steal fish out of the commercial fishermen's nets, tear the hoop nets up, and show a general disregard for the rights of the local fishermen. The problem is compounded by the fact that sportsmen have much more political clout than the commercial fishermen who make only a portion of their living by fishing.

Aside from boundary disputes, fur buying and selling has presented problems in the marshes and swamps for years. In a 1941 account, Edward Kammer reported incidents of violence in the St. Bernard area over trespassing claims. These came about because of a federal government requirement that trappers and fishermen had to get a permit to work in any area not privately owned. From 1924 to 1935, Kammer claimed that the New Orleans *Times-Picayune* reported continual flare-ups. By 1941, the trappers were paying rent to trap on government land and apparently the problems and disputes had been resolved more or less satisfactorily.

Writing in the late 1950s, Carol Ramsey gave an account of a family she stayed with and their attempts to cheat the buyers who had contracted to buy their best furs at very low prices. She joined them on a mock funeral one night as they carried "Tante Chloe" down the river in a coffin to an illegal buyer who paid a better price for their furs.

Other evasions of hunting and trapping restrictions exist. *Outlawing*, which consists of either hunting out of season or hunting illegal game, is fairly common among swamp dwellers. They see no reason

why they should change their hunting habits or stop taking what they
can use. Backwoods Cajuns feel that, once again, sportsmen with
political clout are restricting the hunting that provides the mainstay
of their diet. Malcolm Comeaux relates one game warden's claim to
have arrested almost every man in the village at least once for some
violation or other.

Folk Justice

The strong ties within communities helped to make Cajun culture
very territorial. Before schools and churches provided mitigating
influences, there was often considerable friction between communities. Most settlements had at least one or two nearby rivals, forming a
chain of resentment that could snake across a region for miles. For
the residents of Ossun, it was the Marais Bouleur. For the Marais
Bouleur, it was Pointe Noire. For Pointe Noire, it was Pointe de
l'Eglise. For Pointe de l'Eglise, it was Eunice. For Eunice, it was
Mamou. For Mamou, it was Ville Platte. For Ville Platte, it was
L'Anse des Bélair, and so on. Violence was common throughout south
Louisiana. The reasons were always the same: territoriality, isolation,
a lack of civilizing influences, and a system of justice that did not
necessarily include outside authority.

The earliest descriptions of the Acadians describe them as peaceful, especially in their social events. However, at least throughout the
second half of the nineteenth century and well into this one, the main
location for territorial behavior was the house dance (*bal de maison*)
and later the dance hall. Early weekend dances were neighborhood
affairs held in private homes, attendance at which was by invitation
only. These provided the primary place for courtship. Consequently,
husbands, fathers, and brothers protected the honor of the women
while young men protected their turf. Even in this highly controlled
setting, there could be problems. Interlopers, especially young men
from other neighborhoods, were invariably challenged as soon as they
strained local mores or upset the social order.

Dances rarely passed without incident, because making trouble
was a traditional form of amusement for some. Stories abound about
the neighborhood bully who goes to a dance expressly to test the
system. He might walk in and yell at the top of his lungs, "*Je suis le
meilleur homme dans la place!*" (I'm the best man in the place!) Or he

might walk over to a table and gulp down another man's drink or dance with another man's wife or daughter. A bully from the Marais Bouleur traditionally indicated his presence in the dance halls by sticking his knife in a post or wall and hanging his hat on it. Such expressions of bravado met with either cowardly retreat, which established the bully's machismo, or a fight, which gave him the opportunity to demonstrate it. A fight could be impromptu or quite ritualistic, as in the case of the *bataille au mouchoir,* in which the challenger offered his opponent a corner of his handkerchief and the two went at each other with fists or knives, each holding a corner, until one gave up. Most who remember such tests insist that they occurred because there was not much else to do. One veteran musician explained that men fought "because they liked it. There was no television, no radio in those days. That was their only fun—to see which of them was the best man." A long-time dance hall owner agreed, adding, "Sometimes two of those boys would go to a dance together and, hell, if they couldn't find anyone else to fight with, they fought each other. Those were the days when men were men and women loved them for it." Fighting was a popular sport in most frontier settlements.

For many bullies, the ideal Saturday night consisted of going to a dance in a gang and causing so much trouble that the event had to be called off. This practice was called *casser le bal* (breaking up the dance) or *prendre la place* (taking over the place). Sometimes not even passive nonviolence could save a dance because as most bystanders noted, when the gangs found no one to fight with, they frequently fought among themselves.

Feuds between families added fuel to the fire. They could start with as little as a cow breaking through a fence and last several generations with dreadful results. One particularly gruesome oral history account tells of a house dance in L'Anse des Bélair. When three members of a family involved in a feud with the host family arrived uninvited, the owner of the house decided to let it pass. Soon, however, the visitors were causing trouble, forcing women to dance with them and picking fights with the men. The host approached the three and said, "Listen, nobody wants you here in the first place, and certainly not causing all that trouble. So just get out now."

The three men started walking toward him and backed him against a wall. But when his back hit the wall, the host pulled a pistol from his coat and shot the first one in the chest. Before anyone could react, he shot the second one. By then the third had turned to run, but he was shot in the back. All three men fell dead on the floor. And the host family had so little regard for the men that they simply rolled them under the benches along the walls and continued their dance. They sent for the other family to come pick up their "damned corpses" only after the dance broke up.

This story has some suspicious features, but whether or not it actually happened exactly that way, its oral currency in the region at least fifty years later shows that it is at least psychologically true.

House dances had a certain amount of control built into the system since guests were invited. Dance halls, however, compounded the fighting problem because they were open to the public and frequently drew from two or more neighborhoods. When asked, virtually all Acadians pointed out that if dance halls in one area were visited by people from another area, trouble was inevitable. According to one, "When the men from Marais Bouleur came to Ossun, there was a fight. When the men from Pointe Noire came to Marais Bouleur, there was a fight. And if men from Marais Bouleur and Pointe Noire came to Ossun, there was a big fight." Public halls were frequently the scene of violence and sometimes veritable mayhem. Two feuding families met by chance one Sunday at Maurice Richard's country race track and dance hall in the late 1800s. A terrible fistfight erupted. Things went from bad to worse as combatants went for their pistols and rifles and began shooting. According to the owner's son, the warring factions were forced to cease firing after a while because they could no longer see each other for the smoke. At this point, the mother of one slain fighter rushed to his side and drank the blood spilling from his fatal head wound to prevent it from touching the ground.

Some fight stories are gruesome; some are funny. One story tells of a man who fought often but never won. One night he got the jump on an opponent and was beating him soundly. After a while, the other fellow said that he had had enough. But the loser was having such fun winning a fight at last that he would not stop. This finally angered his opponent who got up and whipped him after all.

Trouble in the dance halls forced many early owners to close; others eventually learned to hire peacekeepers. These were usually the neighborhood's meanest fighters whose efforts dance hall owners sometimes succeeded in channeling onto the side of law and order by pinning a badge on their shirt. The deal was that they could fight as long as it was on the side of the law. Some of these lawmen, constables such as Martin Weber and Joe Hanks, excelled in this "occupational therapy" and became famous for their unwavering (ruthless?) maintenance of order in the dance halls.

Martin Weber's bailiwick included the northwest corner of Lafayette Parish, until relatively recently on the western edge of civilized country. (See Map No. 3) An abundance of ruffians in the nearby Marais Bouleur made it virtually impossible to keep a dance hall open for any length of time (despite the best efforts of owner Sully Babineaux and others), so folks from that area frequently came to Esta Hebert's hall in Ossun and to Forrestier's hall in Vatican. Martin Weber had a habit of announcing his rules once at the beginning of the dance: No fighting, drinking, smoking, spitting, cussing, or wearing of hats in the hall. If anyone had to fight, drink, smoke, spit, cuss, or wear a hat, he should go outside. Mr. Weber did not repeat his rules. He had a hardwood stick and used it liberally to break up fights and take off hats. He surprised cussers, drinkers, and spitters with similar treatment, and often sneaked up behind unsuspecting smokers to crush cigarettes and cigars out on their lips.

Joe Hanks was the constable in the southwestern corner of St. Landry Parish, a no-man's land called the Marais Bouleur. It lay about a mile from Lafayette Parish and across the road from Acadia Parish. The area was already tough when the discovery of oil compounded the problem by attracting Anglo-American drillers and roughnecks from Texas and Oklahoma. Chez Petit Maurice was easily the largest and most popular dance hall of the 1940s. Although it drew from areas as far away as fifty miles, the hall was the first to remain open in the Marais Bouleur, largely due to Hanks's diligent efforts.

Like gunfighters, strong constables had to survive constant challenges. One former dancer recalled a night when a game young man walked into the hall and up to the musicians' stage. He stopped the music and yelled, *"J'emmerde tous les hommes ici, mais pas les femmes!"* (Roughly, "To hell with all the men here, but not the ladies!") Joe Hanks fell upon him immediately, gave him a thorough beating with his stick and threw him outside. On second thought, Hanks decided this was not enough and went outside for the fellow, hauled him back to the bandstand, and demanded that he apologize. The fellow said, *"Je demande pardon de toutes les femmes, mais j'emmerde les hommes encore!"* ("I apologize to all the ladies, but I send the men to hell again!") Joe Hanks gave up on the apology and beat him again.

If they were to survive in such an environment, some men had to find ways of evening the odds. One memorable character was diminutive, and so wisely avoided direct confrontation. He was nevertheless feared far and wide for his legendary skill at throwing a bottle. If he had a score to settle with someone, he simply slipped outside, lined up his victim in one of the windows, and let fly. By the time his opponent regained consciousness, he was safely away. This same man's son was similarly small. Yet he too earned the respect of his larger opponents by virtue of his meanness. On one well-known occasion, he found himself surrounded by an old foe and his friends who called out, *"Grand rond!"* ("Form a circle!") This made the fight official, and thus inescapable. The bigger man pounced on him and was soon kneeling over him, beating him mercilessly. But the smaller man freed one arm, worked his index finger into his opponent's eye and pulled it right out. The big man rolled over covering the bleeding empty socket. The victor struggled to his feet and said, *"Grand rond est fini!"* ("End of the fight!") He walked away untouched through the circle of horrified men. No charges were brought against either party: the fight had been declared official.

Alcée Thibodeaux was a quiet man who insisted that he never looked for trouble, but that if it looked for him, he was not hard to find. A local story has it that one day while playing cards, he reached over and, without getting up, punched a fellow across the table to end his incessant chattering. The fellow flew out of his chair and fell to the floor, out cold. His face had to be splashed with a bucket of water to revive him. The point of the story, however, was not Mr. Thibodeaux's violence, but his prowess in knocking someone unconscious from across a card table without even leaving his chair. No charges were brought against him. On the contrary, his action was considered altogether justifiable and quietly appreciated by all in attendance: strictly speaking, punching someone in the nose is assault, but if it's the only way to shut him up.... This sort of confrontation is not only tolerated, but expected and admired in certain segments Cajun society.

In his recent study of violence in the upland South, Lynwood

Montell discusses in similar terms the difference between a killing and a murder in the popular mind: a murder is considered a crime, while a killing can be deemed an appropriate, although violent, resolution within the system of folk justice. There were two well-known fighters from the Marais Bouleur who generally traveled together and, when they did not succeed in engaging others in a fight, fought each other. One had earned quite a reputation for sneaking behind his victims and opening their stomachs with his Barlow knife. He was eventually shot and killed in a dance hall parking lot by a fellow he had tormented for years. When the sheriff's deputy arrived on the scene, the fellow was reloading his pistol to go after the second outlaw, who had managed to dodge the first six rounds. No charges were pressed. Many members of the community felt that a social problem had been resolved, if only partially.

It is important to understand that these stories are balanced by hundreds of others that portray Cajuns as cooperative, honorable, brave, and good-natured. Moreover, attitudes have changed over the years, and many of today's Cajuns have learned to co-exist peacefully with other people and places. The region undeniably is characterized by a certain amount of violence, but it is easy to misunderstand its nature. Studies by such scholars as John Shelton Reed and Lynwood Montell have shown that violence in the South tends to be confrontational and interpersonal rather than random or gratuitous. The same is true in south Louisiana. People involved in violent situations usually know each other and understand why they are at odds. Assault and even homicide can be considered appropriate resolutions to problems among people who do not always feel it necessary to include institutional law enforcement or judicial agencies in their conflicts. However, it is easy to see that what seems to make perfect sense on a warm Saturday night between two people who share a similar social and cultural background can take on other, more evil meanings when presented out of context.

In order to understand the whole story, it is important to consider the residue of the past in the present. Early literature erred in depicting Cajuns only as pastoral and peaceful. Some recent films and television programs have portrayed Cajuns consistently as violent xenophobes. The truth, of course, lies somewhere in between. Cajun society, like any other, is a rich and complex blend of saints and sinners and everything in between. There remains, nevertheless, a clear sense of folk justice in south Louisiana, which includes a healthy respect for borders and fences. With the advent of literacy, messages that were previously transmitted only orally have been condensed and transferred to signs that hang on those fences. For example, on one fence on the north side of Lafayette hangs the sign: "Trespassers will be shot. Survivors will be shot again." In many places, such as Pointe Noire and the Marais Bouleur, however, written signs remain unnecessary. There is still no need to announce a Neighborhood Watch policy. People remember.

PART THREE

Material Culture

8

Folk Architecture

The origins of Louisiana's Acadian vernacular architecture are little investigated and imperfectly understood. History has eradicated much of the evidence normally available to the architectural historian. The lives of Acadians in the period preceding the settlement in Louisiana were so chaotic that it is extremely difficult to identify specific sources of architectural influence. We are left with little more than a series of educated guesses about the genesis of the Cajun house. It is possible, though, to identify the general cultural influences and to narrow the range of possibilities.

Evidence concerning the houses of Acadian settlers in Nova Scotia is drawn from two sources. Travelers to the area in the period from 1720 to 1755 provided brief descriptions. In addition, a few buildings survive in the areas of New Brunswick where Acadian settlers relocated after the *Grand Dérangement*.

The typical pre-exile Acadian house was built either *pièce sur pièce* (horizontal log construction; Fig. 3) or in earth-fast construction— either *planche debout en terre* (upright planks in the ground; Fig. 4) or in *poteaux en terre* (posts in the ground; Fig. 5). In the first, full dovetail notching was used to tie the ends of the log planks together into a tightly fitting log crib. Originally, wattle-and-daub construction had also been employed for temporary cabins.

The shape of the Acadian house seems to have been relatively standardized. Each building took the form of a rectangle, longer on the front by 30 to 50 percent than it was wide. It was capped with a gabled roof, pitched at 30° to 45°. The Acadian house was comparatively small by European standards. One- or two-room houses were the rule. For most, the width of the house was limited to about sixteen feet. The front door was located near the middle of the long side. Depending on its size, such a house might boast one or two windows in the long walls (Fig. 3), but generally none in its ends.

Figure 3. An Acadian log cottage, New Brunswick (Photo by Georges Escudo)

Figure 4. *Planche debout en terre* construction

Figure 5. *Bousillage entre poteaux en terre* construction

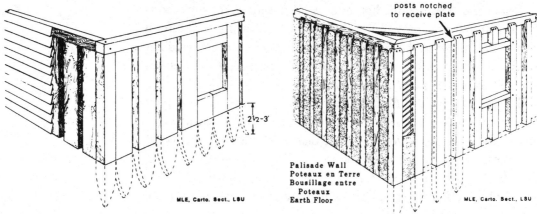

MLE, Carto. Sect., LSU

Palisade Wall
Poteaux en Terre
Bousillage entre
   Poteaux
Earth Floor

MLE, Carto. Sect., LSU

posts notched
to receive plate

Because there was so little room within the house and because families were large, the loft was employed as a boy's bedroom or *garçonnière*. Robert Hale, an English traveler from New England, noted in 1731 that

they have but one room in [their] Houses besides a Cockloft [boy's bedroom], Cellar and sometimes a Closet. Their Bedrooms are made something after [the] manner of a Sailor's Cabbin, but boarded all around about [the] bigness of [the] Bed, except one little hole in the Foreside, just big eno' to crawl into, before which is a Curtain Drawn & as a Step to get into it, there stands a chest.

Furnishings were minimal: a few chairs covered with animal hides, a single rough table, some beds hung with curtains, and a few chests to store clothing. No sideboards or armoirs are reported. China and flatware were both sparse and well worn.

Roofs were generally shingled, though bark was used in earlier days. The eaves of the Acadian house did not extend more than about six inches beyond the walls. There were no galleries, the name given to covered porches. Shingles or clapboards covered the gabled ends of the house and sometimes other exterior surfaces as well.

The comparatively large chimney was built of stone or of sticks and mud. It was located inside one of the end walls or in the middle between two rooms. Cooking was done in the large fireplace.

Reliable information on the earliest Acadian houses in Louisiana is almost as sparse as it is for Acadia. The few historic descriptions that survive make it clear that the folk houses of the Cajuns evolved through several stages between 1765, when they arrived, and about 1900, when traditional folk housing was being replaced by popular and commercial architecture. Nothing like the original houses of the period from 1765 to 1795 survives in Louisiana today. The processes of adaptation and acculturation show clearly in the development of Acadian folk architecture. For convenience, the sequence of changes may be divided into four generations, which will be described in the following sections.

First-Generation Acadian Houses (Palmetto, ca. 1765–1795)

Most of the Acadians who arrived between 1765 and 1795 constructed simple cabins for themselves. The first houses were clearly meant to be temporary. Many were framed from sticks and thatched above and below with palmetto leaves. Palmetto "tents" (A-frames) are recorded as having been constructed by the first settlers in 1785 at Lafourche des Chétimachas on the Acadian Coast. Such cabins lasted only a few years. They were constructed after the style of the huts built by the local Houma tribe (Fig. 6). Antoine Simon Le Page du Pratz, an architect and concessionaire who settled in Louisiana between 1718 and 1734, wrote in 1774:

They set several posts in the ground at equal distances from one another and lay a beam or plate on top of them, making thus the form of a house of an

Figure 6. Palmetto hut, similar to first generation Acadian shelters in Louisiana (Photo Courtesy Fred Kniffen)

oblong square. In the middle of this square they set up two forks, about one-third higher than the posts, and lay a pole across them, for the ridgepole of the building; upon which they nail the rafters and cover them with cypress bark, or palmetto leaves.

The Second-Generation Acadian Cottage (*poteaux en terre,* ca. 1766–1827)

Within a few years after the settlers' arrival, a new semi-permanent type of Acadian house was being constructed everywhere. Most were built as earth-fast structures, either *poteaux en terre*, or *planche debout* (Figs. 4, 5). These were poor structures with dirt floors. The walls were usually covered with split planks set vertically. Some had *bousillage,* a mixture of clay, lime, and Spanish moss, infill in the walls, while others used timber only. Various forms of insulation were used, including mud and paper. The roofs were covered with boards, shingles, or bark. In some cases they were thatched. Second-generation houses were not meant to be permanent, but to last several years until the settler could afford to construct a "proper" cottage. Many settlers, however, were forced to make do with their dirt-floored cabins for many years.

Figure 7. A portion of a view of Decatur Street, drawn in 1765, the year of arrival of the first Acadians (Portion of a sketch by Lieut. Philip Pittman, 3rd (British) Regiment. Courtesy Louisiana State Museum)

Third-Generation Acadian Houses (Timber Frame, ca. 1790–1850)

By the time the first Acadians arrived, a considerable variety of architectural styles existed in Louisiana. In the city of New Orleans, a dominant French Creole vernacular style had been established (Fig. 7). It consisted of a house one room deep and several rooms wide, with a full-length gallery along the front or, occasionally, completely surrounding the structure (Fig. 8). Houses were covered by gabled or, less often, hip roofs of the "umbrella" type. The roof encompassed the gallery and rear service spaces as well as the central rooms of the building.

The plan of the house consisted of a large, near-square central room, the *salle*, roughly eighteen by eighteen feet, and a master bedroom, the *chambre*, roughly fifteen by eighteen feet deep. Even smaller bedrooms, twelve by eighteen feet, might be attached to the ends of this two-room core. Small rooms about ten feet square called *cabinets* were often added to the rear corners of the building and were used for storage or for overflow sleeping. An open porch, the *galerie* (loggia) was set between two rear cabinet rooms. As with Caribbean Creole houses, the houses of New Orleans were often raised above ground level to enhance through ventilation. This was also promoted by the use of multiple double-leaf doors in the front and rear facades of the house in place of European-style windows. All of these features were adopted by Acadians, perhaps because the Creole style of

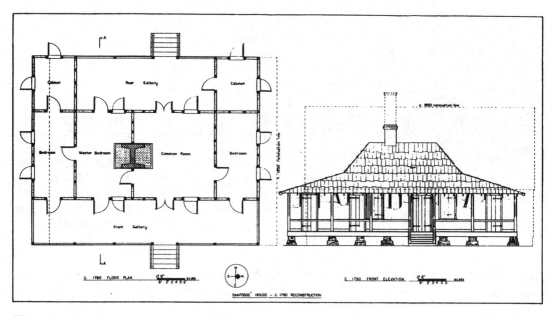

Figure 8. Plan of a typical early French Creole house with loggia (Drawing by Robert Smith)

building represented the dominant style they experienced upon entering Louisiana.

In the countryside there were the huts of the plantation slaves— generally *poteaux en terre* structures (Fig. 9)—and the houses of the French managers. These last were two- to three-room Creole cottages with hip or gabled roofs. In addition, there were the houses of the *petits habitants,* or small farmers, who lived along the banks of the Mississippi River above and below New Orleans. These were also surrounded by galleries and raised above ground level on cypress blocks.

Borrowing from these ideas and relying on the traditions of their past, Acadians established a permanent dwelling style that conformed closely to a common model. They selected a simple, rectangular gable-roofed cottage, constructed in timber-frame. As folklorist George F. Reinecke reported, in the year 1901 examples were still to be seen in the more isolated sections of Acadiana:

Cabane was the name given in early times to all dwellings; it is still applied to those built in the ancient style. In Acadia, Canada, they were called *loge;* in the Antilles, *case.* Houses in the old style still exist in out-of-the-way places on Lake Verret, on the coast, in the great Attakapas and Opelousas prairies and in places where the soil is poor. These little huts dignified with the name of houses are built on blocks, or piers, twenty or thirty inches above the ground level.

Figure 9. A typical
Louisiana slave cabin

In an interview, Acadian Robert Hebert noted that houses were
generally constructed in anticipation of a wedding (Fig. 10):

That's the way people built their houses in the old days, I remember. When
the tide was high they floated cypress logs to the side of the *coteau* [bank of
the natural levee]. . . . Then when a man wanted to get married he began
cutting the wood for his house. He'd roll a log on a scaffold and use a saw to
cut the boards. They'd make boards by hand . . . cut boards, sills, 2x4s, all
by hand. It took a long time, sometimes 3 or 4 years.

According to the anonymous Breaux manuscript, on the prairies or
where cypress woodlots were available:

the wood is hand-sawed and squared with an axe in the woods, before being
brought to the construction site. The building is normally fifteen by twenty
feet, usually of only one big room, but sometimes partitioned or alcoved.
The big chimney is built at the gable end. There are two doors and one or
two windows. The walls and chimney are of *bousillage*, a mixture of Spanish
moss and mud. The preparation is done with the help of friends and
neighbors. Copious refreshments and a heavy meal cooked on the spot by the
womenfolk are the reward for their service.

The third-generation house was constructed *poteaux sur sol* or
with posts on a sill. The sill was raised above the level of the ground

Figure 10. "Cajun Wedding," by Floyd Sonnier

on cypress blocks (Fig. 11). The posts were mortised into the sill and *bousillage* put between the posts. The anonymous Breaux manuscript (ca. 1900) provides an interesting word-picture of the construction of a third-generation folk cottage of the eastern portion of Acadiana:

The *tâche* is a square or round hole for making *bousillage*. The topsoil is stripped off with shovels. Then the hole is excavated with hand tools and the spoilage thrown to the side. At the bottom is laid a coating of "green" [uncured] moss and layers of earth are alternated with further layers of moss. Then the whole is watered so as to soak the earth. Then men called *tâcherons*, bare-footed and with trouser legs turned up, descend into the *tâche*, treading and crushing the mixture until it is of the consistency of mortar. It is then applied to the building frame by *torches* or double-handfuls. Where there is no Spanish moss, prairie grass or hay are poor substitutes.

The wooden uprights of the building frame are indented [with shallow auger or chiseled holes] at intervals of five or six inches to accommodate the *batons* [a lattice of split sticks also called *barreaux*] which are placed between them. The *batons* are thus between two thicknesses of *bousillage* (Fig. 11). When this is half-dry it is smoothed with a shovel-blade, then allowed to dry

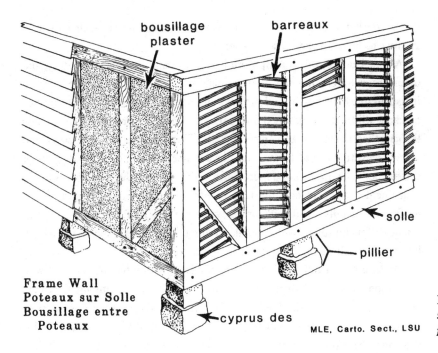

Figure 11. *Poteaux sur sol* wall, *bousillage entre poteaux*

completely, white-washed and then makes a strong and handsome wall, cool in summer and warm in winter.

The roof is made of large pieces of cypress [*merrains*] split with the sledge-hammer and pegged to the rafters. The door-hinges and window fastenings and hinges are also pegged. The chimney is built like the walls, around four *quenouilles de cheminée* [literally, "chimney distaffs," because like the distaff of a spinning wheel, they are inclined inward], 4" x 4" wooden uprights pierced like the *colombes* or wall uprights to receive *batons* and *bousillage*. Earthen chimneys were common in the 1840s but have tended to be replaced by brick (see Fig. 17).

There is no need of a lock; when one goes out, a chair keeps the door closed and informs the public that no one is at home. At the entrance, near the door, are a pail of water, a polished gourd beside it, with which to dip out the water, and a wash-basin or *lavabo*, set on a little shelf fixed to the wall, near which hangs a handtowel of locally-made cloth. The furniture consists of a cypress bed made by just about anybody, for all the *habitants* understand carpentry. There are also a cypress table and chairs upholstered with skins. There are stools and benches. The spinning-wheel for wool and cotton, the loom for weaving the well-known blue-and-red cotonnade take up much room. Roller-beds for the children (*lits-à-roulettes*) are low cots which slide under the big bed at morning and have sticks set up in each corner at evening to hold up the mosquito netting.

As one can see, this [main] room [*salle*] serves as kitchen, dormitory, and dining room. Here too the corn is shelled. Let us not forget the gun, an indispensable object on an *habitation,* hung horizontally over the door on two brackets whittled out in wood and nailed to the wall. From these also hang the gamebag made of *chawi* (racoon) skin. This contains the powderbag and other necessities of the hunt. The powder horn is in fact made of skin or cotonnade. The *racatchias* [spurs] also hang here. [The *racatchia* was an instrument used to receive the lead ball from the barrel of the gun after a misfire. It literally "spurred" or screwed into the lead ball. The gun was essential for hunting wild animals, killing mad dogs, and slaughtering livestock as well as for defending the home.

On entering a rural Acadian house, one is struck by the profusion of wall decoration. There are large and brightly colored prints, among them the family's patron saints, the Wedding of the Blessed Virgin, the Consolatrix of All Afflictions, the Good Shepherd, model of solicitude, carrying on his shoulders the injured sheep. There one sees the affecting story of Geneviève de Brabant. There are sketches from illustrated papers. The chimney walls are papered with all sorts of pictures, clippings from everywhere, badly trimmed, labels from cloth-bolts, liquor bottles, tobacco packages, perfume bottles. The panorama surrounds a statue of the Virgin, perhaps Our Lady of Lourdes, resting on an altar placed on a shelf near which hang a rosary and holy-water font.

The moving of a house or building, called *trainage,* is characteristic of the Acadian country. The house is first placed on long pieces of wood called *rances.* These are set on the axles of large wagons. Oxen in sufficient number, harnessed to this kind of train, pull simultaneously. Whatever its weight, the house is sometimes dragged long distances. The trip is usually made without incident, except for breaking of the ox-teams' harness-chains. Bridges are thrown over smaller streams, ditches filled, fences taken down and rebuilt. Once at the new site, the building is again placed on foundation piers with great skiil. It is in the Attakapas country that this *trainage* is most commonly performed. The labor force consists of volunteers and the operation costs the owner only a few gallons of whiskey, coffee, and an open-air meal.

Houses like the one described in the Breaux manuscript were commonplace through the first half of the nineteenth century, and persisted in rural Acadiana until well into the twentieth century. One thing that is missing from the description of the Acadian house is a

Figure 12. "Morning Dew" by Floyd Sonnier. A third generation Cajun house

gallery. Many third-generation houses were not originally galleried (Fig. 12), though galleries were already being added to some Acadian abodes before the end of the eighteenth century.

Certain similarities can be seen between second- and third-generation Acadian houses in Louisiana and those of Acadia in Nova Scotia. Traditional methods of construction and kinds of furnishings persisted well into the Louisiana experience. At the same time, architectural preferences were changing. The process of evolution from second- to third-generation cottages was witnessed by nineteenth-century observers such as Sidney Marchand:

At the beginning the houses were constructed without floors, other than the alluvial soil of this region. . . . Very poor, [the Acadians] endured all manner of hardships, but, as the years passed, their homes and farms were improved. The more prosperous ones, after 1797, occasionally received *The Monitor of Louisiana*— the first newspaper published in New Orleans and Louisiana. In time some of the exiles built floors of pickets in their homes;

then came small galleries, planked overhead. In time we find them building their cottages "on blocks," or pillars, and the walls were filled with a mixture of mud and moss which was placed between the posts. The exiles called it *"bousillier entre les poteaux."*

Most Acadians adopted the use of raised sills sometime in the late eighteenth or early nineteenth centuries. But as late as 1827 inventories of properties on the Acadian Coast still describe some houses as *poteaux en terre.*

Like the houses of Acadia, the descriptions of early Acadian houses in Louisiana make it clear that they were small. We are fortunate that Marchand saw fit to record descriptions and dimensions of 159 second-and third-generation Acadian houses from St. James, Ascension, and Lafourche parishes. The legal inventories span the period from 1771 through 1803. They provide a useful database for the study of early Acadian houses. Prominent features such as galleries are also recorded. Some typical descriptions are the following:

1771 House on ground, 20' x 14', front gallery, surrounded, covered and floored with *pieux* [split planks].

1773 House on ground, 22' x 16', planked above [roof] and below [walls] with pickets [*pieux*].

1776 House of posts in ground, 25' x 15', gallery on both grand faces [front and rear] covered and floored above and below with pickets.

1780 House on ground, 20' x 10', front gallery, covered with boards, surrounded and floored with pickets.

1790 House of posts in the ground, 30' x 15', with galleries.

1802 House, 26' x 16', built on blocks, two galleries, covered with pickets.

1803 House, 35' x 41' [including galleries], brick chimney.

If one plots the length and width dimensions of one hundred of the eighteenth-century Acadian houses, a rather surprising pattern emerges. The houses conform to a well-defined pattern. They range in width from ten to seventeen feet. The length of the house has little effect on its width—just the opposite of the pattern in Creole houses. Rather, as the Acadian house grows in length (by adding new rooms to the ends), it grows almost no wider (Fig. 13). This pattern is so

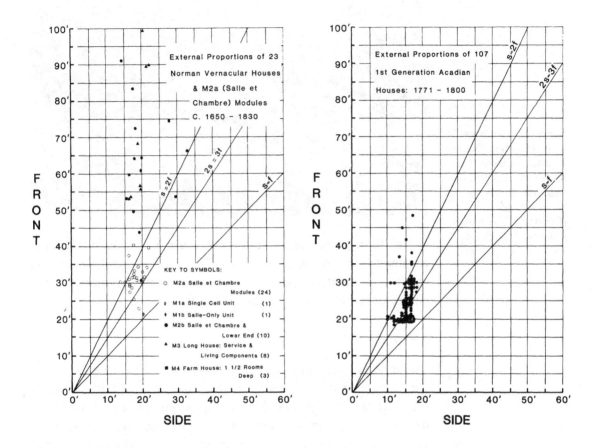

strikingly different from the Louisiana Creole pattern that we cannot help but speculate upon its significance.

It appears that Acadians were uncomfortable in a house with rooms wider than about seventeen feet and that their ideal was a room about fifteen feet wide. Can it be that their years of living in huts and shacks in exile had shaped their spatial preferences in architecture, or is it perhaps a legacy of the cold Canadian north? Another explanation is that what we see laid out on the Louisiana landscape is the medieval French long-house in miniature. Between the eleventh and the seventeenth centuries, peasants in many parts of western France lived in a long-house—a building only one room deep but many rooms wide. Like its ancient teutonic progenitor, the long-house functioned as a combined cow house, hay barn, and residence for humans. As these houses grew longer, they did not grow

Figure 13. Proportions of first and second generation (Louisiana) Acadian and Norman (French) long houses, compared

Figure 14. The boyhood home of Robert DeLapouyade on Bayou Lafourche as sketched by him from memory in the late nineteenth century (Robert De Lapouyade, Courtesy Rare Book Room, LSU Library)

wider. Though wealthier landholders began in the early sixteenth century to expand the Norman long-house into a building one and one-half rooms deep, peasants continued to build traditional long-houses until well into the eighteenth century.

The Creole Architecture of Louisiana

The most popular form of plantation house in 1765 was the raised Creole house with a double-pitch hip roof and encircling galleries (Figs. 8, 14). One of these houses may be seen in the 1765 Pittman drawing of New Orleans, but mostly they constituted a rural form, popular in Pointe Coupee Parish, in Saint Martinville on the Teche, on the German Coast, in Baton Rouge, and also in the Creole communities of Missouri and Illinois. The Acadians could not afford to emulate these structures in the early days of settlement. By the last decade of the eighteenth century, however, there is little doubt that elements of the architecture of these Creole houses were being integrated into the Acadian tradition (compare Figs. 14 and 15). The most important Creole feature to be adopted into the Acadian model was the gallery.

Since the Creole house was far better adapted to Louisiana's tropical climate than the houses of the Acadians (or for that matter, the buildings designed by French engineers in New Orleans), it had already become popular along the banks of the lower Mississippi and the Gulf Coast by the third decade of the eighteenth century. Identical houses were still to be seen when Claude C. Robin traveled up the

Mississippi River from New Orleans in the years 1803–5 (Figs. 8 and 14):

[The houses] are of the most varied form, some built of wood, surrounded by galleries in the Chinese fashion [referring to French Creole houses with double-pitch roofs], others built of brick are surmounted with a gallery in the Italian manner [referring to raised, galleried houses with single-pitch roofs and Tuscan columns supporting their galleries]. . . .

From the city [New Orleans] to Lafourche [Donaldsonville], both banks of the river are lined with houses. From Lafourche to Point Coupee the interval between houses becomes larger. Beyond Point Coupee there are no houses outside of the few settlements at long distances from each other. The houses close to the city (especially those of the sugar planters) are sumptuous. Further away they are smaller and simpler. Some of the houses are of brick with columns, but the usual construction is of timber with the interstices filled with earth, the whole plastered over with lime. These houses have ordinarily only two or three large rooms, but the heat of the climate makes galleries around the houses a necessity. All of them have one, some around all four sides of the house, others on two sides only, and rarely on only one side. These galleries are formed by a prolongation of the roof beyond the walls, but the prolongation forms a break in the angle of the plane of the roof so that the gallery roof rises instead of falling. This produces an effect opposite to the appearance of the Mansard roof. These attached wing-like roofs are supported by little wooden columns, an agreeable effect for the eyes. The galleries are usually eight or nine feet wide. These wide galleries have several advantages. First, they prevent the sun's rays from striking the walls of the house and thus to keep them cool. Also, they form a convenient and pleasant spot upon which to promenade during the day (one of course, goes to the side away from the sun), one can eat or entertain there, and very often during the hot summer nights one sleeps there. In many houses the ends of the galleries are closed to form two additional rooms.

The Fourth-Generation Acadian House
(Creole style, ca. 1790–1920)

Many smaller Creole houses with single-pitched umbrella roofs were also in existence at the time of the Acadian arrival, particularly in New Orleans, but increasingly in the countryside also. It seems that technical problems with the old double-pitch roof caused it gradually to go out of style. Double-pitch roofs leaked and were expensive to construct and to keep in repair.

It would be surprising, indeed, if the dominant Creole architectural pattern had not influenced the growing Acadian tradition, but it appears to have done so remarkably slowly. The Acadians did not simply give up their beloved Canadian house to replace it with the Creole version. Rather, it is clear that they borrowed selectively from the Creole tradition. The borrowing was probably limited at first. The third-generation Acadian house is marked by the use of a single-pitch roof without a full-length front gallery. Even before the turn of the nineteenth century, however, Acadians seem to have begun Creolizing their houses through the addition of full-length front galleries. When this occurred, the fourth generation may be said to have been established. Third- and fourth-generation forms coexisted for many years, with the former gradually disappearing and the latter becoming almost completely dominant by the 1840s or 1850s.

The roofs of third- and fourth-generation Acadian cottages were invariably gabled rather than hipped. A hipped roof was by now the mark of the pretentious Creole. The Acadian retained the ancient (pre-exile) gabled-roof cottage, but adapted it along the lines of the Creole pattern to suit the tropical climate and the economic and social necessities of the new environment.

One way in which the fourth-generation Acadian houses differed from the Creole house was in the use of the loft. All vernacular houses make some provision for expansion. In the Creole house, expansion occurred by enclosing the side galleries of the house to make additional rooms. The Acadian house, however, had no side galleries. The Acadians expanded upward instead. This was probably simply a carry-over of their traditional use of loft space for storage and as a *gârçonnière*. The principal difficulty with this approach for the Acadian was that the loft of the third-generation cabin was not very large or tall. The single-room-deep house was narrow; its rafters were footed only about fifteen feet apart, so little head-room remained in the loft. In the fourth generation, however, the Acadians widened their basic cottage to the front by the addition of a gallery, and to the rear by the addition of a cabinet-loggia range, generally two small rooms with an open porch between them, resulting in a house at least thirty-five feet deep. The house was then capped with an umbrella

Figure 15. Thibodeaux house, Lafayette

Figure 16. A small Cajun house on Bayou Lafourche, eastern style

roof that spanned all of these spaces. This provided much more room in the loft while at the same time keeping the house basically one room deep for purposes of cross-ventilation (Fig. 15).

The loft of the expanded fourth-generation house provided practical living space. It was here in the traditional *grenier,* or grain storage loft (of the French farm house), that the Acadian *garçonnière* was re-established. The young women of the family slept on the ground floor behind the parents' bedroom, while the boys had direct access to the outside from the loft. However, if the family had more girls than boys, the loft might well become a *fillière* instead.

Access to the loft was provided in two different ways (Map 11). In eastern Acadiana, along Bayou Lafourche and on the Acadian Coast, a ladder or a short, steep flight of stairs was inserted within the house itself—usually in a rear room (Fig. 16). In western Acadiana, however, the stairs to the loft were placed on the front gallery (Fig. 15). This may be due to the fact that the more remote western houses were generally smaller in size and placing stairs outside on the gallery saved badly needed space within the house. There may, however, be another reason for the geographical pattern in Acadian stairways.

It was one of the necessities of building in Louisiana that a house be raised above the ground to provide long-term protection for its sills. In the raised Creole house of that period, access to the main floor was gained via a flight of stairs between the ground and the first floor gallery (Fig. 14). The staircase was generally placed directly under the front gallery. By the time the Acadians had arrived in Louisiana, this pattern had become *déclassé* in the area around New Orleans. That area was dominated by settlers from France, and to these relative sophisticates, the inset staircase, the asymmetrical facade, and the sharply broken roof pitch gave the house a rough-hewn and provincial look. Stairs running straight out from the middle of the house in the Palladian manner were thought to be more stylish. In the isolated bayous and on the prairies of western Acadiana, however, the raised Creole house with its stairs tucked under the front gallery was still the most elegant architectural form on the landscape. Acadians therefore saw no reason not to copy an exterior stair to the loft of their cottage directly from this dominant and (at least locally) prestigious form. Thus, the gallery-mounted exterior stairway was adopted more as a symbol of elegance than for any

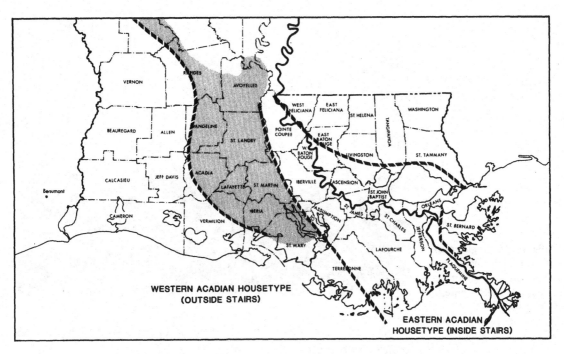

WESTERN ACADIAN HOUSETYPE
(OUTSIDE STAIRS)

EASTERN ACADIAN
HOUSETYPE (INSIDE STAIRS)

Map 11. The distribution of eastern and western Acadian housetypes

specific functional cause. One other factor may have played a part: in the Creole vernacular architecture of Haiti one occasionally finds exterior stairs and ladders leading to the loft of the house.

Acadian cottages also adopted the use of multiple doors in the facade. Like the Caribbean Creole dwellings, the front doors could be opened to direct breezes through the house (Figs. 15, 16).

Yet another Creole feature adopted by the fourth-generation Acadian builder was the rear cabinet-loggia range (Fig. 8). Rear cabinet rooms and inter-cabinet loggias were a feature of the vernacular architecture of both the Spanish and the French West Indies as well as Louisiana. Although the second- and third-generation Acadian houses seem not to have used these for expansion, they were being adopted by many Acadians in the earliest decades of the nineteenth century. With the adoption of full-length galleries, cabinets, and loggias the Acadian house now fell well within the definition of Louisiana Creole architecture.

By the middle of the nineteenth century, the Acadian house had assumed the familiar form that still survives today in the countryside of Louisiana. The fourth-generation house was now characterized by a two-or three-room plan, increasingly identical to that of the small Creole house. Single-room Acadian houses became more and more

Figure 17. Single-room Cajun house on the prairies, ca. 1929 (Photo courtesy Fred Kniffen)

rare, until they almost disappeared altogether—surviving on the prairies into the twentieth century (Fig. 17).

If one separates the various components of the fourth-generation Acadian house, such as *salle-et-chambre* plan, inset gallery, internal chimney, gallery-mounted front stairway, French timber-frame technology, rear cabinet rooms, use of the loft as a *garçonnière*, and the placement of multiple double-leaf doors in the facade, it is possible to trace each element to a separate origin, all of which together reflect the tortured history of the Acadian people.

In the nineteenth century Acadians adopted a new floor plan for the typical two-room cottage (Fig. 16). Along Bayou Lafourche and in the river parishes, a module with two equal-size (or nearly equal) rooms became popular. This was clearly a folk accommodation to the increasing popularity of Palladian/Georgian symmetry of the larger Creole and plantation houses of the state.

In the nineteenth century the big sugar planters were looking for more arable land to bring under cultivation. They began buying up Acadian farms on the natural levees. George Washington Cable described Point Bancée, a settlement of about 150 people who lived in "adobe [*bousillage*] homes with thatched roofs and gables." There seems to have been a natural antipathy between both the culture and the economic system of the Acadians, on the one hand, and the Creole sugar planters, on the other. The inevitable conflict was

Figure 18. Modern slab house in the Cajun style, Lafayette (Photo by Barry Ancelet)

resolved in favor of the planters in most cases. Not only did many Cajuns favor isolation, many were more or less forced to accept it through the power of the industrial agricultural system.

It should not be assumed, however, that all Acadians were subsistence-level peasants. Even in the late eighteenth and early nineteenth centuries, many prospered. Some remained along the natural levees and became planters. In Lafayette Parish, 68 percent of the slave-holders in 1850 were Acadian, with an average of about six slaves per family. Other Acadians turned to raising cattle on *vacheries* on the prairies west of the Teche. Unlike the linear settlements of the bayous, the settlement pattern on the prairies was a dispersed one, with small groups of houses gathered in *anses*, or coves.

The interiors of the houses of the prairie Acadians were neat and presentable. George Washington Cable noted in 1880 that

Madame Baptist Clement wore rawhide shoes [many rural Acadians went barefoot, except on special occasions]. Of house furniture: A showy mantel-piece of stained and varnished wood. Four brown panels in darker colored moulding going around the side of the chimney with red pilasters. Clean hand-scrubbed cypress floor with neat [original obscured—perhaps "cottonade"] mats of plaited rags at the doors and strips of woven rag carpet here and there. The walls and ceiling of plain, unpainted pine. A square army oil cloth for a hearth rag. Neat, plain homes. Locally made wardrobes, turned post bedsteads of stained wood with testers, oak chairs with hide bottoms, white fringed counterpanes made of cotton grown on the farm, and feather beds.

The gallery of the Acadian house is a workshop for both the housekeeper and the breadwinner. The loom, the spinning wheel, the *carot* [?]. From the joists overhead hang the pods of tobacco seed used for next year's planting [tobacco had become popular about 1790].

It is still possible to find fourth-generation Cajun folk houses in many parts of rural Acadiana, though they are fast being replaced with mobile homes and ranch houses built on concrete slabs (Fig. 18). Their distribution coincides well with the boundaries of Cajun country. Many typical nineteenth-century buildings have been preserved in open-air museums, particularly in Acadian Village and Vermilionville in Lafayette and in the Louisiana State University Rural Life Museum in Baton Rouge.

Foodways

In a recent film, *J'ai été au bal* by Chris Strachwitz and Les Blank, the Cajun accordion maker and musician Marc Savoy describes Cajun music as a gumbo made of various ingredients and spices. He demonstrates the development of the sound by adding one element at a time (basic melody, syncopation, embellishment, and so on) until, as he puts it, "it starts to *taste* like a Cajun song." It is no accident that Cajun food (especially gumbo) has often been used as a metaphor for other Cajun cultural features. Like their music, language, architecture, and the Cajuns themselves, Cajun cooking is a hybrid, a blend of French, Acadian, Spanish, German, Anglo-American, Afro-Caribbean, and Native American influences. In addition, the frontier imposed itself on Cajun foodways, forcing the area's cooks to improvise recipes to make ingenious use of what was available to cook and cook with.

The most obvious influence on Cajun cuisine is French. Indeed the people who eventually became Acadians brought with them cooking styles from France, primarily the provinces of Vendée, Poitou, and Brittany. Much of France's fine cuisine is rooted in the need to make the best of a bad situation: examples are the development of cooking techniques designed to tenderize tough cuts of beef and pork, and the creation of sauces designed to make simple foods more appetizing. It is said that the art of French sauce-making was developed during the Middle Ages when peasant and bourgeois housewives developed ways to overcome the poor quality and quantity of available fresh meat. Marinades, spices, and long cooking in covered pots helped tenderize poor cuts and made them tastier. (Marinades helped cure meat of dubious quality.) Long cooking in covered pots also produced sauces that stretched the nutritional and filling value of the dishes.

In Louisiana as in France, fresh pork and beef sausages were

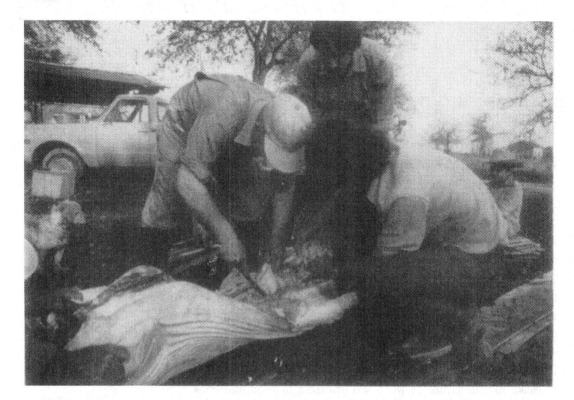

"Boucherie," family hog slaughtering, near Scott, 1978 (Photo by Ginette Vachon)

made for immediate consumption. Before refrigeration, fresh cuts of meat were stored in the coolest available safe spot (sometimes hanging in a well) for a few days. In some areas frequent cooperative *boucheries* (slaughterings) made it possible to have fresh meat on a relatively regular basis. Participants at a *boucherie* let nothing go to waste. Edible internal organs (liver, heart, spleen, kidneys, etc.) were cooked in a *sauce de débris*. Intestines and the stomach were used as casings for sausage and *boudin*. The skin of cows was tanned and used in a variety of ways, such as riding tack and chair bottoms; the skin of pigs was edible, however, and was fried to produce cracklings. Even the head provided the high concentration of gelatinous meats to produce *fromage de tête,* or head cheese, which is more highly seasoned in Louisiana than the version made by *charcutiers* in France.

Louisiana *boudin*, although derived from the traditional French sausage, is quite different from the Gallic *boudin noir,* which is composed primarily of coagulated blood. The French *boudin blanc,* made of pounded chicken breasts, veal, and sometimes sweetbreads, resembles more closely the Louisiana variety, though it is smoother and blander. The Cajuns traditionally made both white and red *boudin*. The white, now the most common variety, is a spicy rice and pork dressing stuffed into casings. Red *boudin*, made from the same rice dressing flavored and colored with blood, is difficult to find on the commercial market today because of State Department of Health restrictions on slaughtering procedures. It can still be found in family and neighborhood *boucheries*.

Chickens, guinea hens, and other domestic fowl were a popular source of meat because of their small size. They could be slaughtered according to need and easily eaten by a family at one meal or two successive meals. Wild game was also a popular source of meat, especially during the winter months when it was plentiful and safe to eat.

Certain meats can be preserved for a limited amount of time. There are several ways to accomplish this, all of which involve a curing process that salts, smokes, or dries the meat. In France, *charcutiers* and *bouchers* produced slabs of cured meats and a wide variety of sausages. This tradition was preserved in Louisiana where individuals made salt pork and beef, *tasso* (a spicy Cajun version of jerky) and a wide variety of sausages, like smoked beef and pork sausage, *andouille* (stuffed large intestines), and *chourice* (stuffed small intestines), and *chaudin* (stuffed stomach), for family consumption. Meat was also preserved for shorter periods of time by submerging small cuts in jars of lard called *pots de graisse* to retard oxidation.

Keeping foods longer than the few days they were fresh was important in filling the gaps during the year. Eventually people developed innovative ways to extend the season on many foods. Fruits and some vegetables were usually preserved by canning them. Beans and foods with high acid content, like tomatoes, had a relatively long shelf life and made popular canned goods. Sometimes these and other vegetables, like cucumbers and *mirlitons* (vegetable pears), were pickled in vinegar with peppers and spices. Locally available fruits—blackberries, dewberries, mulberries, wild cherries, and especially figs—were put up as preserves and used on bread and biscuits, and to sweeten cakes, pies, and cereals.

As in France, bread was an important staple in Louisiana, where it was made from a variety of grain flours. Some, like wheat and rye, were known in Europe, but these grains were difficult to grow in hot, humid Louisiana and expensive to buy even when one could find them in the urban markets. Corn, discovered in the New World with the help of Native Americans, was plentiful and quickly became the grain of choice for making bread as well as cereals such as *couche-couche* (fried corn-meal mush). Even where wheat flour became available, bread did not keep very long, and batches were usually baked at least once or twice a week.

The importance of cheese in France (where there are over four hundred varieties) did not translate to Louisiana. Except for a simple cottage cheese called *caillé goûté*, or dripped clabber, very little cheese was made by the Cajuns in Louisiana. The same appears to have been true of the Acadians even before leaving Acadia; visitors to Nova Scotia before the exile complained about the lack of milk products in general. Early Acadians cooked with oil, often bear oil, instead of butter. This may have been due to the lack of milk cattle in their settlements. In Louisiana, cattle herds were almost always composed of beef stock, usually longhorns, which produced little milk and resisted giving it except to their own offspring. Butter may have been less important to the settlers because most Acadian families originated in the province of Poitou, which lies between France's butter-based cuisine to the north and its olive-oil-based cuisine to the south. Cooking with oil was probably not unknown to them, and when milk products were unavailable, they naturally turned to vegetable oils and animal fats. Perhaps the best known oil-based cooking technique in Louisiana cuisine is the *roux*, flour browned in oil, which serves as the basis for many sauces and gumbos. In southern France, as in Louisiana, *roux* is made by browning flour in oil; in northern France, the flour is browned lightly in butter.

Once in the New World, the French settlers who were to become Acadians found it necessary to relearn many things, including what was good to eat, where to get it, and how to cook it. They learned much of this from the Native American tribes in the area (especially the Micmac) who taught them techniques for acquiring native game and fish, and for growing native fruits and vegetables, especially corn and potatoes. Many of the names for new plants (like *maïs*, corn) and animals (like *chaoui*, raccoon) were borrowed directly from Native American languages. After exile from Nova Scotia, Acadians once again had to relearn what to eat and how to get it in subtropical Louisiana. And again, the Native Americans, especially the Chitimacha and Houma tribes, contributed to their reorientation.

The most obvious example of Native American influence is the cultivation and consumption of corn. This was generally true throughout North America. Once corn was discovered, it quickly became a staple grain. This was not true in France where corn is still thought of primarily as animal feed. In addition to roasting and boiling fresh ears, one of the first uses of preserved corn was a bland corn-meal gruel called *sagamité*. Sweetened and added to fresh milk, this became what the Acadians called *couche-couche*, perhaps because of its resemblance to an African semolina-based steamed mush called *cous-cous*. Spices, onions, and tomatoes were added to stewed fresh corn to produce *maquechoux*.

The practice of cooking with tomatoes and hot peppers shows the influences from Spanish and Afro-Caribbean sources. Cajuns learned to enjoy peppers and *sauces piquantes* as do many others who dwell in the subtropics. The "heat" of the spices actually serves to cool eaters in the long run by making them perspire. Other African influences included single-dish combinations like jambalaya and gumbo. Jambalaya closely resembles sub-Saharan communal rice-based dishes that are eaten by hand, each person rolling a ball of the sticky mixture and popping it into the mouth. Sugarcane, imported from the West Indies, and grown in Louisiana, was used to produce cane syrup, sugar, and a primitive rum called *tafia*. Cane syrup was used by Cajuns as a sweetener and source of calories over many foods, as it was among other poor southern people. It was also used to make cakes, pralines, and a few other confections.

Gumbo, perhaps the most dramatic of the Cajun dishes, has clear African origins, but draws on many other traditions as well. Originally its main ingredient was okra, a vegetable first imported from western Africa where it is called *guingombo*. The spicy cayenne seasoning, typical of subtropical cuisines, represents Spanish and Afro–Caribbean influences. In Louisiana, gumbo is eaten with rice, a crop introduced by the French who harvested what they called providence rice in the flooded lowlands produced by the Louisiana prairie's high claypan. It was grown by slaves and Creole and Cajun yeoman farmers as a supplementary food source, and later made a local staple by German and Anglo-American farmers who moved into the area from the Midwest in the nineteenth century.

Gumbo is now considered festive, but originally it was a cook's way of making do with whatever was at hand: chicken, guinea hen, duck, turkey, rabbit, quail, dove, blackbird, deer, and other wild or domestic meats, alone or in combination. Seafood, once used only in coastal communities, has come into general use with the advent of refrigeration. Shrimp and crab, too delicate to blend well with most meats, are usually used alone or with each other. Oysters, on the other hand, hold their own and are often added to a variety of seafood- and meat-based gumbos. Traditionally, beef and pork are not used in gumbo except in the form of smoked or fresh sausage. Though okra gave its name to the dish, it is not an essential ingredient. A gumbo made with okra is usually called *gumbo févi*. *Gumbo filé*, on the other hand, draws on French culinary tradition for its base, a *roux*. Just before serving, *gumbo filé* is thickened by the addition of powdered sassafras leaves, one of the Native American contributions to Louisiana cooking.

Currently, no food is more representative of Cajun culture than the crawfish. The ancestors of the Acadians and French Creoles may have known about these freshwater crustaceans. Indeed, crawfish are now rare in the streams of France where they have been eaten almost into extinction. Yet until the 1940s and 1950s, though considered edible, crawfish were not commercially available in Louisiana. Nor were they highly prized. In fact, the derogatory name "mudbug," which still repels outsiders until they taste them, was not unknown in south Louisiana even thirty years ago—a time when shrimp and crabs were much more in demand, particularly in towns within easy reach of the coast. People who lived close to crawfish sources, along the Atchafalaya Basin or near prairie lowlands, bayous, and drainage ditches, gathered them from time to time with set nets or drag nets. Recipes were simple: usually crawfish were simply boiled or steamed. Cooks who had help from family members or servants sometimes made bisque. It was not until the mid-1950s, when commercial processing began to make crawfish readily available, that they gained in popularity. They have retained a certain exotic aura, however, and locals like to play upon the revulsion of outsiders faced for the first time with the prospect of eating these delicious but unusual creatures, goading them to suck the "head" (technically, the thorax). A few tails, however, will usually convert the most squeamish unbelievers. As crawfish became commercially available, restaurant chefs and home cooks alike began experimenting with the peeled tails and "fat" to develop recipes for stews, casseroles, and thermidores. The simplest of these new recipes, crawfish *étouffée*, is also the most delicate and most popular. Each season more and more outsiders fall in love with the lowly crawfish, so that the industry now plays a major role in the economy of south Louisiana, exporting to urban areas nationwide and to Europe. Nevertheless, nearly eighty-five percent of the crawfish harvested each year is consumed locally, and some Cajuns wonder how the other fifteen percent is getting away.

The Cajuns discovered some new vegetables when they arrived in Louisiana. They did not know the eggplant, for example, until then, and so had no name for it. They borrowed the Spanish word *berengena,* which eventually became *brème.* To this day the standard French word for eggplant, *aubergine,* is unknown in south Louisiana. The eggplant, which grows very easily in Cajun country, is used in many sorts of dressings, alone or combined with chopped ham, crumbled sausage, browned ground meat, or minced seafood.

An inexpensive source of protein and carbohydrates, beans were once standard fare for slaves and poor whites in the South and the West Indies. Flavoring with sausage was a touch of luxury that came later. The basic ingredients of bean and rice dishes—milled rice, dried beans, and cured ham or smoked sausage—were easy to store over relatively long periods. Beans and rice have followed gumbo and crawfish to become fashionable cuisine in recent times. They are still often served with cornbread, thus duplicating typical nineteenth-century poor southern fare.

Cajuns have been very innovative in developing their cuisine, adapting recipes to available ingredients, including "exotic" meats such as turtle, alligator, nutria, raccoon, possum, and armadillo. Some or all of these may have been eaten by Native Americans, but they were hardly standard European fare, even in the colonies. Yet the Cajuns learned to prepare and eat these and other animals to provide meat in their diet.

The use of turtle meat may been learned from the English, turtle soup being a favorite in Britain. Most parts of the turtle have a rich, pungent taste that makes a little go a long way in stews and soups. Cajuns usually caught turtles by probing the banks of canals and bayous for underwater holes and pulling them out by hand, avoiding the head by feeling the grain of the scales on the back. Increasingly rare, difficult to catch, and even harder to butcher, turtles are an expensive delicacy today.

The alligator, of course, was rightly considered an exotic and

Alligator, now lauded in culinary circles, was once almost trapped into extinction. (Photo by Brad Bigley)

dangerous reptile by early settlers. Prized for its valuable skin, the Louisiana alligator was almost trapped into extinction. Only a few decades ago, it was protected as an endangered species. By the early 1980s, however, the population had grown to such an extent that the Louisiana Department of Wildlife and Fisheries opened a tightly controlled annual alligator hunting season. The alligator has become popular for the surprisingly delicate meat that trappers once discarded after skinning them. Barbecued and fried tail were added to the menus in Louisiana's culinary circles. Meat from other parts of the body is used in soups, stews, and sauces.

Large rodents, like nutria, and other more or less exotic animals, like raccoons, possums, and armadillos, are hardly standard fare in south Louisiana today. Indeed many young Cajuns find the thought of eating them as repulsive as most outsiders do. They *are* edible, though, and can be quite tasty. They also have an obvious shock value, which some aficionados like to play up. These exotic meats are frequently associated with a sort of macho/outdoor/camp lifestyle and consequently are popular among groups of men who eat them conspicuously and boast of eating them to other, less adventurous types. Even the hardiest cooks avoid preparing these highly pungent meats in the confines of a kitchen, preferring to grill or barbecue them outside instead.

Because of the heat, cool drinks have long been popular in south Louisiana. Beer-drinking Anglo-American, German, and Alsatian immigrants fostered a penchant for beer among the Cajuns. The Acadians had learned to make spruce beer in Nova Scotia, since grapes would not grow to make wine there. Grapes did not grow in Louisiana either, though some did make sweet wines with wild berries. Popular nonalcoholic drinks include such standard southern favorites as iced teas (made with a variety of fresh leaves, herbs, and mints) and root beer (originally made with sassafras roots).

Like Cajun culture in general, Cajun cooking continues to adapt to changing times. The most important change, of course, was refrigeration, which made it possible to preserve seafood, meats, and vegetables by cooling or freezing them. This had a great effect on Cajun foodways. Community *boucheries* were no longer necessary as a regular source of fresh meat. *Boudin*, formerly limited to the winter months, now became available year-round, served hot from Japanese rice steamers or microwave ovens in most convenience stores. Seafood and dairy products became more readily and widely available. Along with refrigeration came improved transportation, which allowed the importation of new products such as mushrooms, asparagus, artichokes, and celery.

These changes also affected recipes, which became more complex with a wider variety of foods to choose from. Cajun cooks began to experiment with new ingredients. Oysters were added to chicken gumbos. Celery joined onions and bell peppers as a standard seasoning vegetable. Mushrooms and cheese were added to many dishes. During the mid-twentieth century, chefs at restaurants like Don's, Jacob's, and the Riverside Inn in Lafayette, the Yellow Bowl in Jeanerette, Robin's and Pat's in Henderson, and the Palace in Opelousas developed a sort of Cajun haute cuisine, combining the solid characteristics of simple Cajun country cooking with contemporary ingredients and Creole styles. And the experimentation continues in places like Chez Pastor, the Vermilionville Café, Lafitte's Landing, and many others, as well as in homes throughout south Louisiana. Since the 1950s, there has been a veritable explosion in the uses of crawfish. One can now find crawfish *boudin*, crawfish casseroles, and crawfish au gratin. As south Louisiana grows more cosmopolitan, one also finds crawfish pizza, crawfish tamales, and even crawfish egg rolls! There is a whole industry growing around Cajun cooking. One can

Cajuns have adapted many foods from ethnic groups to create their own distinctive culinary tradition. (Photos by Barry Ancelet)

buy prefabricated *roux*, pre-blended "Cajun" spices, and even frozen "Cajun" dinners. And, of course, since the arrival of chef Paul Prudhomme, whose eccentric creativity has helped bring Cajun cuisine to national prominence, one can find blackened redfish, blackened catfish, and blackened chicken in restaurants from Portland (Oregon) to Portland (Maine) and from Miami to Montreal.

It has been said that Cajuns do not eat to live; instead, they live to eat. Indeed food and its preparation are more important than just nourishment. Cajun cooking has definite performance aspects. Even in the home, cooks expect eaters to comment not only on their food, but on their technique. Dinner guests frequently function as an audience, gathering around the cook to discuss his or her performance along with other topics of social interest. Outside the home, there are entire festivals devoted to the performance of Cajun cooking, such as Lafayette's Cajun Culinary Classic and the Bayou Food Festival. Other festivals focus on one type of food, such as Eunice's Crawfish Etouffée Cookoff, Kinder's Sauce Piquante Festival, and Broussard's Boudin Festival among many others. Even without a specific focus, most festivals feature Cajun and Creole food in some way. One of the not-so-hidden assets of the New Orleans Jazz and Heritage Festival and Festivals Acadiens is that they feed their visitors with culturally and regionally appropriate food.

PART FOUR

Performance

CHAPTER 10

Music and Musical Instruments

Cajun Music

Like jazz, rock, and the blues, Cajun music was improvised in the New World. Along with Cajun cooking, it is one of the most accessible aspects of Cajun folklife. Entertaining and danceable, Cajun music circumvents the language barrier. Like Cajun cooking and Cajun culture in general, Cajun music is a blend of the cultural ingredients found in south Louisiana. The French Creoles shared some western French folk songs with the Acadians. In addition, French Creole immigrants continued to update the repertoire during the eighteenth and nineteenth centuries. Native Americans contributed a wailing, terraced singing style in which vocal lines descend progressively in steps. Black Creoles contributed new rhythms and a sense of percussion techniques, improvisational singing, and the blues. The Spanish eventually contributed the guitar and a few tunes. The violin, which was a popular new instrument in France in the seventeenth century when the French left for the New World, continued to dominate the instrumental tradition until German-Jewish merchants in the area began importing diatonic accordions shortly after they were invented in Austria early in the nineteenth century. The accordion arrived without instructions or cultural baggage. Acadian and black Creole musicians began experimenting with it, discovering how to coax familiar tunes out of this new music-making contraption. Anglo-American immigrants contributed new fiddle tunes and dances, such as reels, jigs, and hoedowns. Singers also translated English songs into French and made them their own. By the turn of this century, these diverse ingredients had steeped long enough in the south Louisiana cultural gumbo pot to become what we now call

Cajun music. (The music developed by Black Creoles along similar lines came to be called zydeco.)

Commercial recording companies like Decca, Columbia, RCA Victor, and Bluebird began recording regional and ethnic music throughout America in the early part of this century for the purpose of selling record players. There was not yet a national music scene. In order to arouse interest in their machines, the companies had to provide the kind of music that people were interested in hearing: their own. To sell record players in south Louisiana, these companies inadvertently recorded the tail end of what turned out to be a formative period in the development of Cajun music—formative in part because it was recorded—as well as subsequent changes in the tradition. Since commercial records were made to be sold, they provided a good barometer of popular trends. They also gave a sort of imprimatur to the musicians they recorded. In south Louisiana, popular music was wholly traditional at the turn of the century, but soon enough recorded musicians began to set the style. Joseph and Cléoma Falcon were fairly well known in the area around their native Rayne, but the release of "Lafayette" in 1928 spread their influence and fame much farther. Everyone wanted to hear the Cajun musicians who had made a record. The newly improvised verses they had added to a new arrangement of an older traditional tune almost immediately became a permanent fixture of the developing core repertoire of Cajun music. Later that same year, Cléoma Falcon's brothers Ophé, Cléopha, and Amédé Breaux made the first recording of what is now called "Jolie Blonde," which they titled "Ma blonde est partie" ("My blonde is gone"). The instrumentation and style of the recording were just as classic as the Cajun waltz was to become, including the accordion, fiddle, and guitar, and a high-pitched emotionally charged singing style necessary to pierce through the noise of early dance halls.

It was during this period, just after the turn of the century, that the stock repertoire of Cajun and Creole music took shape, based on a blend of influences from French, Acadian, Spanish, German, Native American, Scotch-Irish, Anglo-American, and black Creole traditions. Cajun fiddler Dennis McGee's "Valse du vacher," for example, recorded in 1929, is a bluesy description of the life of a cowboy sung in French to the tune of an Old World mazurka. Descriptions of nineteenth-century dance bands had consistently mentioned Cajuns and black Creoles performing together. In the 1920s and 1930s,

Dennis McGee performed and recorded regularly with black Creole accordionist and singer Amédé Ardoin. Together they improvised much of what was to become the core repertoire of Cajun music. Others like Leo Soileau, Mayus Lafleur, Moise Robin, the Walker Brothers, the Segura Brothers, and Angelas Lejeune quickly joined in the first wave of Cajun and Creole musicians to record, improvising what was becoming standard Cajun music.

Then things began to change. By the mid-1930s, the Americanization of south Louisiana was well under way. Accordions began to fade from the scene as string bands like the Hackberry Ramblers and Leo Soileau's Four Aces drifted toward Anglo-American styles, incorporating western swing, country, and popular radio tunes into their repertoires. Rural electrification made sound amplification available to country dance halls, which produced changes in instrumental and singing styles. Yet though traditional Cajun and Creole music was pushed underground by new, more popular sounds, field recordings, such as those made by John and Alan Lomax between 1934 and 1937, show that it did not disappear. These noncommercial recordings also show an older side of Cajun music.

Home music, including unaccompanied singing and solo instrumental pieces, was virtually untapped by commercial recordings, which focused on the more public side of Cajun music. The Lomaxes, for example, made a deliberate attempt to cover the ground that commercial companies ignored. Unlike the commercial companies, which brought musicians out of their cultural contexts to record in urban centers like New Orleans, Chicago, and New York, the Lomaxes went to the musicians' and singers' home turf with a Library of Congress recording machine that made aluminum disks in the field. The Lomaxes avoided popular styles already well documented by the record companies to record unaccompanied singing and solo instrumental traditions, often performed by people who were old then, whose musical style and repertoire reached back well into the nineteenth century and before. They recorded ballads, blues laments, drinking songs, and round dance songs, along with a few fiddle tunes and house dance bands, thus shedding light on the roots of Louisiana French music.

It took the earliest settlers on the Louisiana frontier some time before they were able to afford the luxury of musical instruments. They preserved their musical heritage by humming instrumental tunes for dancing and by singing unaccompanied songs. These songs reflect the French heritage of the Cajuns as well as the influence of their neighbors. Elita Hoffpauir's version of "Tout un beau soir en me promenant" ("One fine evening while out walking"), which she sang for Alan Lomax in 1934, is a version of "La Rencontre au bois charmant" ("The meeting in the enchanted forest"), one of the *bergère* (shepherdess) cycle popular in French and French-American tradition. The song describes a meeting of lumberjacks and a shepherdess who tells them that if they will spare the trees, she will keep their glasses filled with wine:

Tout un beau soir
(Elita Hoffpauir, New Iberia)

Tout un beau soir
En me promenant
O tout du long
Du petit bois charmant.

'garde je vois là-bas,
Je vois venir une bergère.
Ça me fait rappeler
La seule que mon coeur aime.

"Belle bergère,
Jolie bergère,
C'est quoi vous faites
Dedans ces bois?"

"J'ai mes moutons
Dedans ces plaines,
Là où le loup
Me fait souvent ouvrage."

Les beaux bûcheurs,
Ils sont partis au bois,
C'est pour couper
La fleur du bois.

"Ne coupez pas
Ni la souche ni la retraite,
Vous goûterez
Du vin dans mes bouteilles."

One Fine Evening

One fine evening
While out walking
All along
The enchanting little woods.

There I see
There I see a shepherdess coming.
She reminds me
Of the only one I love.

"Beautiful shepherdess,
Lovely shepherdess,
What are you doing
In these woods?"

"I have my sheep
In these plains,
Where the wolf
Often keeps me busy."

The handsome woodsmen
Are going into the woods
To cut
The flower of the woods.

"Neither cut
The stump nor score it
And you will taste
The wine in my bottles."

"En buvons une,
En buvons deux,
En buvons trois,
O s'il le faut."

"Let's drink one,
Let's drink two,
Let's drink three,
Oh if we must."

Elita's father Julian Hoffpauir had a vast repertoire of songs from France and Acadia that ranged from lullabies to drinking songs and included some of the most beautiful *complaintes* (laments) ever recorded, such as his version of "La belle et les trois capitaines" ("The beauty and the three captains"), also known as "La belle qui fait la morte" ("The beauty who feigns death"), well known in France and Canada. This song clearly reflects the morality and sense of honor of another time. In order to avoid the advances of a young captain without jeopardizing the safety of her family, a maiden feigns death for three days to return with her honor intact to her beloved father in the end. Unlike Shakespeare's Juliet, this maiden's plan succeeds:

La belle et les trois capitaines
(Julian Hoffpauir, New Iberia)

The Beauty Who Feigns Death

Le plus jeune des trois
L'a pris pas sa main blanche.

The youngest of the three
Took her by her white hand.

"Montez, montez, la belle,
Dessus mon cheval gris.
Au logis chez mon père,
Je vous emmènerai."

"Climb up, climb up, fair maiden,
Onto my grey steed.
Straight to my father's house
Shall I bring you."

Quand la belle entend,
Elle s'est mis à pleurer.

Upon hearing this,
The fair maiden began to weep.

"Soupez, soupez, la belle,
Prenez, oui appétit.
Auprès du capitaine,
Vous passerez la nuit."

Eat, eat, fair maiden,
With hearty appetite.
Next to the captain
Is where you will spend the night.

Quand la belle entend,
La belle est tombée morte.

Upon hearing this,
The fair maiden fell dead.

"Sonnez, sonnez les cloches.
Tambours, violons, marchez.
Ma mignonette est morte.
J'en ai le coeur dolent."

"Toll, toll the bells.
Sound the drums and violins.
My little girl is dead.
My heart is full of grief."

"Et où l'enterreront-ils?"
"Dedans le jardin de son père
Sous les trois feuilles de lys.
Nous prions Dieu, cher frère,
Qu'elle aille en paradis."

Au bout de trois jours,
La belle frappe à la porte.

"Ouvrez, ouvrez la porte,
Cher père et bien aimé.
J'ai fait la morte trois jours
Pour sauver mon honneur."

"And where will they bury her?"
In her father's garden
Under the three lilies.
We pray to God, dear brother,
That she might enter heaven."

After three days,
The fair maiden knocked at the door.

"Open, open the door,
Dearest and beloved father.
I feigned death three days
To save my honor."

There was still an active unaccompanied singing tradition in south Louisiana as late as the 1930s and 1940s. Groups of singers regularly gathered for weddings, *boucheries*, Christmas and New Year's Day parties, and other extended family and community events to sing traditional French ballads, *complaintes*, and some of the numerous group drinking songs. These included songs such as "Fais trois tours de la table ronde" ("Three times round the round table"), "Toutes les chansons méritent un coup à boire" ("All songs deserve a drink"), and "Trinquons" ("Let's toast"):

Trinquons
(Fenelon Brasseaux, Isaac and Cleveland Sonnier;
Erath)

Trinquons, trinquons,
Mes chers camarades,
Mais oublions jamais
La raison.
Soutenez mon verre
Et me voilà par terre.

Chantez de boire
Du matin au soir.
Que le tonnerre grogne
Et que la muraille recule.
Me voilà par terre
Du matin au soir.

Let's Toast

Let's toast, let's drink,
My dear friends,
But let's never
Lose our senses.
Hold up my glass
And here I am on the ground.

Sing of drinking
From morning to night.
May the thunder grumble
And may the wall fall back.
Here I am on the ground
From morning to night.

Even in this venerable unaccompanied tradition, there is already evidence of the cultural blending process. The tunes of many unaccompanied French ballads recorded in Louisiana are clearly influenced by the blues. There are also new elements in the repertoire that obviously come from places other than France. In Louisiana, the English folk song, "The Old Drunk and His Wife," is called "Mon bon vieux mari." "A Paper [or Packet] of Pins" is called "Un papier d'épingles," and the Louisiana French version of "Billy Boy" is called "Charmant Billy." In 1934 Lomax recorded "J'ai marié un ouvrier" ("I Married a Carpenter"), a remarkable Louisiana French version of an English ballad, "James Harris" or "The Demon Lover" (Child 243). This song, sometimes called "The Carpenter's Wife," tells the story of a woman who is lured away from her family by a sailor who betrays her in turn. In Louisiana French, an *ouvrier* is not a general laborer, as in France, but specifically a carpenter. This Louisiana French version preserves references to the "banks of the Tennessee" from an Americanized version of the song, first published in Philadelphia in 1858:

J'ai marié un ouvrier
(Lanese Vincent and Sidney Richard; Kaplan)

"J'ai marié un ouvrier,
Moi qui étais si vaillante fille,
Mais c'était de m'en dispenser
Sans attraper des reproches."

"Mais quitte ton ouvrier,
Et viens-t-en donc, c'est avec moi.
O viens-t-en donc, c'est avec moi
Dessus l'écore du Tennessee."

"Dessus l'écore du Tennessee,
Quoi-ce t'aurais pour m'entretenir?
Quoi-ce t'aurais pour m'entretenir
Dessus l'écore du Tennessee?"

"J'en ai de ces gros navires
Qui naviguent dessus l'eau
Et soi-disant
Pour t'opposer de travailler."

I Married a Carpenter

"I married a carpenter,
I who was a girl of such means.
But how could I be rid of him
Without reproach."

"Well, leave your carpenter,
And come along with me.
Oh come along with me
On the banks of the Tennessee"

"On the banks of the Tennessee,
What would you have to provide for me?
What would you have to provide for me
On the banks of the Tennessee?"

"I have great ships
Which sail the seas
And supposedly
To keep you from working."

Au bout de trois jours,	After three days,
Trois jours et trois semaines,	Three days and three weeks,
O la belle se mit à pleurer	Oh, the lady began to weep
L'ennui de sa famille.	Out of longing for her family.
"Ne pleure donc pas, la belle,	"Don't cry, Lady,
Je t'achèterai une robe de soie jaune	I'll buy you a dress of yellow silk
Qu'elle soit mais la couleur	The color
De l'or et de l'argent."	Of gold and silver."
"Je ne pleure non pas ton or,	"I do not weep for your gold,
Ni ton or ni ton argent,	Neither your gold, nor your silver,
Mais je pleure ma famille	But I weep for my family
Que j'ai laissée là-bas."	That I left behind."
"Je t'ai pas toujours dit, la belle,	"Did I not always tell you, Lady,
Et quand ce bâtiment câlerait,	That when this ship would sink,
O il aurait une carlet	Oh, its mast
A plus jamais resourdre?	Would never resurface?
"Dessus l'écore du Tennessee,	"On the banks of the Tennessee,
T'embrasserais ton cher et petit bébé.	You would kiss your dear little baby.
O tu l'embrasserais	Oh, you would kiss him
A plus jamais le revoir."	Never to see him again."

Similarly, what eventually developed into the repertoire of Cajun tunes was influenced by the various ethnic groups in the Cajun blend. "J'ai passé devant ta porte" ("I Passed by Your Door"), a popular waltz, appears to be based on a composition for classic guitar by eighteenth-century Spanish composer Frederico Sors. But the most important stylistic influence was from the black Creoles, and most of the influence on the Cajun instrumental repertoire seems to have come from Irish and Anglo-American sources. Cajun musicians played an eclectic mixture of waltzes, *valses à deux temps* (double-time waltzes), *contredanses*, polkas, mazurkas, one-steps, two-steps, reels, jigs, *varsoviennes*, *danses carrées* (square dances), and hoedowns.

Some borrowed material retained the original names, for example, fiddle tunes such as "Chickens Cackling," "Sitting on Top of the World," and "Old Joe Clark." Other tunes were assimilated in whole or in part and now bear French titles. Some of these have now become Cajun dance music standards. In French Louisiana, for example, "The Arkansas Traveler" tune bears the name "Contredanse française," "Old Molly Hare" is the same as "Contredanse de Mamou," "Bonaparte Crossing the Rhine" (also known as "Wreck of the Old Number Nine") is just like "Les veuves de la coulée" ("Widows Along the Creek"), and the melody line of "J'ai été au bal hier au soir" ("I Went to the Dance Last Night") sounds distinctly like the first phrase of "Get Along Home, Cindy."

The first commercial recordings of Cajun music, between 1928 and 1932, already bore the marks of Anglo-American tradition. Joe and Cléoma Falcon, the first to record in 1928, soon began including their own French translations of American popular tunes like "I'm Thinking Tonight of My Blue Eyes" and "Lu Lu's Back in Town." Leo Soileau, who performed on the second Cajun record, "Hey, Mama, Where You At?" with Mayus Lafleur, formed one of the first string bands as the accordion began to lose favor during the 1930s. His Three or Four Aces recorded early country and swing tunes, some translated, some not. His discography, filled with classic Cajun waltzes and two-steps like "The Basile Waltz" and "Petite ou grosse" ("The Little One Or the Fat One"), also includes titles of obvious Anglo-American origin like "My Wild Irish Rose," "Let Me Call You Sweetheart," and "Love Letters in the Sand." Others like "Quand je suis bleu" ("When I'm Blue"), "Je ne me tracasse pas plus" ("I Don't Worry Anymore"), and "Dans ton coeur tu aimes un autre" ("In Your Heart You Love Another") are thinly disguised translations or adaptations of popular songs. The tune to his "Personne m'aime pas" ("Nobody Loves Me"), for example, is the same as "Nobody's Darling But Mine," although he makes no apparent attempt to translate the English lyrics.

In the beginning of this century, Teddy Roosevelt's colonial expansionism and World War I combined to fuel a nationalist fervor that sought to homogenize this country. Clearly, south Louisiana would have to understand and accept its role as a minority in America. Some of the obvious benefits were education, mobility, and the right to participate in the free enterprise system. Unfortunately, the Americanization process lacked subtlety. In south Louisiana, the French language and culture were inadvertently trampled in a frontal assault on illiteracy and isolation. Those who could joined the headlong rush toward the language of the future and of the marketplace. Around the same time, the black-gold rush fueled an economic boom that brought rural Cajuns into a money-based economy just in time for the Great Depression. Nevertheless, Huey Long's roads and bridges made it easier for visitors to get in, and Cajuns to get out, in the cars they were now able to afford with their salaried jobs. They also bought radios, which imported Anglo-American culture over the airwaves. All that came from the outside was quickly imitated and internalized.

If the major cultural influence on Cajun music before had been the blues, it was now Anglo-American music. In the thick of the Americanizing 1930s and 1940s, the accordion faded from the scene and string bands with names like Aces, Ramblers, Merrymakers, and Playboys were the order of the day. They dutifully imitated bluegrass, country and western, and swing, producing such classics as the Hackberry Ramblers' "Une piastre ici, une piastre là-bas" ("A Dollar Here, a Dollar There"), the Oklahoma Tornadoes' bilingual "Dans la prison" ("In Prison"), and eventually the Riverside Ramblers' English-language hit "Wondering." Electrical amplification allowed fiddlers to lighten their bow strokes, and a lighter, more lilting style replaced the intense, mournful sounds of earlier times. Harry Choates was easily the most popular Cajun string band leader of his day. His music no longer imitated western swing, it *was* western swing, and good western swing at that. His first language was French, but he sang the language of swing with virtually no accent in recordings ranging from a swinging remake of the traditional "Pauvre Hobo" ("Poor Hobo") to songs with telling titles like "Rubber Dolly" and "Harry Choates' Special."

After World War II, Cajun GIs returned home and immersed themselves in their own culture. They drank and danced to forget the war. Dance halls throughout Cajun country once again blared the familiar sounds of homemade music in French, but the traditional sound was not unaffected by the years of apprenticeship to America. Trap drum sets, steel guitars, and electric pickups remained part of the new standard instrumentation. Iry Lejeune found inspiration in diverse sources and was an unwitting leader of the revival; his 1948 recording of "La valse du pont d'amour" ("The Love Bridge Waltz") prompted local companies to record the new wave of old music. Along with his spirited renditions of the legendary Amédé Ardoin's Creole blues recorded in the late 1920s and the early 1930s, Lejeune recorded songs inspired by outside sources. His "Bosco Blues" clearly echoes Jimmy Rogers's "I Was a Stranger," also about a loner who walked the railroad tracks, and his "J'ai fait une grosse erreur" ("I Made a Big Mistake") is obviously inspired by American country music.

Following Lejeune's lead, previously popular Cajun musicians dusted off their accordions and began providing music for a generation interested in preserving and reviving its fading heritage. By the 1950s, musicians such as Austin Pitre, Lawrence Walker, Alphé and Shirley Bergeron, Aldus Roger, and many others were once again composing new songs. The influence of American music did not disappear, but now Cajun musicians regained control of the process. The tune of Nathan Abshire's classic waltz, "La Valse de Bélisaire," for example, is based on Roy Acuff's "A Precious Jewel," and "Mon coeur fait plus mal" is an interpretation of "I Don't Hurt Anymore."

In the 1950s, Hank Williams took the country music world by storm. This country singer had a profound effect on Cajun music in general and on D. L. Menard in particular. Menard, who relishes his nickname, "the Cajun Hank Williams," composed a flurry of original Cajun songs in the 1960s, some of them based on Hank's tunes. The tune for his classic "La porte d'en arrière" ("The Back Door"), for example, was adapted from the "Honky Tonk Blues." Williams, whose only son was born in Shreveport while Hank was launching his career on the stage of the Louisiana Hayride, performed often in south Louisiana. It was in those bayou honky-tonks that he encountered the Cajuns and their hybrid music, which in turn affected his own repertoire. One of his biggest hits, "Jambalaya," was based on a lively but unassuming Cajun two-step called "Grand Texas" or "L'Anse Couche-Couche." Interestingly, Williams's song later came home to roost, translated into French and recorded by Aldus Roger and the Lafayette Playboys.

In the 1950s another budding American music form had a profound influence on Cajun music. The sound that English author John Broven has dubbed "swamp pop" is essentially Cajun rhythm and blues or rock and roll. This has found expression in French (as in the music of Belton Richard and his Musical Aces), but full-blown swamp pop is usually sung in English. Some swamp pop performers, like Johnny Allan (Guillot), Warren Storm (Schexnayder), and Rod Bernard, were the sons of Cajun musicians, and their heritage sometimes showed through the rock and roll. Local record compa-

Nathan Abshire at the first Tribute to Cajun Music festival, Lafayette, 1974 (Photo by Philip Gould)

Dewey Balfa at the Festival de Musique Acadienne, Lafayette, 1981 (Photo by Philip Gould)

nies, like Ville Platte's own Jinn Records, were formed to release some of these crossover classics. In 1955, Bobby Page (Elwood Dugas) and the Riff Raffs recorded a rock version of "Hip et Taiaut," a standard Cajun two-step, with blazing saxes and electric guitars instead of an accordion and fiddles, but the song was French and so was the feeling. Rod Bernard hit the charts in 1959 with a song called "This Should Go On Forever" and even appeared on the "American Bandstand" show. Another of his hits was a bilingual version of "Colinda." In 1961, Cleveland Crochet sneaked onto the charts with an accordion rock blend called "Sugar Bee." Joe Barry recorded "Je suis bête pour t'aimer," a translation of his own hit "I'm a Fool to Care." A sort of Cajun Freddie Fender, Johnny Allan has recently recorded several bilingual songs like "One More Time/Une autre chance" and "Little Fat Man/Petit homme gros," but he had perhaps his biggest hit in 1962 with a parody of Johnny Horton's "North to Alaska" called "South to Louisiana."

In the 1960s, traditional Cajun music was again in danger of being overwhelmed by popular commercial sounds. National organizations such as the Newport Folk Foundation, Smithsonian Institution, and the National Folk Festival began to encourage the preservation of traditional Cajun music, sending folklorists and fieldworkers to record the oldest styles and identify the outstanding performers. In 1964, Gladius Thibodeaux, Louis Vinesse Lejeune, and Dewey Balfa were invited to perform at the Newport Folk Festival alongside such well-known folk revivalists as Joan Baez and Peter, Paul, and Mary. They half expected to be laughed off the stage. Even in Louisiana, Cajun music was considered "nothing but chanky-chank" by upwardly mobile Cajuns. Instead, the Cajun musicians received a standing ovation. Dewey Balfa felt that his culture had been validated along with his music. He returned to Louisiana to work with other musicians and cultural activists, determined to bring home the message of this enthusiastic reception.

Other groups followed, performing in cities throughout America as Cajun music became a regular feature on the folk festival circuit. These musicians reinforced Balfa's message. He eventually succeeded in convincing local recording companies to release traditional music alongside their more commercial Cajun records, including that of his own Balfa Brothers family band. He organized a folk-artists-in-the-schools project to introduce Cajun music to students. He also helped to organize festivals and special concerts to provide new settings for Cajun musicians and audiences. Young people were no longer interested in Cajun music, in part because they rarely had an opportunity to hear it. At that time, Cajun music was confined to bars and dance halls that admitted only those of legal drinking age. The results of Balfa's efforts to bridge this cultural generation gap were soon evident. Now, given the choice, some young Cajuns chose to play the music of their heritage.

Yet those young Cajun musicians would have been less than honest if they denied their contact with the popular American music scene. Among the first young musicians to experiment with Cajun music were Zachary Richard and a short-lived though influential group called Coteau. Richard recorded soulful renditions of traditional and original unaccompanied songs and produced innovative rock and country arrangements of Cajun dance tunes for his Bayou des Mystères band. He also discovered that other parts of the French-

Zachary Richard at the Festival de Musique Acadienne, Lafayette, 1982 (Photo by Philip Gould)

speaking world were interested in Louisiana's French music, especially when the sound was jacked up a few notches. Led by Michael Doucet on fiddle, Bessyl Duhon on accordion, and Bruce McDonald on electric guitar, Coteau attracted a substantial young audience with its exciting fusion of traditional Cajun music and southern rock and roll.

Today young musicians continue to improvise new sounds and preserve old ones. Playing Cajun music is no longer a choice made self-consciously; it is part of the regular music scene. One can hear Cajun music in restaurants and on the radio, on television, and at weekend jam sessions. Young musicians have ample opportunities to fall in love with the music of their heritage, many models to emulate, and lots of room to experiment. Zachary Richard has kept his version of Cajun music up to date with contemporary trends including reggae and rap. When internal tensions blew Coteau apart, Michael Doucet concentrated his energies in his other group, Beausoleil, an eclectic group that has added a wide range of influences including classical and jazz to its strong traditional base. Wayne Toups preserves the spirit of his heroes, who include Belton Richard, Lawrence Walker, and Walter Mouton, while developing his own "ZydeCajun" sound, a fusion of zydeco and Cajun styles. Cajun Brew's Pat Breaux preserves the memory of his grandfather Amédé Breaux on the one hand, and translates rock classics such as "Louie Louie" into Cajun music on the other. There is even a heavy metal Cajun group, Mamou, led by Steve Lafleur, which runs traditional waltzes through an electronic maze of synthesizers and wa-wa pedals.

There are also countless others who prefer to follow their own leads. Some musicians, such as Paul Daigle, Johnny Sonnier, and Terry Huval, have produced dozens of new traditional and country-influenced Cajun hits. Bruce Daigrepont has produced stylish new songs in a lighter pop Cajun vein. Others prefer to play in a more classic traditional style. Eddie, Rodney, Homer, and Felton Lejeune carefully preserve the legacy of their family tradition while adding their own contributions to it. Robert Jardell and Mark Mier have based their styles on reverence for the memory of their mentor Nathan Abshire. Some youngsters, such as Steve Riley and Cory McCauley, play in the old-time traditional style, even choosing to perform sitting down, but innovate new harmonies and arrangements. Even Dewey Balfa is composing what he calls "brand new old songs." The process that produced what we have come to call Cajun music continues today as it is renegotiated and reinvented with each performance.

Cajun Instruments

Making music with fiddles and accordions, guitars and triangles, spoons and washboards, Cajun and Creole musicians have become culture heroes as south Louisianans reaffirm their pride in their musical tradition. But the unsung heroes are the traditional instrument makers who have provided performers with the tools of their trade, particularly those who plied their craft at a time when store-bought instruments were either unavailable or prohibitively expensive. Many of these have become master craftsmen who produce some of the finest accordions, violins, triangles, and *frottoirs* (washboards) in the world, contributing to the survival of both the music and culture.

Coteau: Cajun band,
1975 (Photo by André
Gladu)

The western French musical tradition had used brass instruments like the cornet, reeds like the *bombarde*, variants of the bagpipe family like the *biniou* and the *cabrette*, and stringed instruments like the violin. It is unlikely that the early French settlers brought such delicate instruments to the Louisiana frontier, or that Acadians had any in 1765 when they arrived in Louisiana after ten years of wandering. Yet when they arrived in St. Dominigue on their way to Louisiana, the Acadian exiles are reported to have danced to *reels à bouche*, wordless dance music made by their voices alone. By 1780 a colonial report included a violin, and in 1785 a Spanish commandant notes a fiddle and clarinet player named Préjean. Within a generation, musicians using imported and homemade instruments were playing reels, contredanses, waltzes, and two-steps for *bals de maison* (house parties).

It is often said that the only difference between a fiddle and a violin is the music played on it. Thus Itzhak Perlman's Stradivarius became a fiddle when he performed bluegrass during a television special; conversely, many Cajun fiddlers use instruments that would be called violins in a symphony orchestra. Some are fine old Italian, German, or French instruments that reached Louisiana in the migrations of American society. Others were made in America by artisans who patterned their work on that of European masters. Still others were made locally by craftsmen for their own use as well as for their neighbors and friends.

Research for an exhibit sponsored by the Lafayette Natural History Museum in 1984 uncovered the products of Louisiana fiddle makers that date from the nineteenth century. Some of these instruments were homemade imitations, some were finely crafted. Others were harder to place. One blind craftsman from the Marais Bouleur region near Bosco in St. Landry Parish is said to have made pre-Cremonan-style triangular instruments.

Fiddle makers often had to overcome great difficulties in the pursuit of their craft, using pieces of broken bottles as scrapers, for example, until they could acquire proper tools. Young musicians who could not buy or borrow instruments sometimes improvised their first fiddles from wooden cigar boxes, using cypress slats from the barn for necks and bones for pegs. Many faced parental wrath for unraveling window screens to make strings and sneaking thread from the sewing box to supply hairs for bows made of bent branches. Sometimes they even raided the family horse for a few strands from its mane or tail. Wedisson Reed of Eunice whittled instruments from cypress planks and eventually adapted his craft to include top and back plates of spray-painted formica. Paul Devillier of Arnaudville used lumber two-by-fours for his first fiddle and interior paneling for his second. Homemade instruments such as these, born of stubborn desire, symbolize the Cajuns' passion for making music.

The earliest known orchestra-quality violin maker was Emar Andrepont of Prairie Ronde who made over sixty violins around the turn of this century, apparently patterned after the work of a New Orleans craftsman named I. Benoit. One of Benoit's instruments was discovered in the Andrepont family collection. Andrepont used some rather unorthodox techniques. For example, instead of carving his back and top plates from a thick block, he molded thin sheets by soaking them in a well and bending them over a fixed pattern. He was a comfortably well-to-do landowner and apparently made his violins for pleasure, not for money. He consistently refused to sell his instruments, giving them instead to family members who proved equally uninterested in parting with them for cash. They considered them heirlooms and still own the entire collection.

Acadian fiddle makers learned through trial and error, books, and contact with other fiddle makers. Some now produce instruments of excellent quality. These instruments have backs, ribs, necks, and scrolls of curly and bird's eye maple imported from Germany and Czechoslovakia, tops of fine-grained European and Canadian spruce, and fingerboards and pegs of African ebony. Some instrument makers have experimented with indigenous woods; Lionel Leleux has carefully cured rare swamp maple plates for a series of Louisiana instruments, and Adner Ortego uses an interesting collection of salvaged woods including magnolia, black gum, cherry, and walnut to obtain a rich variety of colors and grain patterns. Slender rounds of wood—the best come from the Pernambuco district of Brazil—are fashioned into bows, which are then haired with hanks from horses' manes.

The percussion instruments used in Cajun and Creole music have diverse historical and practical origins. Many were adapted from anything that would make noise when rubbed or struck together. Blacksmiths produced *petits fers*, triangles of medieval French tradition. Reshaped hay or rice rake tines made the best such instruments. The springy tempering of the tines gave them their characteristic clear ringing sound, which traveled far beyond the range of melodic instruments and often provided the only audible music for dancers at the back of Cajun dance halls. Today, triangles are made by dozens of craftsmen, some of whom have perfected even these simple instruments with new techniques for tuning them and preserving their delicate temper.

Some percussion instruments were nothing more than ordinary household items pressed into temporary service to make music. Sometimes stylized versions of these later became pure instruments. Rasps and notched gourds used in Afro-Caribbean music were replaced by washboards, called *frottoirs*, rubbed with thimbles, spoons, or bottle openers. Later, tinsmiths corrugated sheets of metal to create abstract *frottoirs* far removed from their laundry room origins. These musical washboards eliminated the deadening effects of the wooden frame and with newly incorporated shoulder hooks the performers could use both hands to create more complex rhythms. Carved cow bones and bent soupspoons also served to keep rhythm. These were difficult to play because they had to be held just right. This problem was sometimes solved by enterprising musicians who fixed the pieces into the proper position with screws or rivets. A number three washtub became a one-string bass with the help of an old broom handle and a piece of baling twine. (This required drilling a hole in the bottom of the tub, thereafter rendering it useful only as an instrument.) Young fiddlers can observe bowing and fingering techniques while keeping rhythm on an older performer's strings with long thin wooden dowels called fiddlesticks. Paired dowels of the perfect thickness were often put aside as instruments, never to be used as pegs.

Introduced between 1900 and 1920, the guitar is used primarily to provide chords as percussive accompaniment. Several of today's oldest musicians insist that a black Creole named Steve was the first guitar player they remember seeing in the area. In 1928, Cléoma Falcon played a National Steel guitar as her husband Joe played the accordion and sang "Lafayette," the first Cajun record ever released. By then, it had become relatively easy to acquire instruments from mail order catalogs, although young guitar players still improvised instruments with planks and wire strings. One of the first Cajun guitar players, Warnes Schexnayer of Crowley, began making violins in 1921. He later became interested in making guitars and learned to enhance them with inlaid hand-carved pieces of native Louisiana abalone shells as well as imported ivory. Another guitar maker, Harold Romero of New Iberia, contributed to the development of the electric guitar and is credited with several patents.

Pedal steel guitars, an electrified version of the dobro, an acoustic guitar, usually played flat across the lap, have come to play an important melodic role in contemporary dance bands. They entered Louisiana French music tradition during the 1930s and 1940s when Cajuns were electrifying their string bands to play western swing. These complex instruments were adapted but not made in Louisiana until Milton Guilbeau, a plumbing supplier from Lafayette, began building pedal steel guitars using materials available in his warehouse, such as chrome faucet handles, conduits, and shut-off valves.

Invented in Vienna in 1828, the diatonic accordion rapidly became one of the most popular folk instruments in the western world, primarily because of its durability and versatility. Self-accompanying bass chords made it a convenient—and loud—one-man band. In the latter part of the nineteenth century, early versions of the instrument were brought into Louisiana by German-Jewish retailers, such as Mervine Khan of Rayne, who obtained them from New York importers, such as Buegeleisen and Jacobsen. These first imports were bulky, often with several rows of buttons; their cheap tin reeds were set in beeswax and difficult to keep in tune; their flimsy bellows lost air and tore easily. After World War I, a simplified version with a single row of buttons appeared in Louisiana. Though far from perfect (wooden parts were painted black to cover flaws), these greatly improved Monarchs, Sterlings, and later Eagles easily outclassed earlier instruments and quickly replaced them among serious musicians. Smaller, lighter, and louder, these accordions dominated Cajun bands by their sheer volume. Their steel reeds were more durable and easier to keep tuned and their sturdier bellows better able to survive the syncopated exuberance of the times. Limited to a total of twenty notes (ten pushing and ten pulling) arranged on a simple diatonic scale, plus two pairs of accompanying bass chords, these accordions forced musicians to simplify melodies and arrangements.

In the late 1930s, German factories converted to war production and stopped making accordions. In south Louisiana, the dearth of available instruments coincided with social changes brought about by the Americanization of the local culture. Traditional bands, formerly built around the dominant accordion sound, were replaced by western swing string bands as Cajuns and Creoles gravitated toward Anglo-American culture. After World War II, however, returning GIs crowded the dance halls. Performers like Iry Lejeune, Nathan Abshire, Lawrence Walker, and Austin Pitre brought out their long-neglected accordions to satisfy the brand-new demand for old-time music. Musicians without accordions needed instruments. Post-war German accordions were so inferior to Monarchs, Sterlings, and Eagles that the older instruments that had survived a decade of neglect commanded premium prices. The few to be found were carefully refurbished and jealously treasured. As this small supply was exhausted, the ever-increasing demand was filled by local craftsmen who learned to build new accordions by restoring old ones.

The first of these craftsmen, Sidney Brown of Lake Charles, made his instruments of ordinary wood and even masonite, painting them black to copy the "little black gems" from Germany. Valentin

Accordion maker Marc Savoy, near Eunice, 1983 (Photo by Philip Gould)

Lopez, also of Lake Charles, named his Starling accordion in unabashed imitation of the German Sterling. The earliest Louisiana accordion makers used the bellows and reeds from post-war Hohner instruments, with the quality of their instruments being dependent on the quality of the materials they recycled.

Marc Savoy of Eunice developed an early passion for the accordion. He restored a few, began building them, and realized that his instruments could only be as good as his materials. He began using maple and other fine hardwoods, eliminating the need for black paint. The outward appearance of his wood-grain stained accordions shook the faith of those who blindly trusted the black German accordions, but Savoy waged war on black paint and eventually succeeded in establishing natural finishes as the ideal. With tongue in cheek, he did eventually make black accordions—but from polished African ebony.

Yet for all the attention Marc Savoy's finishes received, these changes were minor when compared to those he made on the inside of the instrument. A gifted accordion player himself, he quickly realized that he and most of his colleagues easily outplayed the early versions of his Acadian accordion. He began importing better quality reeds and bellows from Italy and eventually redesigned the inside of the instrument. His ingenious use of decibel meters, electronic tuners, pressure gauges, and his mother's vacuum cleaner led to important innovations in the basic design of the diatonic accordion. A company in Italy has recently begun mass-producing a version of Savoy's Acadian accordion under license from the Eunice craftsman. Savoy has also begun producing double- and triple-row accordions, popular among black Creole zydeco musicians because they include more notes and thus more flexibility, under his Acadian trademark. Today there are several dozen Louisiana craftsmen making accordions, which are used not only locally but worldwide. Their trademarks proclaim their roots: Acadian, Cajun, Creole, Evangeline, Teche, Magnolia, to name but a few. Many have followed Marc Savoy's lead, experimenting with native hardwoods and shell inlays to produce instruments combining beauty and musical quality. It is generally acknowledged today that some of the best button accordions in the world are made in south Louisiana.

11

Games and Gaming

Games

Like most elements of Louisiana French culture, traditional Cajun children's games were usually improvised. Most were very simple, requiring no props; some were based around things easily found around the house or on the farm. Games were also creolized. Some were brought from France, others were adopted from neighboring cultures. Many were made up on the spot and lasted only the time they took to be played. Others were somewhat more durable and were passed on from one generation to the next. In the countryside, children of a fairly wide range of ages played together. Later, schools began to narrow the age distribution of groups as children tended to play within their grade levels.

Games are an extremely regional and highly variable tradition. Since it would be impossible to record all the variant games and names for those games throughout south Louisiana, this section is not intended to be exhaustive. We intend rather to present an overview with examples to show the variety of historical children's games among the Cajuns. Many of these games began to disappear with arrival of television in the 1950s and the increasing popularity of organized sports. Video games have further eroded traditional games. Yet some have been preserved, and children continue to improvise others. Some games have preserved their original French names; others have been translated into English, but remain substantially the same. The following are descriptions of games remembered primarily by adults born from the 1920s through the 1950s.

Infant games mostly include activities parents do with their babies. Consequently, there is much more chance for the transmission of these from one generation to the next. Most are simple and improvised, such as *O mais arrête!* which is essentially a chase game, equivalent to "I'm going to get you!" *Ride le cheval* (ride the horse) is played by a child and a sitting parent who crosses her legs and seats the child on the raised foot, moving it to simulate a galloping horse's motion. This game is usually accompanied by the chant, "petit galop, petit galop" (lope or canter), and is often ended with the word, "Whoa!"

Ring games require a group and are usually played indoors when inclement weather prevents children from going outside. Formerly these were almost exclusively in French. In *cache, cache la bague* (hide the ring), one player hides a small token, usually a ring, in his hands and pretends to pass it to each of the other players, dropping it in the hands of one, all the while saying, "Cache, cache la bague." Afterwards, players must guess which one of them actually has the token, among much bluffing and counter-bluffing.

In *petit mouton, la queue coupée* (little sheep with a cut tail), a player walks around the room holding a handkerchief behind his back, chanting, "Petit mouton, la queue coupée," while walking around the other players sitting in a circle facing the center. At one point he drops the handkerchief behind one of the players. The players must guess when he dropped the handkerchief behind them and catch it. This player continues walking around the circle until he arrives at the place where the handkerchief was dropped to see if it is still there. If it is, he picks it up and resumes his part. If a seated player does notice, he picks up the handkerchief and tries to tag the walker before he reaches his place in the circle.

Another group game is *faire la statue* (be a statue) in which the players move about freely until the leader tells them to stop. They then freeze in position. The leader then picks the most interesting or funniest pose and that person becomes the next leader.

French word games were once especially popular at night and during bad weather when children were forced to stay indoors. *Pin pi po lo ron* is a counting rhyme often used to determine who is going to be "it" in other games. It is also played to determine who will receive some other token reward or punishment, such as banishment to a corner or a *pichenette* (finger thump usually to the forehead). One version (there are many variants) of the chant goes:

Pin pi po lo ron
Va aller faire son pot de lait
Bouillir chez Madame Michelle Aimée.

Si il vient une petite souris,
Foutez-la un coup de baton
Derrière la tête.

Pin pi po lo ron
Goes to make his pot of milk
Boil at Mrs. Michelle Aimée's house.

If a little mouse should come,
Hit it with a stick
On the back of its head.

In this version, each player puts a finger in a circle. The rhyme is performed by a leader who touches a different finger with each syllable. The player on whose finger the rhyme ends must leave the room, and the leader goes to ask if he prefers to return by *plume ou piquant* (feather or thorn). If by *plume*, the player is dragged back into the room by the hair; if by *piquant*, the player is dragged by the foot. In some versions, *plume* indicates tickling as a price for rejoining the group; *piquant*, a pinch, blow, or pichenette. Other versions have the exiled player try to guess a number or a color to reenter.

Another word game, *pim pam*, is a little like an extended knock-knock joke. It sounds like a parody of traditional greeting patterns in which people try to determine extended family connections, and provides an opportunity to catch an unsuspecting partner at the end:

Pim pam.
Qui c'est qu'est là?
C'est moi, Dédé.
Quel Dédé?
Dédé LaCart.
Quel LaCart?
LaCart Boyeau.
Quel Boyeau?
Boyeau Lison.
Quel Lison?
Lison Cochon.
Quel Cochon?
Cochon toi-même!

Knock knock.
Who's there?
It's me, Dédé.
Who's Dédé?
Dédé LaCart.
Who's LaCart?
LaCart Boyeau.
Who's Boyeau?
Boyeau Lison.
Who's Lison?
Lison Pig.
Who's a pig?
You're a pig!

Some word games involve tests of reflexes and cleverness, and are accompanied by gestures. In *pigeon vole* (pigeon flies), each player places a finger on the floor or table before them. A leader calls out various animals and insects: "pigeon vole" (pigeon flies), "papillon vole" (butterfly flies), "moqueur vole" (mockingbird flies), "carencro vole" (buzzard flies), "mouche vole" (fly flies), and so on. Players are to raise their fingers only when the animal named actually can fly. The leader tries to catch players by slipping in other animals or inanimate things that cannot fly: "brique vole" (brick flies), "maison vole" (house flies), "serpent vole" (snake flies), "cochon vole" (pig flies), and so on. Punishment for inappropriately raising or not raising a finger varies from banishment from the game until only one player remains, to punishments such as tickling, pinching, and so on.

Some children developed secret languages, Louisiana French versions of pig Latin. These of course varied from one neighborhood to another, from one circle of friends to another. One version, from the Ossun area, works by adding the first consonant of each word to the syllable *-égué*, which is then tacked onto the end of the word or syllable, as in "u-tégué as-végué as-pégué al-égué-er-légué" for "tu vas pas aller" (you will not go).

Running or chase games require only the participation of several children, usually pitting one person against the rest of the group. In these games, the person chosen to be "it" was traditionally called *le chien* (the dog). Some of these games include *25 bas* (25 low) and *25 haut* (25 high), both variations on tag in which being either on or off the ground is considered safe or "on base." This of course sends children onto and off of tree branches, fences, and outbuildings as part of escaping from *le chien*.

Hiding games have long been popular in south Louisiana. *Cache et fait* is a Louisiana French version of hide-and-seek, where players conceal themselves and the one who is "it" must find them. In some versions players must try to beat the seeker back to the base once they are discovered. Some adults remember hiding too successfully: the other players sometimes stopped looking for them and went on to another game without them. In *cache le fouet* (hide the whip), one player hides a whip or a switch. The other players search for it, with assistance from the hider in the form of hot or cold instructions: "T'es dans le feu" (you're in the fire) or "T'es dans l'eau" (you're in the water). When a player finds the whip or switch, he chases the other players with it, whipping them if he can, until they reach base.

Danses rondes (round dances) are the Louisiana French equivalent of the Anglo-American party songs and dances like "Ring Around the

Rosie" and "Shoo-Fly," in which groups of participants dance to their own singing. These were formerly popular among pre-adolescent children. For many, these dances represented a preliminary step toward courtship because it was the first introduction to dancing and socializing with the opposite sex. In group dances, young people were less individually involved than in paired dancing, which came later. There were special songs associated with these dances. In certain cases, like "Papillon vole" and "Ah, mon beau château," the dancers acted out the lines of the song with stylized movements.

Some games require toys or props. Cajun children once made hand-rolled clay balls of *la terre grasse*, the clay found along bayou and *coulée* banks and dried in the shade to avoid cracking. These balls, called *caniques*, were used when store-bought marbles were not available. Marbles were also improvised from small balls of tightly rolled, hard-tanned leather. Store-bought crystals, *stouns* (agates), and *aciers* (steels) were considered luxuries and were sometimes given as special presents to children after selling the annual crop for cash. Traditional marble games are *grand rond* (big ring), *grand carré* (big square), and *rond fait* (finished ring), all of which involve winning marbles by hitting them out of a set boundary. *La chasse* (the hunt) or *taiau et lapin* (hound and rabbit) can be played with as few as two players and two marbles. One pursues the other by hitting the other's marble. When the shooter misses, the roles are reversed.

Handmade clay balls were also traditionally used as ammunition for slingshots, though these did not need to be as nearly round as marbles. Slingshots were made by hand from the forks of trees, ideally *bois de flèche* (arrowwood or dogwood); two strips of rubber, usually from discarded inner tubes; and a small piece of leather or string. Some children became very skillful with a slingshot and were able to hunt with it. The most skillful were even able to kill birds. A single-armed slingshot, called a *baionnette*, was also used. With pouch on the end of a leather strap or cord, it could be used to hurl clay balls and undoubtedly pre-dated the forked slingshot, which depended on manufactured rubber. Contests were also held to see who was able to fling specially carved pieces of cypress *bardeaux* (shingles) the farthest with a *baionnette*.

Some games required specialized equipment, such as baseball bats and gloves, bought in stores or from *commis voyageurs* (traveling salesmen) if families could afford it. If not, children often made or improvised equipment at home with available materials. Baseball bats were sometimes made of old broom or hoe handles or from whittled *bois d'arc* (osage orange) branches. Balls could be improvised as well: a combination of cotton seeds, corn husks, and pieces of leather covered with leather or stuffed into a sock or small sack often sufficed, as did a ball of tightly wound string or strips of leather. *Bibi la pelote* was a version of hot potato in which such an improvised ball was passed along from one player to another as fast as possible to avoid having it at the end of a secret count or chant.

La vieille truie (the old sow) required the delicate touch of golf and the speed and strength of field hockey, and was widely played. This game can be played by as few as two persons, but usually involves two teams of three or more players. Each side tries to put its ball into the other side's hole, called *faire boire la vieille truie* (making the old sow drink), by hitting it with sticks, while trying to prevent the other side from putting the ball into its hole. In earlier times, the balls were usually small tomato sauce cans or other small roundish objects. This game could easily get out of hand as opponents vying for control of the ball sometimes turned on each other with their sticks. In the days before plastic shin guards, cuts and bruises abounded even when players were trying to concentrate their attention on the ball.

Balls were also used in games like *tant qu'elle est chaude* (as long as it's hot), essentially a version of dodge ball in which a leader rolls a small ball toward a line of three-inch holes. Each hole represents one player. When the ball goes into the hole, it becomes "hot," upon which the player in whose hole the ball has rolled takes it and throws it at the other players. Any player hit with the ball while it is hot is then eliminated. The ball "cools" once it hits a predetermined number of players. The last player in the game wins. In another version of this game, called *la pelote dans le trou* (the ball in the hole), players use sticks to hit the ball.

Still another version of dodge ball was called *la pelote quatre buts* (four-base ball). Four players stand one on each of four bases, arranged in a square about forty feet to fifty feet apart, and toss a ball to each other. Other players stand in the square. If a corner player catches the ball, he is allowed to throw it at a player in the middle. If a middle player is hit, he is out. If a corner player misses or drops the ball when it is tossed, he changes places with one of the players in the middle.

A game called *batons* (sticks) was popular as late as the 1960s. In some areas, children organized neighborhood *batons* tournaments to determine grand champions. The game is played with pointed sticks about two or three feet long. A player starts the game by throwing the stick as hard as possible into the ground. Additional players try to knock over this and other players' sticks by throwing their own sticks into the ground and hitting another stick at the same time. A stick that falls on its own or is not successfully stuck into the ground has only to be audibly nicked by another. In the event a player nicks a fallen stick or knocks a standing stick down while successfully planting his own stick, that player then hits the fallen stick as far away as possible with his own and then attempts to throw his stick into the ground three times. The other player tries to run over and retrieve his own stick and plant it into the ground once. The first to complete his task wins the round while the other is eliminated from the game. The last remaining player wins.

In days before store-bought toys were readily available, children made their own. Even today, children may prefer a homemade toy to a fancy, battery-operated, plastic toy that plays by itself. Makeshift cars are still fashioned out of household debris like sticks, shingles, cans, and cartons. Large cardboard cartons become clubhouses and tunnels. Sometimes other children or household pets find themselves pushing improvised vehicles or store-bought wagons while children take turns driving, often through obstacles. Some toys involve available objects or discarded materials, like pushing an old wheel with a stick, or making darts by sticking loose chicken feathers into a broken corn cob. Homemade *cerfs-volants* (kites) were made with thin strips of wood, paper, and discarded rags when there wasn't enough money to buy one at the store. At one time, commercially produced dolls were rare and quite expensive, so children made their own by stuffing rags with cotton, moss, or corn shucks. Some of these dolls could be quite elaborate, using corn silk (available in black, blonde, and red) for doll hair. Arguably the best *béquilles* (stilts), wooden horses, and tree houses are still made of discarded lumber.

Some games served as informal rites of passage and tests of physical strength and ability; for example, foot racing, arm wrestling, and boxing. Fist-fighting was not only a release of aggression; in many parts of rural Cajun country, it was a popular sport during the days before more peaceable pastimes became popular. It often took

Horse show contestant, near Lafayette, 1978 (Photo by Ginette Vachon)

the form of a contest to determine the best fighter in a given group, such as a dance hall crowd or neighborhood. In the early part of the twentieth century, the energies of fighters were frequently channeled onto boxing teams organized by many south Louisiana towns. (In fact, boxing was one of the first organized sports to take firm root in south Louisiana.) Nevertheless, in some areas, organized bare-knuckle fights continued at least until the late 1960s as contests of strength and ability, as well as to settle scores officially. These were fought in a *grand rond*, a ring of witnesses, under the supervision of a respected member of the community.

Demonstrating skill on horseback was important on the prairie and provided for lots of contests. Formal horse racing is very popular in south Louisiana and grew out of informal horse races often held on country roads on the way home from a visit, a dance, or Sunday Mass, simply to prove who was the best rider and had the fastest horse in the neighborhood. These informal contests were later institutionalized at country tracks where the best riders became jockeys and rode trained horses on a prepared track. Horsemanship was also demonstrated in horse shows featuring rodeo-like events, such as barrel and pole racing, cutting, pleasure riding, and so on. One event, the barrel or buddy pickup, is said to have originated among the Cajuns. This is a timed event in which a rider starts at one end of the arena, goes around a barrel at the other end, and picks up her partner who is standing on the barrel; they then return as fast as possible. Another test of horsemanship, developed in the last few decades, is the annual *tournoi* (tournament) in Ville Platte. Riders dressed in costumes imitating medieval garb ride as fast as they can along a circular track while trying to lance rings hanging from posts around the circle. The rider who captures the most rings in the least time is declared the winner. The *tournoi* has become quite popular among riders in the area who ignore the obvious revival nature of the event and simply judge it to be an interesting test of speed, skill, and the cooperation between a rider and horse.

In south Louisiana, as everywhere else in the United States, horses have been replaced by cars, trains, and planes as the standard means of transportation. Yet horses remain important to many riders, who undergo a great deal of trouble and expense to maintain their mounts. Many of these people are not interested in the specialized training required for successfully competing in horse shows and on the racetracks, but stay in the saddle if only to ride on trail rides. Trail ride clubs can be found throughout Cajun country. The clubs organize mounted journeys through the countryside, on secondary roads and highways, and accompanied by music and the fellowship of people with similar interests. These trail riders preserve elements from older times in a contemporary setting by traveling through the increasingly urbanized landscape at a walking pace, led by a "trail boss" and accompanied by mounted "scouts." They are also accompanied by mounted sheriff's deputies and idling police cars (which must be specially equipped to avoid overheating) whose job it is to supervise the sometimes uneasy relationship between fast-paced automobile traffic and the trail riders. A few rides go from one point to another, but most return to the point of departure for the convenience of those who transport their horses in trailers. Frequently there is a supper and dance at night.

In the bayou areas of south Louisiana, boat races and swimming test water skills. *Pirogues*, the south Louisiana version of the canoe, are especially popular in racing events because of the delicate balance required to stay afloat in them. Another popular event involves two competitors standing on opposite ends of a *pirogue*, each trying to pitch the other into the water. Fishing "rodeos" organized by community groups provide opportunities to test fishing skills and knowledge of the waterways. Prizes are given for largest fish in several classes (bass, perch, catfish, etc.) and for the largest catch overall.

Pistol and rifle shooting matches, called *pategaux*, provide opportunities to demonstrate the skills necessary for successful hunting. The traditional prize for winning a *pategau* is a large goose or turkey. Often the target is a symbolic goose or turkey. The object of the match is to put the most bullets into a hanging target, called the *pategau*, within a limited amount of rounds or time. Another version of the contest involves shooting the string from which the *pategau* is hung.

There are also games and contests designed to test knife handling skills, for example, target throwing onto a wall or tree, or on the ground. *La cambille* (chew the peg) is a game that involves a complex sequence of ways to stick a knife in the ground; the ways vary from one community to another. If a player finishes the sequence without failing to stick his knife, he drives a wooden peg into the ground and his opponent must pull it out with his teeth. Whittling was also a popular form of entertainment that demonstrated skill with a knife. And sometimes whittling was simply a way to kill time after work or between chores.

Gaming

Gaming or gambling sports have long been popular with many adult Cajuns, and one of the most popular is card playing. Many small towns and villages historically had at least one casino where men and women gathered to play a variety of card games. Today, people still gather in bars, homes, and camps for a game of cards. Some of the most popular are *bourré*, poker, euchre, and casino. These games usually involve gambling for money, considered legal in many places as long as the house does not officially take a cut. "Friendly" games are also played for tokens like pecans, buttons, matches, or kernels of dried corn. Couples sometimes play point games, such as rook, hearts, spades, or bridge, after supper at social gatherings.

Other popular table sports include dominoes, checkers, and billiards. These are often located in bars or taverns where men traditionally gather and are often accompanied by drinking. Only recently have these male-dominated activities begun to admit women.

Horse racing has long been a popular form of adult gaming in

Bourré players, Carencro, 1978 (Photo by Ginette Vachon)

south Louisiana. People once depended on horses for daily transportation, and some understandably took great pride in their animals' strength, stamina, and especially speed. On the way home from Saturday night dances or Sunday Mass, all it took for a race was a boast about how fast one's horse was. If someone within earshot thought differently, the race was on, sometimes in the family buggy, more often on horseback—the first one to the big oak tree or the corner wins. Long before the development of parimutuel tracks, such as Jefferson Downs in New Orleans and Evangeline Downs in Lafayette, bush tracks dotted the prairies of south Louisiana. A few still exist. Betting at the bush tracks is between interested parties. The tracks usually feature short, fast races between two or more quarter horses running on straight dirt courses bordered by rails to prevent the horses from interfering with each other. There is little strategy involved; the goal is simply to get a quick start and run as fast as possible. In the days before mechanical gates, races were started by dropping a handkerchief or a rope. Jockeys are frequently light young boys who learn early how to hang on to a bolting mount by grabbing a handful of mane. Some Cajun jockeys, such as Kent Desormeaux and Eddie Delahoussaye, have gone on to distinguish themselves on the national and international racing scenes, but they started the same way. Though there once were tracks in many settlements, one of the most popular of these bush tracks was Chez

Petit Maurice, located near Bosco behind a well-known dance hall of the same name. The track and hall were owned first by Maurice Richard and later by his son Ellis. Automobiles as well as horses raced on this track.

Other adult gaming events that involve animals are cock fighting and dog fighting, with roots in both European and Afro-Caribbean culture. Cock fighting has always been considered quasi-legal, at best. Dog fighting has long been looked down upon by the law and most levels of society, but it nevertheless still has a clandestine following. In both cases the winner is declared when one animal can no longer answer the call to fight, because of lost interest, injury, or death. Among devotees, the breeding, training, and pitting of roosters and dogs are recognized skills.

Cock fighting is done primarily between male poultry or roosters, but can be done between hens as well. Defenders of this activity insist they are only providing a forum for what happens naturally in the barnyard. There are categories of cock fighting named by the presence (or lack) of artificial attachments on the legs of the poultry: natural spurs, metal spurs, gaffes, and blades.

Dog fighting is done primarily between males of a breed called pit bulls, although fights can be arranged between females of this same breed, as well as the males and females of other breeds. Pit bulls are bred and trained for aggressiveness and fighting ability. The breed is characterized by a large head and powerful jaws. Few other species compete with pit bulls. Usually they merely challenge other dogs, but they have been known to attack humans and other animals. Because dog fighting is illegal and does not benefit from the benign neglect afforded cock fighting, it must be done in great secrecy. Outsiders are seldom invited. There is, however, an underground organization, complete with its own publication to report on winners, outstanding breeders, and upcoming events.

Some Cajuns love games of chance so much that they will wager on just about anything: whether a branch will fall on the sidewalk or in the street, whether a spouse will wear a red or blue shirt— *anything*. One of the most popular betting grounds, however, is politics. Some Cajuns have been known to bet huge sums on the outcome of a political race. Yet some of these same bettors would think it ridiculous if they were asked to contribute to a political campaign.

12

Oral Traditions

In the past, Louisiana French oral tradition was studied simply for its reflection of French and African culture. In these terms, the search for traditional tales became little more than a search for Old World vestiges. This was certainly due in part to the area's linguistic singularity as well as to past trends in folklore scholarship, which placed a premium on the discovery of long, European-style fairy tales collected by the Grimms in Germany, or Afro-Caribbean-styled animal tales. Alcée Fortier's almost exclusive emphasis on animal tales among New Orleans black Creoles in his landmark 1890s collections stressed the Louisiana/Africa connection. In the 1920s and 1930s, Calvin Claudel and Corinne Saucier sought out magic tales and numbskull tales (about the humorous misadventures of fools) in an attempt to demonstrate the Louisiana/France connection. Like her predecessors, Elizabeth Brandon in the 1940s collected material that also focused on the links with French traditions, though she did record other tale genres in an effort at thoroughness. Those connections do exist; however, to present only the stories that exemplify these ties distorts the image of Louisiana French oral tradition. The repertoire of folktales in French Louisiana can be divided into two general categories: vestiges and active oral entertainment.

Vestiges of Early Oral Tradition

Animal tales and magic tales (*Märchen*) are often the only genres represented in earlier collections. These folktales are usually part of the inactive repertoire of Louisiana French storytellers; they lack currency and are often heard only by the likes of a persistent folklorist who might ask for them specifically. They are, nevertheless, an important and respected part of French Louisiana's traditional heritage. The tales are immediately recognized by folklorists as research finds, while the tellers of these tales are invariably revered as bearers of tradition both by folklore collectors and by their neighbors and friends alike. Folklorists are sent to them with a standard formula of referral: "You ought to go see Mr. X. He knows a lot of old stories."

All examples used here are transcribed from the collection of taped interviews on deposit in the University of Southwestern Louisiana's Center for Acadian and Creole Folklore. (All type numbers refer to the second edition of Antti Aarne's and Stith Thompson's *The Types of the Folktale: A Classification and Bibliography*.)

Animal Tales

Animal tales require that a storyteller and his audience accept certain conventions a priori. The essential element is that animals can take on human characteristics: they can speak and reason, weep and laugh. This kind of characterization often involves a simplification of roles. Each animal can become the incarnation of a human trait: ruse (the rabbit, the fox, the turtle), stupidity (the wolf, the bear), evil (the spider, the monkey), brute strength (the elephant, the lion). By investing characters with these attributes, the storyteller can often indirectly criticize society without mentioning names.

Louisiana French tales that cast animals as characters are generally from two sources. Some resemble fables in the French tradition of the *fabliaux* and the *Roman de Renard*. It is possible that some tales came from teachers who read the fables of La Fontaine to entertain schoolchildren; some of these would then eventually have entered oral tradition when they were remembered and retold by those children after they were grown and had children of their own. Some tales even include a mild moral statement at the end, perhaps reminiscent of their origins. The moral of the following tale, a variant of international tale type 59 *The Fox and the Sour Grapes*, found in Aesop's and La Fontaine's classic collections of fables, is very well known, but the tale itself has not been widely collected. In the Louisiana version, the moral is obvious, but left unspoken.

Le Renard et le Raisin
(*Evélia Boudreaux, Carencro*)

Le renard était dans le bois où ils habitent et, toujours, il avait beaucoup faim. Et il était

The Fox and the Grapes

The fox was in the woods, where they usually live, and anyway, he was very hungry.

après chercher pour trouver du manger. Et il a vu des belles grappes de raisins haut d'un arbre. Et il s'est dit à lui-même, "Ça serait beaucoup bon, ce raisin. J'aimerais beaucoup d'en manger. Il est un peu haut. Je vais essayer de sauter et essayer de l'attraper."

Et il sautait et il sautait, mais il venait pas près du raisin, et il s'est découragé.

Il dit, "Je peux pas l'attraper. Ou," il dit, "je le veux pas quand même." Il dit, "Il est trop aigre, quand même." Il dit, "Je le veux pas."

Et il est parti. Il s'en a été.

And he was looking to find some food. And he saw some beautiful bunches of grapes high in a tree. And he said to himself, "Those grapes would be very good. I would like to eat some of them. They are rather high. I'll try to jump and try to catch them."

And he jumped and he jumped, but he didn't come close to the grapes, and he became discouraged.

He said, "I can't catch them. Or," he said, "I don't want them anyway." He said, "They are too sour anyway." He said, "I don't want them."

And he left. He went on his way.

Easily the most popular animal tales in Louisiana are those in the Bouki and Lapin cycle. These tales have origins in the French *fabliaux*, but their most direct origins are African. The name of the foil character, Bouki, means "hyena" in the Oualof dialect of Senegal, where that animal is cast in the same role opposite the cleverer hare. Bouki and Lapin (the rabbit) have counterparts in West Indian lore (where Bouki, Malice, Macaque, Anansi, or Nancy is paired with Lapin or Rabbit) and in the black American (Brer Fox and Brer Rabbit) tradition. There are other minor characters, including the elephant, the snake, the cat, the dog, and the turtle. It is interesting to note that despite French Louisiana's obvious cultural connection with the West Indies the spider (Anansi) is unknown among the Cajuns and Creoles.

In French Louisiana, there has been a great deal of cultural contact between black Creoles and white Cajuns, and these stories are told by members of both groups. The following tale is a variant of type 47A *The Fox Hangs by His Teeth to the Horse's Tail*, often told to explain the origin of the harelip (hare laughs so hard at his duped victim that he splits his lip). This tale, which seems to be especially popular in black tradition, with versions reported from Africa, the West Indies, and the South, has also entered Cajun tradition, as illustrated in this version told by a white Cajun storyteller from St. Martin Parish, an area heavily influenced by black Creole culture.

Tiens bon, Bouki
(Martin Latiolais, Catahoula)

Hang on, Bouki

Tu vois, il y a un *joke* pour Bouki et Lapin aussi.... Ils étaient à la chasse dans le bois. Et, ça fait ils ont vu un ours après dormir, couché après dormir. Ça fait, Lapin (il bluffait tout le temps Bouki, tu vois), il dit à Bouki, "Attrape sa queue!"

Ça fait, Bouki a parti. En peu de temps, il approchait l'ours. Il a fait un tour après la queue. Ça a réveillé l'ours, il y a pas de doute. L'ours a parti avec.

Lapin était à côte, il disait, "Tiens bon, Bouki! Tiens bon, Bouki!"

Il dit, "Comment tu veux moi, je tiens bon, mes quatre pattes, elles touchent pas par terre?!"

D'après moi, l'ours était après courir manière vite. Bouki, il touchait pas par terre!

You see, there's a joke about Bouki and Lapin, too. . . . They were hunting in the woods. And so they saw a bear sleeping, lying down asleep. So Lapin (he was always fooling Bouki, you see), he said to Bouki, "Catch his tail!"

So Bouki left. In a little while, he was near the bear. He twisted the bear's tail once around his hand. This woke the bear, of course. The bear took off with him.

Lapin was nearby, saying, "Hold him, Bouki! Hold him, Bouki!"

He said, "How do you expect me to hold him when not one of my four feet are touching the ground?!"

I believe the bear was running pretty fast. Bouki wasn't even touching the ground.

Even in the obviously French- and African-influenced animal tales, one can see the effects of the south Louisiana melting pot. In the traditional French tale (for example, "The Division of the Crops"), the hero, typically the youngest son, dupes the ogre or devil into dividing their communal crops by what grows above and below the ground. When they plant potatoes, the young hero offers the impressive vines above the ground to his witless victim. The dupe then insists on reversing the deal the next year. The hero agrees and suggests planting grain, usually wheat. In Africa, hunters or hunting animals divide the game they have killed together. The clever one gets the outside (meat), the other, the inside (entrails). In the Cajun and Creole versions, the main characters are Bouki and Lapin, from West African tradition, but the plot, about dividing the potato and corn crops, is basically French with an American modification.

Animal tales have been well collected in Louisiana in the past, but today they are fading from the repertoire. They can still be heard in some areas, especially in the parishes east of Lafayette (St. Martin, Iberia, and St. Landry) where Creole culture is strong, and much less so in the predominantly Acadian and *petit Créole* parishes on the

Evilia Boudreaux, story-
teller, Lafayette Parish,
1979 (Photo by Philip
Gould)

southwestern prairies. Even when a teller of animal tales can be
found, one must ask for them to hear them. These stories, which
were once apparently quite popular among all age groups, seem now
to be performed only for children and tenacious folklorists.

Magic Tales

The fast pace of modern life has gradually eroded the popularity
of the magic tale. This genre, filled with kings and castles, princes
and princesses, fabulous treasures and impossible tasks, heroes and
horrors, tends to be multi-episodic and long. These stories flourished
in the days before radio and television, when families and friends
filled the long evenings with stories and songs. These days, people
don't take time to listen to such oral masterpieces. Consequently, the
magic tale has been replaced by shorter forms like the joke and the
tall tale, which can be told in passing. Today the long stories are
heard almost exclusively by folklore specialists who have to look long
and hard to find them. Even so, versions of such long magic tales as
"St. Genevieve de Brabant" ("The Innocent Slandered Maiden"),

"Petit Poucet" ("The Dwarf and Giant"), and "Fin Voleur" ("The Master Thief") have been recorded in south Louisiana since 1977. These long tales are always impressive when encountered in the field. They often show clear connections to European tradition, yet are invariably adapted to the Louisiana experience. In the following tale, a variant of type 513B *The Land and Water Ship*, a typically French and Franco-American hero, Jean l'Ours, is helped by his marvelous companions to win the hand of the princess and the riches of the kingdom. He proves to be a gracious winner, giving the king his special possessions in return, and a lake to fish in during the king's "retirement." A part of the Grimms' collection (nos. 71 and 134), this tale is very popular in French and Franco-American tradition. (It is also known in Africa, where it is told with animal characters.)

Jean l'Ours et la fille du roi (*Elby Deshotels, Rydell*)

Le roi était beaucoup, beaucoup riche. Il était millionnaire un tas de fois. Et il était beaucoup jaloux, beaucoup jaloux. Il avait une belle fille. Elle avait des grands cheveux jaunes, et les yeux bleus. Et il quittait pas personne parler avec sa fille. Et il avait tout le temps dit qu'il aurait fallu que quelqu'un la gagne pour la marier.

Et il y avait un jeune homme, son nom, c'était Jean l'Ours. Et il a déménagé au ras de chez le roi un jour. Et Jean l'Ours avait beaucoup de la capacité. Et il était beaucoup glorieux de ça il avait. Il avait les plus beaux cochons il y avait. Tout ça Jean l'Ours avait, c'était le meilleur. Et il croyait qu'il avait le meilleur coureur il y avait. Et dans son organisation, il avait le Grand Coureur, le Grand Tireur, le Grand Souffleur, et le Grand Crieur... et le Bon Entendeur; il entendait beaucoup bien.

Ça se fait, un jour la fille du roi a été, elle s'est baignée. Il y avait un beau lac, et elle allait les après-midi; elle s'est baignée.

Jean l'Ours and the King's Daughter

The king was very, very rich. He was a millionaire many times over. And he was very jealous, very jealous. He had a beautiful daughter. She had long blond hair and blue eyes. And he let no one speak to his daughter. He had always said that he who would marry her would have to win her hand.

And there was a young man named Jean l'Ours. And one day he moved in next door to the king's house. And Jean l'Ours was very gifted. And he was very proud of what he had. He had the most beautiful pigs in the land. All that Jean l'Ours had was the best. And he thought he had the best runner in the land. In his organization, he had Great Runner, Great Shooter, Great Blower, and Great Crier—and Great Listener; he heard very well.

So one day the king's daughter went to take a bath. There was a beautiful lake, and she went every afternoon to take a bath. And Jean l'Ours came close and he threw pebbles at her.

Et Jean l'Ours approchait, et il a tiré des pierres après.

Elle lui dit, "Jean l'Ours, je connais c'est toi qu'es là. Mais," elle dit, "si mon père t'attrape, il va couper ton cou!"

Il dit, "Je suis venu ici, la fille du roi, pour te demander pour me marier." Il dit, "Je t'ai pas jamais vue, mais je connais que t'es réellement une belle fille." Il dit, "Je veux te marier."

"Bien, mais," elle dit, "tu peux pas me marier." Elle dit, "Je peux pas te marier autrement que mon père me dit que tu m'as gagné. Mais," elle dit, "si tu veux prendre tes chances..."

Ça se fait, un jour, il y a eu un encan de cochons, et le roi a arrivé avec une belle bande de cochons. Et il a commencé à dire comment ses cochons étaient beaux, et comment ils estiont gros, ils estiont ci, ils estiont ça. Et Jean l'Ours lui a dit, "Mon roi, c'est pas des beaux cochons que vous avez." Il dit, "Vous devriez voir les miens."

Ça se fait, il l'a invité, et le roi a été, et surement ceux à Jean l'Ours étaient un tas plus beaux que les siens.

Et un jour, il a rejoint le roi dans le bois, il était à la chasse. Et Jean l'Ours avait tué deux gros chevreuils. Et le roi avait pas de rien. Il avait pas tué rien. Il dit à le roi, "Si t'aurais des chiens de chasse, des taïaux comme ça moi, j'ai, tu pourrais tuer un chevreuil."

Le roi dit, "J'ai les meilleurs taïaux il y a qui chassent."

Ça se fait, Jean l'Ours a lâché ses taïaux, et dans peu de temps, ils ont ramené un chevreuil, et ils l'ont tué. Et il dit à le roi, "J'aimerais marier ta fille."

She said to him, "Jean l'Ours, I know it's you. But," she said, "if my father catches you, he'll cut your throat!"

He said, "I came, daughter of the king, to ask you to marry me." He said, "I've never seen you, but I know that you are a very beautiful girl." He said, "I want to marry you."

"Well," she said, "you can't marry me." She said, "I can't marry you unless my father tells me that you've won me. But," she said, "if you'd like to take your chances...."

So one day there was a pig auction, and the king arrived with a beautiful band of pigs. And he started saying how his pigs were beautiful, and how they were big, they were this and they were that. And Jean l'Ours told him, "My king, those pigs that you have are not beautiful." He said, "You should see mine."

So he invited him, and the king went and sure enough, the pigs of Jean l'Ours were indeed much more beautiful than his own.

And one day, he met the king in the woods, he was hunting. And Jean l'Ours had killed two big deer. And the king had nothing. He had killed nothing. He said to the king, "If you had hunting dogs, hounds like mine, you might be able to kill a deer."

The king said, "I have the best hounds in the land."

So Jean l'Ours let loose his hounds and in no time at all they returned with a deer and they killed it. And he said to the king, "I would like to marry your daughter."

The king said, "Jean l'Ours, you can't marry my daughter. It would take thousands and millions of dollars, and jewels and everything in the world to have my daughter."

Le roi dit, "Jean l'Ours, tu peux pas marier ma fille. Ça prendrait des mille et des millions de piastres, et des bijouteries, et tout ça qu'il y aurait dans le monde, pour ma fille."

Jean l'Ours, il dit à le roi, "Je vas te parier que mon coureur peut courir plus vite que le tien." Et le roi avait le plus beau coureur, le plus vite il y avait. Il pouvait courir vite comme le vent. C'était un grand sauvage.

Ça se fait, un jour, ils ont eu un rendez-vous. Ils ont fait un rendez-vous et Jean l'Ours avait amené tous ses hommes avec lui. Il faulait ça court cinq cents milles. Ça se fait, Jean l'Ours avait son Grand Coureur, et le roi avait son Grand Sauvage.

Ça se fait, quand le pistolet a craqué, le Grand Sauvage a parti loin devant le coureur à Jean l'Ours. Et dans l'après-midi tard, ils ont vu le sauvage qu'était après revenir et ça voyait pas l'homme à Jean l'Ours. Ça se fait, Jean l'Ours a appelé son Bon Entendeur. Il lui dit, "Mets ta tête sur la terre, peut-être tu vas l'entendre. Il est peut-être après dormir."

Ça se fait, le Bon Entendeur a mis sa tête par terre. Il dit, "Je peux pas l'entendre. Il y a trop de train." Il dit, "L'herbe est après élever." Ça se fait, il a été dans le brûlé, ayoù il y avait pas d'herbe. Il a mis sa tête, il dit, "Je l'entends, il est après ronfler."

Ça se fait, il dit à Bon Tireur, "Grimpe dans la tête du grand pin, et vois si tu peux le voir." Ça se fait, il a grimpé dans le grand pin; il l'a vu. Il avait sa tête dessus un noeud de bois gras. Et il a pris sa mire, il était au dessus de deux cents milles. Il a pris sa bonne mire avec sa grande carabine; il a tiré et il

Jean l'Ours said to the king, "I'll bet you that my runner can run faster than yours." And the king had a fine runner, the fastest of all. He ran as fast as the wind. He was a great Indian.

So one day they met. They arranged a meeting and Jean l'Ours brought along all his men with him. They had to run five hundred miles. So Jean l'Ours had his Great Runner, and the king had his Great Indian.

So, at the crack of the pistol, the Great Indian took off far in front of Jean l'Ours's runner. And late that afternoon, they saw the Indian coming and they couldn't see Jean l'Ours's man. So Jean l'Ours called his Great Listener. He told him, "Put your head on the ground, maybe you will hear him. Maybe he's sleeping."

So the Great Listener placed his head on the ground. He said, "I can't hear him. There's too much noise." He said, "The grass is growing." So he went to a burned spot, where there was no grass. He put his head down, he said, "I hear him, he's snoring."

So he said to Great Shooter, "Climb to the top of the tall pine and try to see him." So he climbed the tall pine; he saw him. His head was resting on a pine knot. And he took his sight, he was over two hundred miles away. He took his best sight with his great rifle; he shot out the pine knot from under the head of the Great Runner.

And the Great Crier cried, "The Indian is coming very fast. It's time. You must come."

And Jean l'Ours's man took off running, but he had Great Blower with him, too. Before the Indian arrived, he said to Great Blower, "Listen, couldn't you blow us a sea," he said, "something to stop him?"

a ôté le noeud de bois gras dessous la tête du Grand Coureur.

Et le Grand Crieur, il a crié, "Le sauvage est après venir si vitement. C'est l'heure. Faut tu viens."

Et l'homme à Jean l'Ours a parti pour courir, mais il avait son Bon Souffleur avec lui. Avant le sauvage a arrivé, il dit à Bon Souffleur, "Ecoute, tu pourrais pas nous souffler une mer," il dit, "quelque chose pour l'arrêter?"

Il dit, "*Well*, il est assez au ras," il dit, "faudra je souffle juste dedans une narine parce qu'il y aura un tremblement de terre et," il dit, "je vas tout tuer tout le monde il y aura alentour d'icitte." Ça se fait, il a mis son doigt sur un bord de son nez et il a soufflé dans une narine, et ça a fait une crevasse qu'avait des mille de pieds de creux. Et les pierres et tout ça, ça tombait.

Il dit à son Grand Souffleur, "Resouffle," il dit, "une petite orage, un ouragan, pour l'empêcher d'arriver." En même temps, le Grand Coureur à Jean l'Ours a cassé la ligne, ils estiont moins qu'un demi-pouce de différence, mais il avait gagné.

Ça se fait, Jean l'Ours était planté. La fille du roi, elle est venue, elle s'est envoyée dedans ses bras. Elle dit, "Jean l'Ours, tu m'as gagnée. Je suis pour toi. T'as tout mon amour."

Ça se fait, le roi, il a dit, "Jean L'Ours, faudra tu viens avec moi à la maison." Il dit, "J'ai des choses je veux te donner." Ça se fait, il l'a amené dans sa maison. Et il l'a amené dans une grande chambre qu'il y avait beaucoup, beaucoup des valises tout le tour de la chambre. Et il a ouvert ces valises, et ils estiont pleins des bijouteries, des rubis,

He said, "Well, he's so close." He said, "I'll have to blow through only one nostril because, otherwise, there will be an earthquake and," he said, "I'll kill everyone in the vicinity." So, he put his finger on the side of his nose and blew through one nostril, and he blew a crevice that was thousands of feet deep. And rocks were falling all around.

He said to his Great Blower, "Blow again," he said, "a little storm, a hurricane, to prevent him from winning." At the same time, the Great Runner of Jean l'Ours broke the finish line, winning by less than one-half inch, but he had won.

So there was Jean l'Ours. The king's daughter came and threw herself into his arms. She said, "Jean l'Ours, you have won me. I'm all yours. You have all my love."

So the king said, "Jean l'Ours, you must come with me to my house." He said, "I have some things I want to give to you." So he took him home. He took him into a large room where there were many, many cases all around. And he opened those cases, and they were filled with jewels, rubies, and all that you can imagine that was worth millions and millions of dollars. He said, "Jean l'Ours, I give you this." And he said, "I give you my castle." And he said, "I give you all that I have; it's all yours."

And Jean l'Ours said, "I thank you for all you've given me but," he said, "I have something I want to give you, too." So he gave him his dogs. He gave him his bulls. He gave him his pigs. And he gave him a wide river to fish in. And Jean l'Ours had the king's daughter.

That's the end of the story of Jean l'Ours and the king's daughter.

et tout ça qu tu peux t'imaginer qui valait des millions et des millions de piastres. Il dit, "Jean l'Ours, je te donne ça." Et il dit, "Je te donne mon *castle*." Et il dit, "Je te donne tout ce que j'ai; c'est pour toi."

Et Jean l'Ours, il a dit, "Je vous remercie pour ça que vous m'as donné, mais," il dit, "j'ai quelque chose que je veux vous donner, moi aussitte." Ça se fait, il lui a donné ses chiens. Il lui a donné ses boeufs. Il lui a donné ses cochons. Et il lui a donné une grosse rivière pour lui pêcher dedans. Et Jean l'Ours avait la fille du roi.

Ça, c'est la finition du conte à Jean l'Ours et la fille du roi.

Some magic tales have partially disintegrated as they have fallen out of favor. The following tale, a fragment of type 301A *The Quest for the Princess*, is perhaps one of the most widely known stories in the world. It also was collected by the Grimms and is well known in French and Creole traditions. The descent of the hero into the hole is at least as old as the tale that inspired *Beowulf* and parts of Voltaire's *Candide*. Except for the princess herself, this Louisiana version has most of the essential elements of the story, including the descent into the hole to escape violence and the reemergence from the land at the bottom of the hole on the wings of a bird of prey that requires meat to be able to fly the hero out of the hole. Eventually the hero is forced to cut a piece of his own flesh when he runs out of sheep to feed the bird. This short account is all that remains of a story that was once probably much longer.

Barbe-Bleue et Barbe-Rouge
(Lazard Daigle, Pointe Noire)

Il y avait deux hommes, Barbe-rouge et Barbe-bleue, des hommes avec des grandes barbes. Ils s'avaient battu. Il y avait un qui avait battu l'autre. Barbe-bleue s'avait fait battre. Et il avait de la grande barbe.

Ça fait, Barbe-rouge l'a pris et il lui a

Bluebeard and Redbeard

There were two men, Redbeard and Bluebeard, men with long beards. They had fought each other. One had beaten the other. Bluebeard had been beaten. And he had a long beard.

So Redbeard took him and separated his

séparé la barbe et l'a passée par dessus d'une branche dans un arbre et l'a amarrée. Et il avait les mains d'amarrées et les pieds d'amarrés, et la barbe amarrée après l'arbre. Il était pendu en haut-là.

Il s'a débattu, débattu jusqu'à qu'il a tombé. Il s'a dépris. Et il avait peur de l'autre. Il s'a fourré dans un trou dans la terre et quand il a été dans le trou, il s'a aperçu qu'il était dans un autre pays-là. Et il a resté un bout de temps, puis là, l'ennui l'a pris. Il était seul. Il voulait s'en revenir, mais il pouvait pas, parce qu'il avait pas moyen de sortir. Il lui aurait fallu des ailes d'oiseau pour sortir.

Ça fait, il y avait un gros, gros, gros z-oiseau qui restait là. Et il a été joindre le z-oiseau. Le z-oiseau lui a dit, "Ouais je peux te sortir, mais ça va prendre de quoi. Il faudra tu me donnes à manger. Ça va prendre cent moutons."

Ça fait, il y avait des moutons alentour, dans ce gros trou, dans ce pays-là. Ça fait, il a tué cent moutons et il les a amarrés de quelque manière et puis ça a parti.

En allant en haut, à tout moment, le z-oiseau disait, "Donne-moi du mouton!" Et il lui passait un morceau de mouton, et "Donne-moi du mouton!" Quand il a arrivé en haut, il y avait plus de moutons. Juste pas assez de moutons pour le sortir. Il a fallu qu'il se coupe un morceau après sa jambe à lui pour le dernier morceau. Autrement il l'aurait réchappé.

beard and passed one end over a branch and tied him to the tree. And his hands and feet were tied together, and he was tied by the beard to the tree. He was hanging there.

He struggled, struggled until he fell. He freed himself. And he was afraid of the other man. He hid in a hole in the ground and when he went into the hole, he realized that he was in another world. And he stayed a while, then he got lonesome. He was alone. He wanted to go home, but he couldn't because he didn't know how to get out. He would have needed wings like a bird to get out.

So there was a big, big, big bird that lived there. And he went to meet the bird. The bird said, "Yes, I can take you out, but it will cost you. You will have to feed me. It will take one hundred sheep."

So there were some sheep nearby in this big hole, in this other world. So he killed one hundred sheep and he tied them up somehow and they took off.

On the way up, every now and then, the bird would say, "Give me some mutton!" And he would pass it a piece of mutton. And "Give me some mutton!" When he made it up to the top, there were no more sheep. Not quite enough to get him out. He had to cut from his own leg for the last piece. Otherwise, he would have fallen back.

Active Oral Tradition

When Corinne Saucier concluded her introduction to *Folk Tales from French Louisiana* with the statement that her collection of thirty-three

Old talkers, Lafayette, 1938 (Photo by Russell Lee, Farm Securities Administration collection, Library of Congress)

stories was small, but "representative...of our Southern Louisiana form of oral literature known as folklore, a heritage that is disappearing in our mechanized age," she was thinking of oral tradition in narrow terms. The Louisiana/Old World connection, so important to past Louisiana scholarship, may now be fading, but oral tradition in general certainly is not. It has evolved, following the American trend, in the direction of the shorter joke form, the tall tale, and the "true experience" story. These fall into the category of active oral entertainment. Tellers of these stories are not always revered; more often, they are taken for granted, or sometimes even scarcely tolerated, and their stories are considered nonsense. Yet these are the modern jesters who provide a community with important social needs: laughter within their own context and self-criticism through humor. Their tales occur naturally and spontaneously, without solicitation and even despite protests. They thrive in bars and barbershops, outside church services and service stations, at wakes and cake sales, wherever people gather. If these genres are included in Louisiana French oral tradition, then the folklore of the region has adapted to the mechanized age and is in no danger of disappearing. On the contrary, the Cajuns and Creoles esteem and encourage good tellers and "liars." One can hardly avoid hearing, in groups of two or more French-speakers, "*T'as entendu le conte pour...?*" ("Have you heard the one about...?").

Jokes

The joke is by far the most popular oral genre in Louisiana. Like most Americans, Cajuns and Creoles delight in telling short, funny stories. Jokes have not suffered the negative influences of the mass media and continue to animate nightly visits and gatherings of all sorts. Often Louisiana jokes are localized versions of internationally known stories, but early scholars showed little interest in them, perhaps because they offered little overt evidence of Louisiana's French or African past. Yet they are a living testimony to the French fact in Louisiana because they are told in French by choice, often despite their origins in Anglo-American tradition.

If jokes count in the oral repertoire, the latter can hardly be said to be disappearing. Even surrounded by computers and televisions, people feel a need to tell stories. They have adapted the repertoire and style to suit the fast pace of modern times and they continue to relate quick jokes that may reflect on their cultural heritage in ways that are just as interesting as the more venerable genres. Jokes can be expanded by good talkers with a little time on their hands almost to the length of magic tales.

One of the most popular characters in Louisiana French jokelore is the small, clever trickster who succeeds in extracting himself from difficult situations by means of his wit and a clever ruse, always taking care to avoid a direct confrontation.

La jument verte
(Felix Richard, Cankton)

The Green Mare

Ils m'ont dit, à Church Pointe, il y avait arrivé.... Des années passées, c'est comme je te dis, il y avait du monde là qui avait des coeurs. Et il y avait un bougre, un vieux garçon. Il avait jamais essayé à sortir, parce que son père, il continuait à l'écharlanter.

"Ecoute, garçon. T'aurais un goût d'aller au bal, et t'aurais un goût de rencontrer des filles, peut-être te choisir une fille pour ta femme, mais," il dit, "écoute. C'est pas tout ça, non. T'as pour avoir assez de quoi, quand tu vas te rencontrer une dame, en tout cas tu te décides de te marier, peut-être pas

They told me, in Church Point, something happened.... Years ago, as I was telling you, there were people there who had heart. And there was a guy, a bachelor. He had never tried to go out, because his father constantly needled him.

"Listen, son. You think you would like to go dancing, and you would like to meet girls, maybe pick a girl to be your wife. But," he said, "listen. That's not everything, you know. You've got to have means when you will meet a lady, in case you decide to marry her, maybe not long afterwards." He said,

longtemps après." Il dit, "Quoi c'est que tu vas soigner cette femme-là avec? T'as pour avoir de quoi pour avoir une femme. T'as pour avoir un cheval et un boggué, ça c'est sûr, et," il dit, "t'as pour avoir de l'argent. Ça fait, tu peux pas aller te marier avec les poches vides."

Ça fait, il a écouté son père et il était derrière pour se faire de l'argent. Il pouvait pas rentrer sa récolte assez vite. C'était mettre ça à la banque et puis il la comptait souvent. Et un de ces jours, il allait venir à en avoir assez, et il pourrait aller au bal.

Ça fait, il était rendu vieux garçon. Encore dans le temps, l'argent était rare. Il pouvait pas s'en trouver un tas. Il travaillait tout ça il pouvait, sur tous les côtés. Quand il avait pas d'ouvrage chez lui, il travaillait à faire des fossés, et le diable et ses cornes.

Ça fait, un bon jour, il y a quelqu'un de ses *partners* qui lui dit, "Ecoute, voir. Moi, je crois t'es après manquer le *show*." Il dit, "Quand tu vas t'apercevoir. . . . T'es après écouter ton papa-là, c'est bon. O, c'est une belle chose. C'est rare les enfants qui écoutent leur père, d'une certaine manière, aussi bien que ça. Mais, écoute. Il y a une limite dans cette affaire. Mais," il dit, "tout à l'heure, tu connais quoi ce qui va arriver? Tu seras rendu trop vieux, quand tu vas aller au bal. C'est des jeunes filles qui restent-là." Il dit, "Les vieilles sont toutes parties. Il y a quelqu'un qui les a pris. Ça fait, toutes celles-là qui seront là seront un tas plus jeunes que toi. Quelle c'est, tu crois, qui voudra de toi? Tu seras trop vieux. Tu pourras pas t'en trouver une. Ça fait," il dit, "écoute. Avant tu manques le bateau, tu ferais mieux venir au bal, et puis c'est comme ça que tu vas trouver une femme."

"How will you take care of that lady? You've got to have means to have a wife. You've got to have a horse and buggy, that's for sure. And," he said, "you've got to have money. So you can't go off and get married with empty pockets."

So he listened to his father and he got to work making money. He couldn't get his crops in fast enough. It was straight to the bank and he counted his money often. And someday he would have enough, and he would be able to go to the dance.

So he became an old bachelor. In those days, money was rare. He couldn't find a lot of it. He worked as hard as he could, everywhere. When he didn't have work on his own farm, he worked digging ditches, and every damn thing.

So one day, one of his friends said to him, "Listen, here. I think you're missing the show." He said, "Before you know it. . . . You're listening to your father now, and that's good. Oh, that's a wonderful thing. It's not often that children listen to their father, in a way, as well as that. But listen. There's a limit to it." He said, "Soon do you know what will happen? You're going to be too old when you finally go to the dance. It's young girls who go there." He said, "The old ones are all gone. They are all taken. So all the ones who will be there will be a lot younger than you. What young girl do you think will want you? You're going to be too old. You won't be able to find one for yourself. So," he said, "listen. Before you miss the boat you had better come to the dance, and that's how you will find a wife."

So, naturally, he wasn't like those young boys who have to hitchhike to the dance or

Ça fait, lui, naturellement, il était pas
comme ces jeunes petits bougres-là qui allaient
au bal sur un *ride* ou quelque chose comme
ça. Lui, il avait son boggué neuf. Et puis,
il avait une belle bêtaille noire. Ça sortait pas
de l'écurie, cette affaire. Ça fait qu'il a décidé
d'aller au bal à la pointe. Il a été bonne
heure, juste après le soleil couché. Ça fait,
il y avait un poteau de lumière dehors qui
était allumé. Et il a figuré, "*Well*, je vas
mettre mon boggué là, et ma bêtaille en bas
de la lumière-là. Ça fait, je suis sûr il y a
rien qui va les toucher. Il y a des constables
ici. Aller mettre mon boggué dans le noir
là-bas, eux peut massacrer mon boggué.
Quelqu'un peut couper le *top* ou . . ." tu
connais.

Ça fait, pour être sûr que rien arrive,
il l'amarre au poteau ayoù la lumière était.
Ça fait, quelqu'un est arrivé, ils ont vu
cette belle bêtaille et ce beau boggué.
Il avaient jamais vu ça, tu connais. Il y
en avait, des bons boggués, mais ça avait
pas de boggué, pas comme lui. Bougre-là,
un petit brin de poussière et il fallait
il le lave.

Ça fait, tout à l'heure, il s'avait amené
une topette, tu connais, dans le bas du
boggué. Dans le temps, c'était du *moonshine*
et tu pouvais pas boire ça dans la salle. Pas
proche! Et il avait chaud dans la salle. Il était
après avoir un bon temps. Ça fait, il décide
il aurait été dehors et puis se ramasser un
petit coup de ce *moonshine* il avait, et puis
voir à sa bêtaille et son boggué. Il arrive là-
bas. Eux avaient peint sa jument verte avec
de la peinture. Non, mais, monde, monde,
monde! Quand il a vu ça, ça l'a foutu en
feu, tu vois.

something like that. He had a brand new
buggy. And he had a beautiful black horse.
It hardly ever left the stall. So he decided
to go to the dance at the point. He went
early, just after sunset. So there was a lamp
post outside that was lit. And he figured,
"Well, I'll put my buggy there, and my horse
under the light. So then I'm sure nothing
will touch them. There are constables here.
If I were to put my buggy over there in the
dark, someone could destroy my buggy.
Someone could cut the top off or. . . ." You
know.

So to be sure that nothing happened, he
tied up to the post where the light was. So
someone came by and saw that beautiful horse
and that handsome buggy. They had never
seen them, I guess. There were some nice
buggies around, but no one had one like his.
That fellow would wash it if it got a speck
of dust on it.

So later—he had brought along a flask,
you know, in the buggy. (In those days, it
was moonshine and you couldn't drink it in
the dance hall. Not at all!) And he was hot
in the dance hall. He was having a good time.
So he decided he would go outside and take
a little hit of the moonshine he had and check
on his horse and buggy. He got there.
Someone had painted his mare green, with
paint. Man, man, man! When he saw that,
it just burned him up, you see.

So he comes back into the dance hall.
He climbs up onto the musicians' table. He
stops the music. He raises both hands in the
air. He started announcing that he couldn't
imagine who in the world had done that to
his horse, right there under the light for all
to see. He said that someone had come and

Ça fait, il revient dans la salle. Il monte sur la table de musiciens. Il arrête la musique. Il lève ses deux mains en l'air. Il a commencé à annoncer qu'il pouvait pas voir dans le monde qui dans le tonnerre qu'avait fait ce qu'ils avaient fait avec sa bêtaille, droit là, à bic-à-blanc en bas de la lumière. Il dit que quelqu'un a venu peindre sa bêtaille vert. Il dit, "Qui-ce qui aurait fait ça?" Et puis il se cognait l'estomac, tu connais, comme s'il avait devenu un taureau tout du coup.

Tout à l'heure, il s'en vient un bougre en travers de la salle qui avait la chemise déboutonnée avec le jabot grand ouvert, avec les culottes qui étaient après pendre un peu bas et il avait le mouchoir juste manière enfoncé dans sa poche. Il vient au ras de la table de musiciens-là. Il avait son estomac plein de crins, tu comprends. Il se cogne dans l'estomac comme ça. Il dit, "C'est moi le boulé qui a peint la jument." Il dit, "Quoi ce que t'as pour dire pour ça?"

"Mais," il dit, "j'ai venu pour te dire qu'elle est sèque. Elle est parée pour une seconde couche."

painted his horse green. He said, "Who would have done that?" And he was hitting his chest as though he had suddenly become a bull.

After a while, a fellow came across the hall, his shirt unbuttoned and his collar opened wide, his pants hanging low, with a handkerchief stuffed into one pocket. He came up to the musicians' table. He had a chest full of hair, you understand? He beat his chest like this. He said, "I'm the bully who painted the mare." He said, "What do you have to say about it?"

"Well," he said, "I came to tell you that she's dry. She's ready for a second coat."

Usually the joke is much quicker, based on a clever or absurd retort.

Les oeufs craqués
(*Adley Gaudet, Bayou Pigeon*)

Il y avait une femme dans Lafayette. Elle a été à la grocerie. Elle dit à Monsieur Viator, elle lui a demandé voir combien est-ce qu'il vendait ses oeufs. Il dit, "Trente-cinq sous la douzaine pour les bons, mais," il dit, "les massacrés, ceux-là qui sont craqués, c'est vingt-cinq sous la douzaine."

Elle dit, "Comment ça serait de m'en craquer trois ou quatre douzaines?"

The Cracked Eggs

There was a lady in Lafayette. She went to the grocery store. She said to Mister Viator, she asked him how much he wanted for his eggs. He said, "Thirty-five cents a dozen for the good ones, but," he said, "the broken ones, those that are cracked, are twenty-five cents a dozen."

She said, "How about cracking me three or four dozen?"

An obvious reflection of Louisiana's French heritage is found in jokes based on French-language puns. The following story is based on the confusion of the homonym phrases: *le fer*, the iron, and *le faire*, to do it. Variants of this story are told in many parts of the French-speaking world, including France, Belgium, Quebec, and New Brunswick.

Le fer dans le lit
(Evélia Boudreax, Carencro)

Une fois, il y avait une vieille fille et elle avait fini par trouver à se marier. Et c'était une excitation beaucoup dans la maison! La vieille maman était veuve et elle voulait sa fille trouve à se marier, mais ça prenait du temps.

Ça fait, finalement, le jour a arrivé pour le mariage. Après le mariage, ils ont eu la célébration. L'heure était arrivée pour les mariés aller à leur chambre. La maman savait que sa fille avait tout le temps les pieds froids. Et elle avait l'habitude de chauffer un fer à repasser et le mettre dans son lit, pour réchauffer ses pieds le soir. Ça fait, la maman voulait d'être vaillante et bonne pour la fille. Elle a chauffé le fer, et elle l'a mis dans le lit. Mais le marié s'est aperçu du fer dans le lit. Et il connaissait pas quoi c'était. Il a levé les couvertes, et il a trouvé le fer. Et il a demandé à la mariée pourquoi le fer était dans le lit. Elle a dit, "Pour réchauffer mes pieds." Elle dit, "Mes pieds sont tout le temps si froids."

Mais la maman, tellement elle était excitée, avait l'oreille à la porte pour écouter quoi qu'allait dans la chambre des mariés. Et tout d'un coup, le marié a jeté le fer par terre, en disant à la mariée, "Tu as plus besoin le fer pour réchauffer tes pieds!"

La maman dit, "Qu'est-ce que c'est ce train?"

The Iron in the Bed

Once there was an old maid who had found herself a husband at long last. And excitement filled the household! Her old mother was a widow and she was eager for her daughter to find a husband, and it had taken a long time.

So finally the day had come for the wedding. After the wedding, there was a celebration. The time had come for the newlyweds to go to their room. The mother knew that her daughter's feet were always cold. And she had a habit of heating an iron and putting it in her bed to keep her feet warm at night. So the mother wanted to be nice and good for her daughter. She heated the iron and put it in the bed. But the groom noticed the iron in the bed. And he didn't know what it was. He raised the covers and he found the iron. And he asked the bride why the iron was in the bed. She said, "To keep my feet warm." She said, "My feet are always so cold."

But the mother was so excited that she had her ear to the door to listen to what was happening in the newlyweds' bedroom. And suddenly the groom threw the iron on the floor, saying to the bride, "You no longer need the iron to warm your feet!"

The mother said, "What's that noise?"

The daughter said, "Mom, he doesn't want the iron [le fer] in the bed!"

Elle dit, "Maman, il veut pas le fer dans le lit!"

"Mais," elle dit, "mais, chère, si il veut pas le faire dans le lit, fais par terre!"

"Well," she said, "Dear, if he doesn't want to do it [le faire] in the bed, do it on the floor!"

Other jokes reflect the Cajuns' cultural heritage more indirectly. The following story is a version of the international type 1476 *The Prayer for a Husband*, which usually includes a young troublemaker who overhears an old maid's prayer and demands of her several ridiculous tests. She, thinking his voice is that of God or a saint, complies. In a version from Quebec, the old maid prays at the foot of St. Joseph's statue. Upon hearing the voice of the young trickster, she jumps onto the statue of St. Joseph, causing it to fall on her, to which she exclaims, *"Débarque donc, St. Joseph. T'es pire qu'un jeune!"* ("Get off, St. Joseph. You're worse than the boys!") This irreverent response comes from the very heart of Québecois culture where the mere mention of religious trappings (*calice [chalice]*, *hostie [host]*, *tabernacle*) makes for good cussing. In a parallel version of this story from New Brunswick, the old maid hides in a chicken coop to pray. When she lifts her head in prayer, chicken droppings fall into her mouth, at which she exclaims, *"Bonne Ste. Viarge, j'ai reçu vos grâces, b'en c'est amer!"* ("Good St. Virgin, I have received your graces, but how they are bitter!") This response is a remarkable reflection of the downtrodden Acadian culture of the Canadian Maritime provinces.

At first glance the following Louisiana French version does not seem to be successful. It depends on the confusion between the owl's hoot and the English *who*. The storyteller, Mrs. Clotile Richard, had heard the story in English, but had not felt the need to change the cry of the bird to something that would have made sense in French—like the killdeer's "kee kee," for example, which could be confused with the French *qui*. For her, it was not at all surprising that God might speak English; most people in power usually did. Her response unconsciously reflects the social context of the storyteller who lives in a bilingual world. The old maid reacted in French to what she mistook for God's "Who?" in the same way that Mrs. Richard herself did when speaking with her own grandchildren who addressed her in English.

La vieille fille qui voulait se marier
(Clotile Richard, Carencro)

C'était une vieille fille qui voulait se
marier. Et puis, elle avait pas d'avantage. Ça
fait, elle avait été consulter sa grand-mère.
Ça fait, sa grand-mère l'a dit, "Mais, si tu
prierais les soirs auprès d'un chêne," elle dit,
"ta prière pourrait être exaucée."

Ça fait, la vieille fille est allée prier . . .
prier. Il y avait pas de réponse à sa prière.
Ça fait, un soir, elle dit, "Je vas prier avec
plus de ferveur!" Elle s'est mis d'à genoux,
près du chêne, mis sa tête contre le chêne.
"Mon Dieu!" elle crie, "faîtes-moi la grâce
que je peux me marier!"

Il y a un vieil hibou qui fait, "Hou
houou!"

"Ah," elle dit, "Grand Dieu! Partant que
c'est un homme," elle dit, "envoyez-moi le
tout de suite!"

The Old Maid Who Wanted to Get Married

There was an old maid who wanted to
get married. And she had no luck. So she
had gone to talk to her grandmother. So her
grandmother told her, "Well, if you were to
pray every night next to an oak tree," she
said, "your prayer might be answered."

So the old maid went to pray . . . and pray.
There was no answer to her prayer. So one
night, she said, "I'll pray with more fervor!"
She got down on her knees, next to the oak,
put her head against the oak. "My God!"
she cried, "do me the favor of sending me
a husband!"

An old owl went, "Hoo hooo!"

"Ah," she said, "Great God! As long as
it's a man," she said, "send him to me right
away!"

Some stories reflect cultural concerns quite directly. The following
story, a variant of type 1628 *The Educated Son and the Forgotten
Language*, is known in many areas where a new language threatens
the existence of an older one. It has been collected in many parts of
the world, including Lithuania, Sweden, France, Germany, Italy,
Hungary, Russia, and Canada. In a version from Ile Maurice in the
Indian Ocean, the young man asks in French *"Qu'est-ce que c'est?"*
("What is it?") pointing to a crab at the marketplace. When the crab
pinches him, he regains his native Creole to curse it. In this Louisiana
version, a rake handle on the mouth is what it takes to jar the young
Cajun's memory.

Jean Sot à l'école
(Clotile Richard, Carencro)

Jean Sot avait été à l'école pour apprendre
l'anglais. Ça fait, il a revenu *back* pour visiter
son père et sa mère, et il faisait comme s'il
comprenait plus le français.

Ça fait, il a été au jardin (son père et sa

Jean Sot at School

Jean Sot had gone to school to learn
English. So he came home to visit his father
and mother and he acted as though he no
longer understood French.

So he went out into the garden (his father

mère faisaient jardin) pour visiter. Et puis, il voit les rateaux et la pioche. Ça fait, il voulait demander à sa mère ce que c'était cet outil, pour travailler le jardin. Et puis, en même temps, il met son pied sur le rateau. Le rateau a revenu *back*, l'a frappé sur la bouche. "Ah!" il dit. "Mon fils-de-putain de rateau!"

"Ah," elle dit, "mon garçon, je vois ton français commence à te revenir!"

and mother were working in the garden) to visit. And saw the rakes and the hoe. So he wanted to ask his mother what this garden tool was called. And at the same time, he stepped on the rake. The rake handle came back and hit him on the mouth. "Ah!" he said. "Mon fils-de-putain de rateau!" ["Son-of-a-bitchin' rake!"]

"Ah," she said, "my son, I see your French is beginning to come back to you!"

Another important, though often overlooked, category of joke is the dirty joke. These range from the mildly naughty to the grossly obscene, and they make up a considerable part of the repertoire of actively told jokes in south Louisiana. Yet in the past, few fieldworkers collected them, either because tellers were unwilling to risk offending the sensibilities of visitors or because folklorists working in Louisiana saw little value in reporting these stories. One collector, a very distinguished East European woman, even declared that Cajuns did not appear to have bawdy songs or stories in their traditional repertoire. In retrospect, it is easy to see that her Cajun informants were simply being polite; they avoided telling or singing things that they felt might offend her. The following story is an example of humor on the farm, based on a very earthy understanding of the realities of life and the motivation of sex, even in supposedly dumb animals.

La truie dans la berouette
(Claude Landry, Bayou Pigeon)

The Sow in the Wheelbarrow

T'as entendu cil-là pour le Cadien. Il s'avait marié. Il restait loin, loin, loin dans la campagne. Son premier voisin était deux miles, sûr. Et il avait quelques volailles. Il avait une truie. Il avait un mulet et un cheval. C'était juste lui et sa femme, tu sais? Ça fait, ils ont convenu qu'ils auraient élevé des petits cochons.

Ça fait, sa femme dit, "Mais, Bèbe, t'as pas de verrat."

"Non, mais," il dit, "notre voisin là-bas,

You heard the one about the Cajun. He got married. He lived far, far, far out in the country. His nearest neighbor lived at least two miles away. And he had a few chickens. He had a sow. He had a mule and a horse. He and his wife lived alone, you know? So they decided they would raise pigs.

So his wife says, "But, Honey, you don't have a boar."

"No, but," he says, "our neighbor over there, he raises pigs. He has a boar over

lui, il élève des cochons. Lui, il a un verrat là-bas." Il dit, "Je vas emmener la truie là-bas et puis la *breed*.

Ça fait, *sure enough*, l'homme, à matin, il a parlé avec son voisin. Son voisin dit ça, "Mais sûr, emmène la truie là-bas dans ton char."

"Mais," il dit, "j'ai pas de char."

"Mais," il dit, "comment est-ce que tu vas l'emmener?"

"Mais," il dit, "tout ce que j'ai, c'est une berouette."

"Mais," il dit, "mets-la dans la berouette et puis emmène-la là-bas dans la berouette."

Ça fait, *sure enough*, le lendemain matin, il se lève bien de bonne heure. Il met la truie dans la berouette. Elle pesait à peu près deux cents livres, tu sais? Il s'en a été sur le fond du *gravel road* à peu près deux miles, à pousser cette berouette avec cette truie là-dedans.

Il arrive là-bas. Ils la mettont dans le parc avec la mâle. Le mâle l'a grimpée. Le bougre lui dit ça, "*Well*, ça devrait être bon." Il rentre *back* la truie sur la berouette. *Back* deux miles là-bas chez lui.

Le lendemain matin, il se lève. Il va là-bas au parc regarder. Il vient *back* dans la maison. Sa femme dit ça, "Quoi il y a, Bèbe?"

"*God dog!*" il dit, "je connais pas quoi ce qu'il y a, mais on a pas de petits cochons encore."

Elle dit, "Mais peut-être que ça a pas pris."

"Peut-être pas," il dit. "Demain matin, je vas faire la même chose."

Back en haut du chemin. *Breed* la truie encore. Il va. Il regarde dans le parc. Pas

there." He says, "I'll take the sow over there to breed her."

So sure enough, the man, in the morning, he spoke to his neighbor. His neighbor says, "Well, sure, bring the sow over in your car."

"But," he says, "I don't have a car."

"Well," he says, "how will you bring her?"

"Well," he says, "all I have is a wheelbarrow."

"Well," he says, "put her in the wheelbarrow and bring her over in the wheelbarrow."

So sure enough, the next morning, he got up very early. He put the sow in the wheelbarrow. She weighed about two hundred pounds, you know? He went to the end of the gravel road, about two miles, pushing that wheelbarrow with that sow in it.

He arrived there. They put her in the pen with the male. The male mounted her. The fellow said, "Well, that ought to do it." He loaded the sow back in the wheelbarrow. Back two miles to his house.

The next day, he gets up. He goes to the pen to see. He comes back into the house. His wife says, "What's the matter, dear?"

"God dog!" he says. "I don't know what's the matter, but we don't have any little pigs yet."

She says, "Maybe it didn't take."

"Maybe not," he says. "Tomorrow morning, I'll do the same thing."

Back on the road. Breed the sow again. He goes. He looks in the pen. Still no little pigs. He says to his wife, "I don't know what's wrong."

So he loads the sow in the wheelbarrow. Pushes for two miles. He comes back.

de petits cochons encore. Il dit à sa femme, "Moi, je connais pas quoi, ça il y a de *wrong*."

Ça fait, il embarque la truie dans la berouette. Pousser *back* pour les deux miles. Il revient *back*.

Le lendemain matin, il se lève de bonne heure. Il dit à sa femme, "Bèbe, écoute. Moi, je vas te dire la franche vérité. Moi, je suis fatigué." Il dit, "Comment ça serait que tu irais voir au parc là-bas, voir si on a pas de petits cochons à ce matin."

"Mais," elle dit, "*okay*, Bèbe." Ça fait, elle va là-bas. Lui, il était toujours couché dans le lit. Elle revient *back*.

"*Well*," il dit, "quoi ce que . . . ? On a des petits cochons?"

Elle dit, "Non, Bèbe, mais la truie est après t'espérer dans la berouette!"

The next morning, he gets up early. He says to his wife, "Baby, listen. I'll tell you the truth. I'm tired." He says, "How about you going out to the pen to see if we don't have any little pigs this morning."

"Well," she says, "okay, baby." So she goes out there. He was still in bed. She comes back.

"Well," he says, "what about it . . . ? Do we have any little pigs?"

She says, "No, baby, but the sow is waiting for you in the wheelbarrow!"

Tall Tales

The tall-tale tradition is also very popular in Louisiana where there is a distinction between *une menterie*, a lie meant to amuse, and *un mensonge*, a lie meant to deceive. When Mamou storyteller Revon Reed pointed out to a group of visiting French journalists that Cajuns are "artistic liars," he was not referring to their mendacity, but to their penchant for *le conte fort*, the whopper. While animal tales are concentrated in the Creole parishes east of Lafayette, tall tales are most popular on the southwestern prairies, where the Cajuns' lives were greatly influenced by the American frontier.

Most tall tales are set in a familiar context, often on the farm. Sometimes they are based on a tacit understanding between tellers and audiences to suspend reality for a tale or two. Other times, they are deliberately set up to shock the audience by manipulating familiar reality.

Tall tales are perhaps most interesting when competition develops between several tellers who try to see which of them can most deftly

Stanislaus Faul, story-
teller, Crankton, 1984
(Photo by Philip Gould)

stretch the limits. Indeed there are even stories concerning this sort
of competition. This tale, a variant of type 1960D *The Great Cabbage*,
is an excellent example of this structure, sometimes called the *Contest
in Lying* (type 1920A).

La grosse pomme de chou et la chaudiere (*Stanislaus Faul, dit Tanisse, Cankton*)	*The Big Head of Cabbage and the Pot*

Une fois, il y avait deux camarades, mais
il y en a un, il était menteur, menteur,
menteur, mais ça s'adonnait bien. Ça fait, le
grand menteur, il a été au Texas, lui. Et il
s'avait convenu il aurait été rester au Texas.
Ça fait, il dit à l'autre, il dit, "Viens avec
moi. Allons rester au Texas. Il y a de la
bonne terre là-bas. Il y a moyen de faire des
récoltes, ça fait drôle."

"O," l'autre dit, "non, moi, je fais ma
vie ici. Moi, je veux pas aller là-bas. Je vas
m'ennuyer." Il dit, "Je pourras pas rester."

"O, non!" Il dit, "Tu t'ennuyeras pas."
Il dit, "C'est des belles places." Enfin, il dit,
"Moi, je suis *gone* rester."

"Mais," il dit, "va. Si c'est bon, plus tard,
je vas peut-être aller."

Ça fait, le bougre a été. Il a déménagé
là-bas. Dans l'année d'après, il a revenu faire

Once there were two friends, but one of
them was a terrible liar, but they got along
well. So the big liar went to Texas. He
decided he would go to live in Texas. So he
tells the other one, "Come with me. Let's
go live in Texas. There's good land there.
Great crops are possible there."

"Oh," the other says, "no, I'm making
a life for myself here. I'm not going out
there. I'll be lonely." He says, "I won't be
able to live there."

"Oh, no!" He said, "You won't be lonely."
He says, "There are beautiful places." Finally,
he says, "I'm going there to live."

"Well," he says, "go. If it's that good,
later I might go."

So the fellow went. He moved out there.
During the next year, he came back on a
trip around here. He borrowed a horse to

une promenade par ici. Il a emprunté un cheval pour lui *ride*. Il a passé en avant de chez l'autre bougre, et son camarade était après rabourer.

Il arrive. Il dit, "Pourquoi t'es après graffigner toujours la vieille terre?"

"Ah, bien," il dit, "je suis après faire ma vie."

Il dit, "Tu viens là-bas au Texas. C'est là il y a de la bonne terre."

"Mais," il dit, "comment. Quoi c'est vous autres fais?"

Il dit, "Ecoute. Je vas te dire une chose." Il dit, "Il y a un homme, il a fait une pomme de chou." Il dit, "Il a cent têtes de moutons, et les cent moutons vont se coucher à l'ombre en bas de cette grosse pomme de chou."

L'homme lui dit, "Mais, c'est sûr une belle pomme, j'imagine."

Ça fait, le bougre a continué à raconter toutes sortes des affaires, tu connais, comment il avait vu, quoi il avait entendu.... Un bout de temps, mais là, c'est que c'était rendu à midi. L'homme voulait s'en aller dîner, lâcher pour aller dîner. Le bougre lui dit, "Moi, depuis je suis *gone*," il dit, "quoi t'as vu de nouveau?"

"Mais," il dit, "j'ai vu cinquante z-hommes après faire une chaudière." Il faulait, dans ce temps-là, tu connais, il faulait ça cogne, ça visse ça. Il dit, "Avec chacun un marteau assez loin à loin qu'un entendait pas l'autre cogner."

"O, mais," il dit, "quoi ils vouliont foutre avec une pareille grosse chaudière?"

"Mais," il dit, "cuire ta pomme de chou!" Ça lui a donné la chance d'aller dîner.

ride. He passed in front of the other fellow's house and his friend was plowing.

He stops. He says, "Why are you still scratching that old dirt?"

"Ah, well," he says, "I'm making a living."

He says, "Come to Texas, that's where the good land is."

"Well," he says, "how do you mean? What do you all grow?"

He says, "Listen. I'll tell you one thing." He says, "There's a man who grew a head of cabbage." He said, "He has one hundred sheep and the hundred sheep sleep in the shade under that big head of cabbage."

The man says to him, "Well, that's surely a nice head, I imagine."

So the fellow continued to tell him about all sorts of things, you know, that he had seen, that he had heard.... For a while, but then it got to be noon. The man wanted to go home to eat, knock off to eat. The fellow says to him, "Since I've been gone," he says, "what new things have you seen?"

"Well," he says, "I saw fifty men making a pot." In those days, you know, they had to beat them, rivet them. He says, "Each with a hammer so far apart that they couldn't hear each other striking the pot."

"Oh, well," he says, "why the hell did they want to build such a big pot?"

"Well," he said, "to cook your head of cabbage!" That gave him a chance to go and eat.

There is also a tradition called *le menteur démenti*, in which the liar is forced to reduce his story, often with comical results (type 1920D). In this story, the liar finally rebels against his detractor when pushed too far, questioning the very purpose of telling a story if it can't include a little stretching.

Le chasseur de chaoui
(Witness Dugas, Lafayette)

The Raccoon Hunter

Il y avait un bougre qui allait à la chasse. Et il avait tout le temps un nègre avec lui pour approuver ça il tuait. Quand il mentissait, il faulait tout le temps lui haler sur sa queue de capot. Ça fait, il a tiré un chaoui. Et il disait qu'il avait dix pieds de queue. Le nègre hale sur sa queue de capot. Il dit, "Pas aussi long que ça, *Boss*."

Ça fait, il tourne de bord. "Mais," il dit, "peut-être pas dix pieds, mais," il dit, "sûr sept pieds."

Le nègre lui hàle sa queue de capot encore. Il dit, "Peut-être pas sept pieds, mais," il dit, "sûr cinq pieds."

Il le hale encore. "Mais," il dit, "quoi? Tu veux je le laisse avec pas de queue?"

There was a fellow who went hunting. And he always had a black man with him to confirm what he killed. When he lied, the black man pulled on his coattail. So he shot a raccoon. And he said it had a tail ten feet long. So the black man pulled on his coattail. He says, "Not that long, Boss."

So he turns around. "Well," he says, "maybe not ten feet but," he says, "at least seven feet."

The black man pulls on his coattail again. He says, "Maybe not seven feet but," he says, "at least five feet."

He pulls again. "Well," he says, "what? Do you want me to leave it with no tail at all?"

"Pascal" Stories

Lying traditions are sometimes localized, as in the case of the Pascal stories found in the town of Mamou. These stories are not performances of fixed texts. Instead they are spontaneous oral creations, often conversational in nature, which form a system of exaggerations, lies, and nonsense that is quite popular among those who participate in the daily storytelling sessions in the bars along Sixth Street in Mamou. Pascal stories are the result of a group effort, with individual parts contributed by members of the group as they alternately take the floor. Each talker helps shape the story by contributing narrative material that applies to the current theme. Occasionally, one especially imaginative person may hold the floor and perform alone for several minutes. Invariably, however, someone will eventually challenge him, contribute further to his idea, or even take over the floor with a change of subject if the performance begins to falter. It is the obligation of the talker to create his story spontaneously, to invent an idea appropriate to the Pascal tradition, and then to develop it according to the "rules," which are defined by the expectations of the other members of the group.

In the world of the Pascal story, the main character is usually Pascal himself. There are several variant explanations for the origin of the character, although all versions refer to a real-life person as the inspiration for the legendary hero. Some maintain that Pascal is named after a former state trooper, Pascal Guillory, who lived in the Mamou area and was allegedly overzealous in his enforcement of the speed limit. Hence the story about Pascal catching speeding drivers by riding his converted bicycle on telephone or power lines and descending ahead of the speeders. Among countless adventures, he clips along on it at a cool 700 miles per hour and cuts tornadoes in two with a razor blade mounted on the handlebars.

Pascal, the hero, is most often described as tall and very thin. He is a hero in much the same way that Brer Rabbit is in the trickster tales, champion of the *niche* (practical joke) and successful rascal. Other characters in the tradition include Jim and Mayo Israel and Olide. Pascal's friend and right-hand man, Jim Israel is himself often the central character of the stories. His importance is not due to any special descriptive feature, but rather to his innumerable exploits. Jim is constantly involved in some grandiose project such as going to the moon (in any number of outlandish ways) or reflooding and resalting the Pacific Ocean after drying it up to plant rice. Pascal's neighbor, Olide, shared in many of the early exploits of the tradition and was apparently more popular years ago than at present. He is the brother of Tante Auroc and the boyfriend of the infamous Tante Coque. In spite of a heart transplant to his back (to avoid *mal au coeur*), he died unexpectedly at the tender age of 123 on his birthday, February 32nd. Tante Coque is generally referred to as a wicked old witch. According to some reports, she is indeed well placed in the hierarchy of witches. In all reports, she hates Pascal fiercely and is obsessed with his undoing. Mayo Israel, Jim's brother, is often cast as the goat or the fool who offers a foil for Jim and Pascal. For example, in a tale describing the division of the moon, Mayo was initially duped into taking the dark side, although he unwittingly profited from the dark, rich soil in the long run.

Pascal et son bicycle
(Elvin Fontenot [EF], Hube Reed [HR], et Alexandre Manuel [AM], Mamou)

EF: Pascal, c'est pas lui qu'avait rentré dans la mer en bicycle?

HR: Il allait vite.... Mais, ouais, il a été à l'Angleterre, là-bas. Quand Lindbergh a monté l'aéroplane pour aller, il était après espérer Lindbergh là-bas. Lui, il allait, il allait assez vite, c'était.... Il allait sur la mer!

BA: Sur son bicycle?

HR: Sur son bicycle. Il a jamais eu un *flat*. Il cognait trois ou quatre baleines, des petites baleines. Il y en avait une, elle était à peu près un mile de long.

AM: Jim a été à Tokyo, lui.

HR: Jim a été avec Tojo et Tokyo Rose.

AM: Il avait appelé là-bas au téléphone de la Californie et ça a *ring* deux ou trois fois et il s'a répond.

HR: O, ouais! Faut ça *ring* trois fois.

AM: Il a descendu de son bicycle et il s'est répondu lui-même, quand il a arrivé au téléphone.

HR: Quand il a appelé là-bas, avant ça peut élever le téléphone, il s'est répond lui-même.

AM: Ouais. Il était rendu de la Californie.

HR: Et là, c'ètait pas un bébé, mais il avait le vent avec lui, tu connais? Là le courant, toute l'affaire... mais, écoute! Il pagotait, ouais, cher! Ses jambes étaient sûr grosses comme mon cigare, mais il mettait du quatorze dans les souliers.

Mayo sur la lune
(Irving [IR] and Revon Reed [RR], Mamou)

IR: Il y avait pas d'eau là-bas sur la lune, quand ils ont arrivé, mais Mayo a fait de l'eau! Mayo travaillait pour l'affaire d'eau.

Pascal and His Bicycle

EF: Pascal, isn't he the one who went into the ocean on a bicycle?

HR: He was very fast.... Well, yes, he went to England. When Lindbergh boarded his plane to leave, he was already waiting for Lindbergh over there. He went so fast, it was.... He rode on the sea!

BA: On his bicycle?

HR: On his bicycle. He never had a flat. He would hit three or four whales, little whales. There was one that was only about a mile long.

AM: Jim went to Tokyo.

HR: Jim went with Tojo and Tokyo Rose.

AM: He had telephoned over there from California and it rang two or three times, and he answered his own call.

HR: Oh, yes, it had to ring three times.

AM: He got off his bicycle and he answered himself, when he reached the telephone.

HR: When he called over there, before anyone else could answer, he answered himself.

AM: Yes. He had arrived from California.

HR: And then, he's no slouch, but he had the wind at his back, you know? And the current, and everything....But listen! He was really pedaling! His legs were surely as big as my cigar, but he wore a size fourteen shoe.

Mayo on the Moon

IR: There was no water over there on the moon, when they arrived there, but Mayo made water! Mayo used to work for the waterworks.

RR: Il travaillait pour *Mamou Waterworks*. Il a trouvé de l'eau sur la lune?

IR: Mayo va prendre une qualité de pierre il y a dessus la lune et il reste peut-être cinq gallons d'eau. Ça connaît pas comment longtemps, mais il boit peut-être deux gorgées par jour. Et il va cracher sur une de ces pierres-là, ça fait une rivière, une rivière que l'eau coule partout, il paraît. Il a fait un gros *pond* l'autre jour, le dernier gros crachat il a fait-là, quand il a fait la rivière. Ça tombe là-dedans. C'est tout de l'eau fraîche. Et à tout moment, il éteint le soleil là-dedans. Il l'éteint le soir. C'est pour ça tu le vois pas.

RR: He worked for Mamou Waterworks. He found water on the moon?

IR: Mayo takes a certain kind of rock that is found on the moon and there might be only five gallons of water left. No one knows how long, but he drinks maybe two swallows a day. And he goes to spit on one of those rocks, and it makes a river, a river with water running everywhere, it seems. He made a big pond the other day, the last big spit he made, when he made the river. It falls in there. It's all fresh water. And every once in a while, he puts out the sun in there. He puts it out at night. That's why you don't see it.

In addition to the fictional characters, real-life persons are often cast in the Pascal stories. Those fictionalized are usually prominent talkers, as in the case of Hube Reed, who tells of his desire to have a sea turtle's heart transplanted on his right side, so that when his own heart failed, he would simply switch over to the transplant and live another few hundred years. (Compare type 660 *The Fabulous Transplants*.)

L'opération à Hube
(Hube Reed [HR] et Alexandre Manuel [AM], Shorty [S], Mamou)

Hube's Operation

HR: Quand je vas mourir (j'ai fait mon *will* l'autre jour), je veux ça prend rien que ma tête. Et les côtes, que ça donne ça aux chiens. Je vas aller chez Simon-là, je veux il me donne une de ces petites boîtes à souliers-là. Je vas mettre ma coyoche en dedans-là, rien qu'avec assez pour une petite cravate. Fermer les n-oeils. Si il met des *four bits*, Alex, prends-les pas, non! Quitte-moi monter avec mes taxes en haut-là.

AM: Je te garantie, si je suis cassé, je vas les prendre les deux.

HR: C'est comme ça je veux aller. Et je parie Shorty croit pas ça, non. Tu me crois ou tu me crois pas?

HR: When I die (I made my will the other day), I want them to take only my head. And they can give my ribs to the dogs. I'll go to Simon's, I want him to give me one of those little shoe boxes. I'll put my noggin in there, with just enough for a little necktie. Close my eyes. If they put two quarters, Alex, don't you take them! Let me go up there with my taxes.

AM: I guarantee you, if I'm broke, I'll take them both.

HR: That's how I want to go. And I'll bet Shorty doesn't believe that. Do you believe me or not?

s: Je te crois pas.

HR: C'est dur à croire qu'il me croit pas. Mais je vas me faire opérer la semaine qui vient. Je vas me mettre une cervelle d'éléphant. Là, tu oublies jamais. J'auras pas besoin de mon petit livre pour écrire ces *notes*-là.

AM: Un éléphant?!

HR: Tu vois, hier, je voulais dire quelqu'un pour il vient souper. J'ai oublié. Et là, je veux me faire mettre un coeur de caouane bord-là. [Geste désignant le côté droit.] Tu connais ces caouanes de mer-là, ça vit trois cents années, ça. Ça fait, quand ce maudit va arrêter de battre comme ça-là, j'aurais un petit bouton-là, "Proupe!" Et ce coeur de caouane va commencer, ces caouanes de mer-là qu'a des ailes, manière. Là, je veux pas me raser. Comment tu crois, j'aurais un bébé de barbe, trois cents années?

s: I don't believe you.

HR: It's hard to believe that he doesn't believe me. But I want to be operated on next week. I want to have them give me an elephant's brain. That way, you never forget. I won't need my little book to write my notes.

AM: An elephant?!

HR: You see, yesterday, I wanted to tell someone to come and eat supper. I forgot. And then, I want them to give me a turtle's heart on this side. [Gesture indicating the right side.] You know those sea turtles, they live three hundred years. So that when this bastard stops beating, I'll have a little button, "Proupe!" And that turtle heart will start, those sea turtles that have wings, sort of. Then I don't want to shave. Don't you think I'll have a beauty of a beard in three hundred years?

Legendary Stories

Legendary stories appear frequently in the Louisiana French repertoire. The most popular of these describe buried treasure and the unusual or supernatural phenomena that accompany attempts to unearth it. There *is* in fact quite a bit of treasure buried in Louisiana. During the Civil War, some people buried their valuables to protect them from Yankee raiders and vigilantes alike. A traditional mistrust of banks among the settlers of French origin caused some of them to hide their valuables. Sometimes these wary folks died without telling anyone in the family where their fortunes were buried, so the goods remained for others to find. The activities of pirates or corsairs like Jean Lafitte also contributed to the stock of Louisiana buried-treasure stories.

This type of story, known the world over, often includes references to ghosts and other spirits. One explanation holds that these spirits are the souls of people who were somehow implicated in the burying of the treasure and seek to preserve it for family members. Another describes the pirates' tradition of killing one of their number or an animal and burying him or it with the treasure to protect it from interlopers. This malevolent spirit usually provides the intrigue for these stories. Here, a treasure seeker has hired someone who claims to be able to control the evil spirits that would drive his party away.

Le controleur d'esprits et le boeuf (Samuel Gauthreaux, Cecilia)	*The Spirit Controller and the Bull*

A Charenton, dans le nord du lac Charenton, il y avait ce vieux Indien qui s'appelait Jim. Et ils ont demandé à vieux Jim ayoù un certain chêne avec une marque au nord du lac. Et vieux Jim a dit il connaissait.

In Charenton, north of Lake Charenton, there was an old Indian named Jim. And they asked old Jim where there was a certain oak tree with a mark on the north side of the lake. And old Jim said he knew.

Ça fait, ils ont été. Ils ont commencé à fouiller. Et dès qu'ils ont fouillé un bout, il y avait un gros boeuf qui s'en venait en travers de le bois avec la flamme qui lui sortait du nez.

So they went. They started digging. And as soon as they had dug a while, a big bull came through the woods with flame coming from his nose.

Ça fait, ça a passé. Et ça a juste touché la pelle de le bougre qu'était après fouiller, et tout la bande a échappé. Ça fait, dès que le bougre a regardé, tous les autres étaient *gone*. Ça fait, il a *gone* aussi.

So it passed. And it just touched the shovel of the fellow who was digging, and the whole gang took off. So as soon as the fellow looked around, the others were gone. So he left, too.

Et le bougre dit à l'Indien, *"Well,"* il dit, "faudra je retourne en ville après un contrôleur d'esprits." Ça fait, il dit, "Je vas revenir *back*."

And the fellow says to the Indian, "Well," he says, "we'll have to go back to town to get a spirit controller." So he says, "I'll come back."

Ça fait, quelque temps après, il a revenu *back*, mais c'était dans le temps qu'il y avait ces vigilants-là, tu connais, les Ku Klux Klan. Et sa femme croyait que c'était ça le monde qui voulait causer avec lui. Ça fait, sa femme a pas voulu il va avec eux. Ça fait, le contrôleur d'esprits-là, il dit à l'Indien, "Est-ce que tu nous livres ta part?"

So some time later he came back, but this was in the days when there were vigilantes, you know, the Ku Klux Klan. And his wife thought that's who wanted to talk to him. So his wife didn't want him to go with them. So the spirit controller says to the Indian, "Do you give us your share?"

Et l'Indien dit, "Ouais, *go ahead*, vous autres peux l'avoir."

And the Indian says, "Yes, go ahead, you can have it."

Ça fait, il ont été. Ça fait, quelque temps

So they went. So a little while later, the Indian says to my late father.... He was going through the woods not far from there. So he decided he would go to the north side of

après, l'Indien dit à pauvre Pap. . . . Il était après passer dans le bois pas loin de là. Ça fait, il a décidé il aurait été dans le nord du lac pour voir, tu connais. Le trou était là, et la caisse, et les marques de piastres étaient dessus les bois qu'ils ont cassé de la caisse. Ça fait, ils l'ont trouvé. Le contrôleur d'esprits l'avait fait. Faut croire il a contrôlé le boeuf-là, le boeuf avec la flamme. Mais ça dit la flamme sortait dans le nez et ça pouvait l'entendre s'en venir dans le bois. Ça entendait le bois craquer, tu connais, dès qu'il sautait. Plus ça craquait fort, plus près il venait, jusqu'à il arrivait côté d'eux.

the lake to see, you know. The hole was there, and the case, and the imprint of coins was on the wood they had broken from the case. So they found it. The spirit controller had done it. He must have controlled the bull, the bull with the flames. But they say that the flames came out of its nose and they could hear it coming through the woods. They heard the wood cracking, you know, with each jump. And it cracked loudly, the closer it came, until it arrived next to them.

Most treasure-hunting legends are harrowing adventure stories filled with ghosts and evil spirits. Some of them, however, can be almost humorous misadventures, like the following story about another spirit controller who proved to be less than effective.

Le controleur et sa bible
(Leonard Gauthreaux, Cecilia)

The Spirit Controller and His Bible

J'ai été rencontrer un vieux homme à Marrero, et il m'a conté une histoire. Il a été chercher pour un trésor avec d'autres hommes. Et il y avait un contrôleur qu'avait amené une bible pour contrôler les *spirits*. Et quand ils arraivaient à la place, ils ont vu un gros cheval s'en venir à travers du bois avec un homme dessus, et quand il a descendu, c'était plus un homme qu'était sur le cheval. C'était un chien. Et il dit le chien a venu se frotter sur ses jambes. Il dit il grognait. Il dit, le chien, il connaît le chien était après le toucher, mais il sentait pas à rien. C'est comme si c'était juste du vent. Et il dit ils se sont tous sauvés. Il a perdu son chapeau et ses lunettes et il a tout déchiré son linge. Et jusqu'à le contrôleur s'est sauvé et il a jamais vu sa bible après ça.

I went to meet an old man in Marrero and he told me a story. He went to search for a treasure with some other men. And there was a controller who had brought along a bible to control the spirits. And when they arrived at the site, they saw a big horse coming through the woods with a man on it, and when he got off the horse it wasn't a man anymore. It was a dog. And he says that the dog came to rub itself against his legs. He says it growled. He says, the dog, he knew the dog was touching him, but he couldn't feel anything. It's as though it was just a wind. And he said they all ran away. He lost his hat and his glasses and he tore his clothes. Even the controller ran away and never saw his bible again.

Not all Louisiana legends have to do with buried treasure. Some stories are actually local versions of internationally known legends, such as the following tale, a variant of type 752B *The Forgotten Wind*, about a man who wanted to control the weather.

L'homme qui demandait la pluie
(Stanislaus Faul, dit Tanisse, Cankton)

Il y avait un homme, et il aurait toujours voulu avoir et que les autres aient pas. C'était un homme, tu connais, qui était glorieux. Il voulait se faire accroire mieux que les autres.

Il était après travailler son maïs. Le Bon Dieu passe, Il dit, "T'as du joli maïs."

"Ouais, mais," il dit, "*boy*, s'il pourrait avoir la pluie comme je voudrais, là je ferais du maïs."

Bon Dieu dit, "Mais quand t'aurais besoin de la pluie?"

"Ah, mais," il dit, "à soir, une bonne pluie, et une pluie tous les temps en temps...."

"Mais," Il dit, "'garde, t'auras de la pluie à soir et à chaque fois que t'auras besoin de la pluie," Il dit, "juste dis tu veux de la pluie tel temps, et tu l'auras."

"O, mais," il dit, "là, je vas faire du maïs, si je pourrais croire ça."

Il dit, "Tu l'auras. *Go ahead.*"

Ça fait, le Bon Dieu a parti. Le soir, il y a venu une bonne pluie, juste comme à peu près qu'il voulait. Droit à la barrière qui séparait l'autre clos (c'était du monde pauvre qui restait là, faire du petit maïs), il y a pas eu de la pluie du tout.

Quelques jours après, il dit, "Là, une bonne pluie encore," il dit, "là, mon maïs viendrait." La pluie a venu, comme il voulait. Les autres, pas de pluie. Sec, leur petit maïs était jaune.

The Man Who Wanted Rain

There was a man, and he always wanted to have things, but he wanted no one else to have them. He was a man who was, you know, proud. He wanted to appear better than everyone else.

He was working in his cornfield. The Good Lord passes. He says, "You have beautiful corn."

"Yes, but," he says, "boy, if only it could rain like I'd like, then I'd grow some corn."

The Lord says, "Well, when would you have it rain?"

"Ah, well," he says, "tonight, a good rain, and a little rain every once in a while...."

"Well," He says, "look, you'll have rain tonight and each time you need rain," He says, "just say you want rain at a certain time and you will have it."

"Oh, well," he says, "now I'll grow corn, if I could believe that."

He says, "You'll have it. Go ahead."

So the Lord left. That night, there came a good rain, just about how he wanted. Right across the fence at the edge of his field (some poor people lived there, growing a little corn), there was no rain at all.

A few days later, he says, "Now, another good rain," he says, "then my corn would come." The rain came, like he wanted. The others got no rain. Dry, their corn was yellow.

Boy, he was excited. He says, "I'm going to have corn; the others won't have any."

The others, when it was time, when the

Boy, il était content. Il dit, "Moi, je vas faire du maïs; les autres en fera pas."

Les autres quand ça a venu temps, le Bon Dieu a voulu, Il a donné une pluie à eux-autres, ça a fait des épis de maïs. Mais son maïs à lui a juste fait des champignons. Une petite affaire blanche à la place des épis de maïs. Il a fait pas une graine de maïs.

Lord wished it, He gave a rain to them, which formed the ears of corn. But his corn just made buds. A little white thing where the ear of corn should be. He didn't grow a single grain of corn.

Ironically, the best-known Louisiana French legends are also the least told. Legendary figures like the *loup garou, feux follets*, and *chasse galerie* are known by many. Consequently a simple reference is usually all that is needed to conjure the legend. Several forms of bogeymen are used to frighten children. One is *Madame Grands-doigts*, who is said to come at night and pull the toes of naughty children with her long, bony fingers. Another is *la tataille*, a beast who comes to take naughty children away and even eat them up. Cajuns and Creoles alike tell of *cauchemar* or *couchemal*, which rides people in their sleep, causing them to feel suffocated and distressed, and of *gris-gris*, evil spirits or spells cast on one person by another. To these widely known dangers individual families add their own idio-syncratic bogeymen—baboons and raccoons, cows and cats, bulls and bears.

Cajuns also tell of *feux follets*, a Louisiana French version of will-o'-the-wisps or foxfire. They are described as mysterious lights floating in the night, which cause unwary and overcurious observers to become lost in the woods or on the prairie, sometimes forever. *Feux follets* are said to be the wandering souls of unbaptized babies who lure travelers away from roads in the dark. It is said that one way to avoid their influence is to open a three-bladed knife and stick it into a post or tree. The *feu follets* will then become attracted to their own reflection in the blades, allowing the person to escape.

The *loup garou*, the Louisiana version of the werewolf, does not need to be shot with a silver bullet to be killed, as in Europe. In some tellings, he needs only to be made to bleed to be transformed into human form. Other Cajun changelings include *hibou garou* (man transformed into owl), *chien garou* (man into dog), and *chat garou* (man into cat).

Louisiana also has legends and beliefs that include stories about God walking on earth, unrepentant men rooted to the ground, and babies' cauls (membranes) announcing special psychic powers.

In Quebec, the sound of thunder is called *la chasse galerie*, and is said to be the shouting of damned lumberjacks who sold their souls to the devil in exchange for the ability to paddle their canoes in the air, to return from the woods to visit their girlfriends in town. The Louisiana *chasse galerie* resembles the original French version of the legend, which describes thunder as the crying of wild huntsmen who were damned for hunting on Sunday.

La chasse-galerie
(*Stanislaus Faul, dit Tanisse, Cankton*)

La chasse-galerie, c'est un homme qui avait été à la messe dimanche matin, tu connais. Et l'église était dans la prairie. Et il y a quelqu'un avec des chiens qui les avait suit. La messe était juste bien commencée, les chiens ont sorti au ras de la porte ayoù il était assis avec un lapin, à courser un lapin. Il a sorti dehors et il a parti à la course derrière lui aussi et il est après galoper toujours.

C'est ça ils ont appelé la chasse-galerie. Pendant des années, il a galopé sur la terre, mais asteur, il peut plus. Ça va dans l'air, ça. Mon père et mon beau-frère ont resté un soir un arpent avant de rentrer dans la savane à l'écouter passer. "Hou, hou, hou," ils écoutaient, comme si c'était des cloches et des chaînes. Supposé, il passe dans chaque pays tous les sept ans.

The Wild Huntsman

The *chasse galerie* is a man who had gone to Mass Sunday morning, you know. And the church was in the prairie. And someone with dogs had followed them. Mass was just getting started, the dogs came out with a rabbit, after a rabbit, near the door where he was sitting. He went outside and he started running after it, too, and he's running still.

That's what they called the *chasse galerie*. For years, he ran on the earth, but now he can no longer. He goes through the air. My father and my brother-in-law stayed out one night an *arpent* away from the pasture just listening to it pass. "Hoo, hoo, hoo," they heard, as though there were bells and chains. Supposedly, it comes to each country every seven years.

Experience Stories

Often ignored for their lack of traditional pedigree, personal experience stories deserve a place in the description of Louisiana French oral tradition. Unlike historians and folklorists, storytellers must entertain their audiences if they are to keep the floor. An original incident is related, expanded, polished, and embellished, eventually to become a full-blown story, with a beginning, development, climax, *dénouement*, and an ending. There are characters and roles. Historical truth becomes less important than psychological truth in the mind of the tellers and their audiences. Facts are molded,

if necessary, to fit the shape of the developing story. Sometimes, events are remembered as they might or *should* have happened. These accounts are often masterpieces of oral tradition, frequently requested by an eager audience of family members and friends who delight in hearing them told and retold. Often storytellers feel it necessary to remind listeners that "this is no tale; this is true." Yet their stories become tales in form and function, if not in origin.

Sometimes experience stories develop a humorous event. The following story concerns the common practice on the Louisiana frontier of ruffians taking over a dance hall for their own amusement on Saturday nights. This same story, told invariably as true, is said to have happened in a multitude of dance halls throughout south Louisiana.

Victor et Arthur essaient de casser le bal
(Adley Gaudet, Bayou Pigeon)

Victor and Arthur Try to Break Up the Dance

Vieux Victor Vaughn était un batailleur, tu sais, c'était un bon batailleur. Il était connu, vieux Victor Vaughn. Et un des cousins à Pap, vieux Arthur Gaudet. Ils ont été pour casser un bal un soir. Le cousin à Pap dit à vieux Victor, "Vic, allons casser le bal à soir."

Il dit, *"All right!"*

Il y avait un jeune homme et il était petit. Il avait juste à peu près cinq pieds, vieux Jake Mayeux. Et ça, c'est correct, ouais! C'est un *joke* dans une manière, mais c'est vrai.

Il dit, "Vic, moi, je vas rentrer en dedans-là, et toi, mets-toi à la fenêtre en dehors et comptes-les." Il dit, "Moi, je vas les passer en dehors."

Ça fait, vieux Jake s'en vient en dansant. *God damn!* Il l'attrape par le col et par la ceinture. *"Boy,"* il dit, "c'est pas rien pour passer vieux Jake en travers." Jake pesait à peu près quatre-vingt-dix livres, tu sais. Il le passe en travers la fenêtre. Il tombe en dehors.

Old Victor Vaughn was a fighter, you know, he was a good fighter. He was known, old Victor Vaughn. And one of Pop's cousins, old Arthur Gaudet. They went to break up a dance one night. Pop's cousin said to old Victor, "Vic, let's go break up the dance tonight."

He said, "All right!"

There was a young man who was small. He was just about five feet tall, old Jake Mayeux. And this is true! It's a joke in a way, but it's true.

He said, "Vic, I'll go in there and you go outside next to the window and count them." He said, "I'll throw them outside."

So old Jake comes along dancing. God damn! He catches him by the collar and by the belt. "Boy," he said, "it's nothing to throw old Jake out." Jake weighed about ninety pounds, you know. He throws him through the window. He falls outside.
Vic says, "One!"
Boy, four or five men jumped on him.

Vic dit, "Un!"

Boy, il y a quatre ou cinq qui lui ont tombé dessus l'autre. Lui, il était grand, Arthur Gaudet. Ils l'ont sacré à travers de la fenêtre. Il tombe dehors.

Vic dit, "Deux!"

"Euh, euh...Vic!" il dit, "Compte pas ça icitte. C'est moi!"

Arthur Gaudet was big. They threw him out the window. He falls outside.

Vic says, "Two!"

"Uh, uh...Vic!" he says, "Don't count this one. It's me!"

Stories about contraband runners abound in Louisiana, especially those about the ones who got away from the federal agents. Many of these stories are based on the same principle as the animal tales, with the wily moonshiner pitted against the government revenue agents who usually fall into the role of the dupes. There is also an element of the outlaw hero in the stories. Most listeners sympathize with the moonshiner who succeeds in evading the larger forces of the government.

Les revenues
(Andrew Chautin, Gillis)

Un jour, j'arrivais au camp, et je m'étais aperçu qu'il y avait quelque chose qui était *wrong.* J'ai vu des pistes dans la boue que j'étais pas accoutumé de voir. Ça fait, j'étais à cheval et il y avait pas de selle, pas rien sur le cheval. J'avais justement mis la bride en haut et puis j'avais amarré après la barrière du camp. Et les *revenue men* étaient cachés depuis l'avant-jour pour m'espérer.

Ça fait, j'ai arrivé là. J'ai descendu. J'ai amarré le cheval avec la corde après la barrière. Quand j'ai descendu, il y a deux des *revenues* qui ont galopé en allant à moi avec deux pistolets qui ressemblaient longues comme ça. [Geste pour indiquer environ un mètre.]

J'ai sauté sur ce cheval. Et c'est un cheval qui était nerveux puis vite. Et le cheval s'a aperçu qu'il y avait quelque chose qui était *wrong.* Quand j'ai monté en haut de lui, j'ai pas eu le temps pour démarrer la corde après

The "Revenue Men"

One day, I was arriving at the camp, and I noticed that there was something wrong. I saw tracks in the mud that I was not accustomed to seeing. So I was on horseback and there was no saddle, nothing on the horse. I had just a bridle and I had tied up to the fence around the camp. And the revenue men had been hiding since before dawn waiting for me.

So I arrived there. I got off. I tied the horse to the fence with the rope. When I got down, two of the revenue men ran toward me with pistols that looked as long as this. [Gesture to indicate about a yard.]

I jumped on that horse. And it was a spirited and fast horse. And the horse noticed that something was wrong. When I jumped on it, I didn't have time to untie the rope from the fence. And the revenue men started running toward me and they would have caught me. When I saw that, I thought the

la bride. Et les *revenues* ont pris à galoper en allant à moi et ils m'auraient attrapé. Quand j'ai vu ça, j'ai jonglé le plus court je peux faire, c'est ôter la bride du cheval et rester en haut. Ça fait, j'ai poussé la bride et j'ai ôté ça de dans sa tête. Le cheval a tourné et puis ça a parti. Il passait en travers des éronces et il sautait avec moi monté sur son dos. Il avait la queue de collée en arrière de mon épaule après se sauver.

Et ils nous ont pas attrapés. Hé, j'avais peur, donc.

quickest thing I can do is to take the bridle off the horse and stay on. So I pushed the bridle off its head. The horse turned and took off. He went through brambles and jumped with me on his back. His tail was flat against the back of my shoulder as he ran away.

And they didn't catch us. Hey, I was scared, though.

The Language and Ethnicity of Humor

Generally, the stories told in French represent that part of Cajun oral tradition which comes from the inside. The present stress on the language from Anglo culture places a considerable strain on the tradition. Many of the stories that can be translated are now being told in English. As a rule, storytellers don't make value judgments concerning cultural and linguistic preservation. More important to them is the appropriate reaction of their audiences. They will instinctively tell a story in the language that gives the punch line the most chance of making people laugh. Yet a vast amount of the repertoire continues to be told in French for a variety of reasons. First, many of the best storytellers feel more confident in French. Their timing and vocabulary are stronger in their native language. Further, the French language sometimes functions as a convenient secret code with which one can selectively isolate one's audience. Thus adults can eliminate children, and insiders can eliminate outsiders from their potential audiences. Finally, French is an important identity marker with which to underscore one's origins and cultural allegiances. Thus many storytellers, especially politicians and businessmen, elect to tell their stories in French as an overt expression of their Cajun or Creole ethnicity.

Not all jokes are told in French, however. Now many are told in English, some of which are just funny stories from the international stock of traditional humor that has been around for centuries. Some jokes are translated from the French to reach new and younger audiences. Old jokes are adapted to describe current events almost immediately. Nevertheless, the best humor tends to be rooted in community values. We are often most ticklish in our most sensitive spots. Consequently, Cajun humor can serve as a social, cultural, and linguistic barometer.

Toward the turn of this century, as Cajuns were undergoing Americanization in earnest, jokes began to reflect social changes, poking fun at the rural Cajuns confronted for the first time with modern ways. Soon, however, self-deprecating humor paralleled the social stigma that came to be attached to all aspects of Cajun culture. One of the basic assumptions of ethnic jokes about Cajuns was that they were impossible to educate. Most Cajuns had never been to school until the 1916 mandatory education act began to bring them into the classroom. Then their inability to speak English made them appear dull and recalcitrant. The following joke describes a "typical" first day at school for young Cajuns who found themselves forbidden to speak their native language on the schoolgrounds.

Say Two
(Larrell Richard, Ossun)
My father sent me to school in the first grade and I came home after only twenty minutes. When my father asked me why I wasn't in school, I told him, "I came home because that's all there was. The teacher said everybody had to talk only English. There were a few who understood, but most of us didn't know what she was saying. Then she said something about numbers and said, 'Say one.' A few people around the classroom said, 'One.' Then she said, 'Say two.' So we all got up and left."

Get it? For the benefit of nonfrancophone readers, the punch line is based on the confusion between the bilingual homonyms "Say two" and "C'est tout" (that's all), and plays on the assumed eagerness of Cajuns to be rid of schooling as soon as possible. The joke also assumes the functional bilingualism that eventually resulted from the educational system in question. Standard written English presents additional problems to the Cajun stereotype, who is barely literate at best:

Did you hear about the Cajun who was on his way to Houston? He saw a sign in Lake Charles, "Do not pass on bridge," so he turned around and went home. (Rick Dugas, Lafayette)

Even their now-celebrated cuisine once gave Cajuns trouble:

Hold the Rice
(Alex Giroir, Pierre Part)

A Cajun boy went to school at LSU, and he was very concerned about hiding his origins. He paid attention to the way he dressed and the way he spoke and everything. One day he decides to go out to eat at McDonald's. He checks to make sure he has left his boots at home, then he goes in and says carefully, "I would like a hamburger, please."

The waiter says, "You want that all the way?"

"Hell, no! Hold the rice!" he says. "What you think I am, a Cajun?"

Sexuality is a sensitive subject, and sexual ineptitude is among the worst possible insults for any culture. Consider the following riddle:

Q: Do you know what Cajun foreplay is?
A: *Chère*, you sleeping? (Anonymous patron in a bar, Scott)

Since World War II, changes on the political, educational, and popular scenes have rehabilitated the Cajun self-image, complete with French-language education in the schools and French programming in the media. This transformation is reflected in current oral tradition in both French and English. Texas and Texans figure prominently in an ongoing border battle in Cajun humor. The Cajuns underwent Americanization with Texas for a neighbor; everything that was bigger and better about America was right there across the Sabine River. Jokes about Texans and Cajuns were inevitable.

How Long Did It Take?
(Alex Giroir, Pierre Part)

A Cajun taxicab driver in Baton Rouge picked up a Texan on his way to the airport. When they passed by the LSU football stadium, the Texan said, "What's that?"

The Cajun said, "That's Tiger Stadium."

The Texan said, "How long did it take y'all to build it?"

The Cajun said, "Oh, about five years."

The Texan said, "Oh, we've got a bigger one in Austin that only took one year."

As they passed the state capitol, the Texan asked again, "What's that building?"

The Cajun said, "That's the state capitol."

"And how long did it take y'all to build that?"

The Cajun said, "About three years."

The Texan said, "We're got one in Austin that only took six months." The Cajun had just about enough of this, you know. Then they drove past the Mississippi River Bridge. The Texan said, "How long did it take y'all to build that bridge?"

The Cajun said, "I don't know. It wasn't there this morning."

Even hell is no match for the renewed Cajun spirit:

Cajuns in Hell
(Fred Tate, Mamou)

A busload of Cajuns went over a cliff and all were killed instantly. When they got to heaven's gate, St. Peter was informed by God that there had been a mistake. They weren't supposed to come until next week. There was no room yet in heaven. So St. Peter sent them down to hell, just temporarily, until their places in heaven could be prepared. A few days later, Satan came to the pearly gates to talk to St. Peter. "Listen," he said, "don't you think you could take those Cajuns off my hands?"

St. Peter said, "What's the matter? They giving you trouble?"

"Well," Satan said, "first they had a *fais do-do* [house dance]. Then they had a *banco* [raffle]. Now they're having a bingo. They're trying to raise money to air-condition the damn place!"

There is no clear dividing point between the attitudes of the past and those of today. The entire spectrum of jokes can be heard in the current repertoire. Cajun culture, like any other, preserves some favorite old stories, while responding almost immediately to contemporary situations with new and recycled humor.

The Cajun Who Went to Harvard
(Rick Dugas, Lafayette)

A young Cajun went to school at Harvard. He didn't know his way around, so he asked directions of somebody on the street. "Where's the library at?" he asked.

"You must be new at this institution," the other fellow said with a very proper Ivy League accent. "One never ends a question with a preposition."

"Excuse me," the Cajun said. "Where's the library at, asshole?"

The Louisiana French repertoire is heavily influenced by the American context in which Cajuns have lived for over 350 years. The connections between Louisiana and France, and Louisiana and Africa, are undeniably important, especially in the oldest genres. But the social, geographic, and cultural connections between Louisiana and America are also very important, especially in the most contemporary genres. Louisiana is not only part of the French-speaking and Creole-speaking worlds. It is also a part of the American South, of the Gulf Coast, of the Caribbean Basin, of the Mississippi Valley, of the American West, of the political United States, and of the New World.

When we reflect on the style of life that Cajuns forged for themselves in the late eighteenth and nineteenth centuries, we realize just how completely the orally transmitted aspects of their culture dominated. And yet, we also see how culturally mixed was the world they lived in. In the more isolated areas of the state, the traditional rural lifestyle persisted well into the twentieth century. The Cajun family lived in a world that reflected both the traditions of France and the realities of Louisiana.

While any generalization about Cajun culture can always be contradicted by the enormous diversity within it, we can outline a set of ways that were characteristic of the lifestyle of many rural Cajuns in the nineteenth century. As in their former French and Canadian homelands, hospitality and conviviality were foremost, with the house acting as the center of social life. Neighbors gathered periodically at *boucheries, coups-de-main,* weddings, and funerals. *Bals de maison* (house dances) were held often, attended mostly by young people. *Veillées* (evening visits) were intensely anticipated by all. People regularly traveled many miles by *voiture* (which may have been a *bateau*) to visit their friends. Oral entertainment— games, folk stories, music, and gossip—were the highlights of the evening. Guests sometimes stayed overnight before returning home. In summertime, cotton curtains were hung around the perimeter of the gallery to create an outdoor room for overflow sleeping. Speech, etiquette, music, games, dance, worship, and other customs and habits reflected those of French peasants and Acadian families.

Food was an essential ingredient of all major social gatherings, including even dances and funerals. The foodways were dominated by hardy American foodstuffs—corn, rice, beans, cane syrup, melons, peanuts, and potatoes, but prepared in the distinctive styles of the French Creole or Cajun. Highly spiced Creole food was unusual before the end of the nineteenth century, although gumbos and wild game were regular elements of the cuisine.

To own more than one party dress or suit of formal clothing was rare, but what was owned was well cared for and important for formal visits, church attendance, and dances. Almost everything was made by hand. Material culture came predominantly from local innovation rather than French derivation. Houses were decorated with handmade furniture constructed of local materials. The furniture was simple in decoration, highly functional, and durable. Very few household objects survived the dislocations and moves from Acadia or from France. The interiors of the typical one- or two-room house mostly contained locally made objects with a sprinkling of commercial goods and imports. Blankets, sheets, quilts, and curtains were woven in the house by the hardworking womenfolk. Sewing, spinning, weaving, and carding might be practiced on the *galerie* of the house. In some seasons the *galeries* were hung with bunches of tobacco and strings of dried fruit, spices, and medicinal herbs.

The lifestyles of the men combined hard work in the local fields with wide-ranging adventures in the region—throughout the bayous, swamps, prairies, and coastal estuaries. Profound knowledge of the environment was required. Hunting, fishing, trapping, and gathering, each demanding complex techniques and understanding, provided periodic relief from the drudgery of farming and the monotony of a locally grown diet. Much time was spent out of doors, traveling or tending to the fishing traps, trotlines, gardens, livestock, and fields.

What lessons may we—today—bring away from this rich and surprisingly distinctive society? What do we learn from the Cajuns' odyssey, with its tragedies and eventual triumphs? We end by raising several, perhaps by now obvious, points:

Cajun culture is now popular and prestigious in America. Almost anywhere in the United States one is likely to discover a restaurant proudly advertising "Cajun cuisine" (though the fare is often unrecognizable to native Cajuns). Cajun music is now performed to enthusiastic audiences on the stages of major theaters and folklife festivals. Many thousands of people travel annually to Louisiana to enjoy its distinctive cultural diversity—the style of life Louisianans refer to as our *joie de vivre*. But this enormous popularity was not always the case. Within the last thirty years, Cajun culture was popularly vilified as belonging to ignorant peasants. "Coonie," "coon ass," and even "Cajun" were not always terms of endearment, especially when employed by Anglos. Indeed, if one recalls the enormous difficulties the Acadian people have undergone to preserve their culture, it is amazing that the culture has survived at all.

More than that of most peoples, Acadian culture experienced repeated and often powerful attempts to eradicate it. As an ethnic and social class the Acadians were sorely tested by persecution and warfare in Poitou, before departing for Acadia (Nova Scotia) in the seventeenth century. Once in the New World, they were isolated and left virtually unsupported by the French crown for more than a century. Between 1745 and 1755 the British attempted to anglicize the Acadian peasants of Nova Scotia by demanding they give up their religion and culture, and by settling Scots pioneers among them. When this did not work, the British simply dispersed as much of the population as their troops could lay hands on. Acadians were shipped in small groups to distant and widely separated locations, and put to work under the most difficult circumstances. Upon finally arriving in Louisiana in extreme poverty, Acadians were again dispersed to isolated frontier communities by the Spanish government. In the American period, Acadian children were forbidden to speak their native language in the schools of Louisiana—a misguided policy that almost erased the Acadian dialect. Until recently, government support for anything Acadian was grudging at best. Yet somehow through it all Acadian culture survived and even prospered.

How was this possible? Several contributing factors should be mentioned. The first is the particular strength of the core institutions of Cajun society—the family, religious values, and oral heritage and language. Somewhere along the line the Acadians worked out a system of family and social life that created extreme loyalty to the central institutions of Acadian culture—the family itself, the religion as a folk institution (though not necessarily as embodied in the clergy), and the language as a vehicle of communication. These institutions they refused to forfeit, even under the most pressing circumstances. They lie at the heart of what the introduction to this volume calls a "tenacious sense of ethnicity." Other things could change, but the informal patterns of family life, communication and oral tradition, socialization, and belief have held remarkably stable until the present.

The second point is that much of what popularly passes as Cajun culture in the United States is of very recent vintage. Cajun cuisine, as served in the fine restaurants of Paul Prudhomme (K-Paul's) and John Folse (Lafitte's Landing), is now known throughout the country. Folse was even invited to serve his famous Cajun dishes in Moscow in 1989. But the cuisine of these fine chefs bears only superficial relationship to the food they were served at home as children. They and other chefs have modified and refined the cuisine described in Chapter 9 and turned it into something distinctive. Like progressive jazz, its distinctive flavor and forms lie in the folk traditions of its people, but they have been modified in the past generation to appeal to the sophisticated tastes of a mostly urban population.

The same may be said of Cajun music, now also popular on the national level. As pointed out in Chapter 10, twentieth-century Cajun music retains little of its early nineteenth-century character. In this century it has been repeatedly modified with new forms of instrumentation (accordion, guitar, drums, amplification) and by repeated influxes of music from other traditions (Anglo country folk-dance music, blues, country and western, western swing, popular, rock'n'roll, and even reggae). The fact that a visitor who was at home with the music of the country *bal de maison* in the 1850s would hardly recognize the music of a Cajun band in the 1990s hardly matters at all. The willingness of the Cajuns to radically transform their peripheral traditions, while holding tightly to their core traditions, is something Acadians have been good at for a very long time. Indeed, Cajun culture might well be termed an incorporating culture, because of the large number of foreign institutions it has been willing to make its own during the past two centuries.

Thus there is a pattern to Cajun adaptability. The more superficial aspects of their heritage are open for endless experimentation and transformation. New foods, new clothing, new houses, new music and dances, new sports and games, new jokes, and new jobs are acceptable and even desirable. But the more intangible and unstated aspects of Cajun culture have remained stable—family values, important allegiances, and styles of communication.

In this book we have treated the history of Cajun culture as if there were a basic contrast between a more traditional nineteenth-century form and a more modern and less folksy late twentieth-century form. Yet any such dichotomy is just a convenient illusion. In fact, Acadian culture has been constantly revised and modified since its earliest days, and particularly since the period of settlement in Louisiana. What its principal critics—the Creoles and Anglo sojourners of the nineteenth century—interpreted as Cajun "backwardness" and "conservatism" were, in fact, largely based upon perceived differences in economic standing (multiple smallholders in a region of large plantations) and cultural differences (practices out of accord with urban Creole standards). The Acadians arrived in Louisiana with hardly more than the clothing on their backs. The small holdings they were granted ensured that economic marginality would result. From the beginning, therefore, Cajun culture has depended on a kind of bootstrap welfare starting from very poor conditions. From the beginning Cajuns engaged in massive and unashamed borrowing from their neighbors. At the same time they experimented with practices and material traits and reformulated them in the light of new conditions. Selective borrowing, syncretism, innovation, creolization, and adaptive reinterpretation provided an enormously successful springboard for what has appeared to some in the outside world as a miraculous Cinderella-type transformation: from brute peasant to sophisticated bearer of a rich and fascinating set of alternate American traditions, all in a handful of generations.

In fact, Acadian lifestyles have *always* adjusted well to the environment in which they found themselves. For example, in the wetlands or prairies of rural southern Louisiana, whatever innovations were needed to support the values of Cajun culture, those were established anew. Year in and year out, it has been adaptability that has brought about Cajun success.

One final point concerns the problem of characterizing any complex culture with a few descriptive statements. Cajun culture is at least as diverse as other cultures of its size. It has never been monolithic. When we describe a typical rural way of life of the *petit habitant*, we necessarily ignore the Cajun planter who planted sugarcane with forty slaves, the Cajun merchant who ran a dry goods store, the Cajun fisherman, and the Cajun cowboy, to say nothing of the banker, the lawyer, the gas station owner, the university professor, and the urban housewife. Yet each of these Cajuns also carries something of the lifeways and values described in this book, while simultaneously participating in the general American lifestyle. Just as important, Cajun culture continues to improvise responses to contemporary pressures and opportunities and, as such, is as complex as any living society.

Pre-Acadian Louisiana History

General histories of Louisiana date back to French colonial times. These treatises provide insight into the ways in which Native Americans and Europeans became acculturated to each other and to the climate and terrain of Louisiana. Most notable are Antoine Simon Le Page du Pratz's 1774 *Histoire de la Louisiane* and the Pénicault narrative *Fleur de Lys and Calumet*. P.F.X. de S.J. Charlevoix's *Journal of a Voyage to North America* (1761) did much to imbue Louisiana and the New World with utopian hues, which French writers of the pre-Romantic and Romantic literary movements quickly elaborated during the eighteenth and nineteenth centuries.

While these highly personal accounts may lack objectivity they do provide a compelling look at colonial attitudes and events. The same holds true for the multitude of personal memoirs written by the founders of the new colony. *A Comparative View of French Louisiana, 1699 and 1762: The Journals of Iberville and Jean-Jacques Blaise D'Abbadie* (Carl Brasseaux, ed.) permits just such a look at the Louisiana the Acadians journeyed towards from their forced internments after their expulsion from Acadia.

The Acadian Migrations

The Acadian migration to Louisiana is revealed in later general histories from a nineteenth-century perspective by Charles Gayarré (*History of Louisiana*, 1851–52) and by François Xavier Martin (*The History of Louisiana from the Earliest Period*, 1827). Good twentieth-century analyses are in Marcel Giraud's four-volume *Histoire de la Louisiane Française* and Joe Gray Taylor's *Louisiana: A History*.

There is an abundance of information about the Acadian deportation from Nova Scotia. The classic work is Oscar W. Winzerling's *Acadian Odyssey*. Dudley LeBlanc's *Acadian Miracle* and *True Story of the Acadians* reveal as much about their politician/impresario/entrepreneur author as they do about the tragic exile. Some interesting primary source material has been brought together in *The Acadian Deportation: Deliberate Perfidity or Cruel Necessity* by Naomi Griffiths. William Rushton covers many aspects of the Acadians' gradual transformation into Cajuns in his *Cajuns: From Acadia to Louisiana*.

The University of Southwestern Louisiana's Center for Louisiana Studies is an important source of many books and treatises about this period. In particular, Carl Brasseaux's ongoing investigations, detailed in his *Founding of New Acadia, 1765–1803*, *In Search of Evangeline*, and many other works, provide a window into the massive quantity of available archival records, contemporary accounts, and historical interpretations of the Acadian diaspora.

Bona Arsenault's definitive genealogical source, *Histoire et généalogie des Acadiens* incorporates revealing details of life in Acadia/Nova Scotia as well as a very thorough compilation of Acadian ancestry. *Acadian Exiles in the Colonies* by Janet Jehn accounts for the many Acadian families spread among British, French, and Spanish colonies. Acadian genealogy in Louisiana is dominated by the massive compendia of Donald Hebert, whose *South Louisiana Records* and *Southwest Louisiana Records* together comprise almost fifty volumes, with more on the way.

Folklife

C.C. Robin's *Voyages à l'intérieur de la Louisiane* (1807) is the archetypal reference for students of Acadian folklife. It contains vivid descriptions of dances, celebrations, and daily life.

During the late 1800s and early 1900s many scholarly reflections on Cajun and Creole lifestyles emerged. The rich material of Alcée Fortier (*A History of Louisiana*, "The Acadians of Louisiana and Their Dialect," *Louisiana: Sketches*, *Louisiana Folktales*), Lafcadio Hearn (*Gumbo Zhèbes*, *Louisiana Cuisine Creole*), and Lyle Saxon (*Gumbo Ya Ya*, *Old Louisiana*) provide not only clever presentations of Cajun and Creole customs but also extremely palatable literary reading. George Washington Cable's books, including *Old Creole*

Days, *The Creoles of Louisiana*, and *Creoles and Cajuns: Stories of Old Louisiana*, give a Creole (and sometimes condescending) view of Cajun ways.

And, of course, mention must be made of Henry Wadsworth Longfellow's *Evangeline* (1882) whose idealized and sensational portrayal of Acadian life, from deportation in Nova Scotia to shelter in Louisiana, brought the Acadians' story to the attention of the English-reading public. Even today the Evangeline myth represents much about Cajuns and Acadiana, as evidenced in the many businesses and products that bear her name. Carl Brasseaux traces the development of the myth in his *In Search of Evangeline: Birth and Evolution of the Myth*.

The development in recent decades of folklife and folkways as a legitimate subject for scholarly study did much to improve knowledge of Cajuns and Creoles. *Louisiana Folklife*, edited by Nicholas Spitzer, is a comprehensive outline of the heritage of modern Cajun and Creole life. Similar wide-ranging studies have been pursued by folklorist Barry Ancelet, whose many essays, articles, and lectures focus on all kinds of subjects from language and literature to music, movies, education, and festivals. Glenn Conrad's *Cajuns: Essays on Their History and Culture*, though narrower in scope, collects several enlightening essays on a variety of related topics.

Captivating photographic portrayals of Louisiana are found in Philip Gould's books, *Les Cadiens d'Asteur* and *Louisiana: A Land Apart*. Photographs in the latter are accompanied by the delightful and insightful text by former Louisiana state folklorist, Nicholas Spitzer.

Architecture and Furnishings

Comprehensive surveys of Cajun and Creole architecture have long been absent from Louisiana studies. Overviews usually deal mainly with plantation homes and buildings that do not truly represent the Cajun lifestyle. Fortunately many detailed studies exist of specific houses and communities, thanks to architectural enthusiasts and historic preservation societies.

Excellent studies of Acadian dwellings can be found in essays by Fred Kniffen, "Louisiana House Types," and Robert Heck, "Building Traditions in the Acadian Parishes." Milton Newton's *Louisiana*

House Types: A Field Guide is a good supplemental work on Louisiana architectural styles.

The art of building with *bousillage* is ably covered in Yvonne Phillips's article, "The Bousillage House." Lauren Post devotes several pages to Cajun houses and farmsteads in the book *Cajun Sketches*. Warren Robinson outlines typical Cajun architectural styles in "Louisiana Acadian Domestic Architecture."

Milton Newton's *Atlas of Louisiana* contains excellent depictions of Louisiana house types and their distribution around the state. He also includes related information on settlement patterns and numerous maps showing the cultural and physical geography of the state. Through his publications, Jay Edwards has established himself as an authority on Louisiana French vernacular architecture. Of particular interest is Edwards's report to the Jean Lafitte National Historical Park of Louisiana, *A Survey of Louisiana French Vernacular Architecture*, which was the first detailed, large-scale survey of Louisiana's French vernacular architecture. His book *Louisiana's Remarkable French Vernacular Architecture*, along with his essay "Origins of the Louisiana Creole Cottage" in *French and Germans in the Mississippi Valley: Landscape and Cultural Traditions* (Michael Roark, ed.) were the first published studies devoted specifically to both Cajun and Creole origins and the development of Louisiana's French vernacular architecture.

Robert Smith is an invaluable resource for Cajun architecture and furnishings. His association with Jack Holden has produced an excellent compilation of household furniture in *Early Louisiana Furnishings 1700–1830*. Several of Smith's presentations and studies can be found at the Fred B. Kniffen Cultural Resources Lab, Department of Geography and Anthropology, LSU.

Wetlands Culture

There is less historical material on Louisiana Cajuns' wetlands culture, probably because bayou villages and prairie farms were much more visible and accessible to the traveling observers who documented nineteenth-century Cajun life.

The best book on swampers' lifestyles is Malcolm Comeaux's *Atchafalaya Swamp Life*. Christopher Hallowell describes swamp life in *People of the Bayous: Cajun Life in Lost America*, as do Roy Hyde in *Rural Family Organization on Bayou Plaquemine* and Edward Kammer in *Four Southwestern Louisiana Parishes*.

Cypress lumbering is documented in libraries at Morgan City (photographic archives) and Houma (oral history recordings) in southeast Louisiana. George François Mugnier's *Louisiana Images* features photographs taken in the 1890s, many of which show swamp dwellings and occupations.

Cajun saltwater fishing culture is perhaps most easily studied by inference. The destruction of Chenière Caminada, then the Louisiana Gulf Coast's largest fishing village, by a hurricane in 1893 spawned a host of books, articles, and even poems, each of which took at least a token glance at life in such a place before covering the gruesome details of the storm itself. Loulan Pitre, Jr.'s *Chenière Caminada avant l'ouragon* makes a detailed statistical analysis of the economic and ethnic structure of the town on the eve of the storm. Kate Chopin's novel, *The Awakening*, is also partly set in the same pre-hurricane village.

It should be added that the Center for Traditional Boat Building at Nicholls State University in Thibodaux, Louisiana, is conducting much good research on boat types and construction as well as fishing techniques. C. Ray Brassieur's "The Louisiana Sailing Lugger: Survival of Traditional Form and Method" is the first publication to result from this research project.

Some of the best historical material on Cajun market hunting, fishing, and trapping remains the series of booklets issued by the Louisiana Department of Wildlife and Fisheries.

Domestic Life

Apart from the commentaries of literary travelers in Acadiana, very few primary sources exist on Cajun and Creole clothing and materials. Unfortunately, some scholars have been tempted to base their analysis of cloth colors and weaves entirely on one or another of these travelers' narratives. Conclusions drawn from a single passing reference by a casual observer have led to claims for an impossibly large rainbow of hues in what was in fact a rather limited Cajun palette of dyes.

What little is known for certain can be found in studies such as Louise Brown's "Louisiana Costume from 1700–1900," and in the selective memories of Cajuns themselves. Acadian weaving and dyeing receive more thorough treatment in *L'Amour de Maman* by Leonard Huber and in Sophia Ward's "Acadian Spinning, Dyeing, and Weaving."

Folk medicine has been a perennial subject for reports written for Louisiana university classes. As this book goes to press, new studies on *traiteurs*, the folk healers of Cajun culture, have emerged, including those by Paul Tilyou of LSU Medical School and John Lançon, an honors graduate from USL. Extensive interviews with *traiteurs* are archived on video in Côte Blanche Productions' *"En Bas du Bayou"* collection and on audio in the same company's "Memories of Terrebonne" collection, both housed at Nicholls State University Library in Thibodaux.

Music

There are a handful of very good books on Cajun music, all published in the 1980s. Ann Allen Savoy's *Cajun Music: A Reflection of a People* puts the emphasis on the music, while Barry Ancelet and Elemore Morgan, Jr., organized *The Makers of Cajun Music* around the musicians. Both approaches prove appropriate and both books give exhaustive yet entertaining histories of the music in modern times. Barry Ancelet's recent *Cajun Music: Its Origins and Development* describes the cultural processes that generated what we now call Cajun music. *Travailler, c'est trop dur: The Tools of Cajun Music*, also by Ancelet, filled a gap in books on Cajun music by focusing on instruments rather than songs or personalities.

John Broven's *South to Louisiana* concentrates on music since the advent of recording. His scope is broader, embracing not only Cajun music and black/French zydeco, but also blues, jazz, and the local rock and roll variant known as swamp pop.

Johnnie Allan's *Memories*, part insider's memoir, part historical scrapbook, gives a more personal view of the subject by someone who was an important force in south Louisiana music. Jeanne and Robert Gilmore's *Chantez Encore, Folksongs of French South Louisiana* provide sheet music for a good selection of Cajun songs.

Commercially recorded Cajun music began in the 1920s with

artists like Cléoma and Joe Falcon. Such early efforts done by national labels, as well as ethnographic recordings by Alan and John Lomax, eventually gave way to those of regional recording companies. Still active, and long dominating the genre, are Floyd Soileau's Swallow Records in Ville Platte, J.D. Miller's Kajun Label in Crowley, and Carol Rachou's La Louisianne Records in Lafayette. George Khoury's Khoury label and Eddie Schuler's Goldband label in Lake Charles are no longer active.

Two national folk and ethnic music specialists, Rounder Records of Cambridge, Massachusetts, and the San Francisco Bay Area's Arhoolie Records both have significant Cajun music sections in their catalogs. Of special note are the Arhoolie reissues of very old Cajun recordings on its Old Timey label. In addition, many mainstream record companies have a Cajun artist or two rounding out their country and western catalogs.

Language

In the 1920s, 1930s, and 1940s a wealth of theses and dissertations on Cajun French were written for Louisiana State University. These works (for the most part unpublished) typically examine the subdialect of a specific town or parish, with heavy emphasis on variance from standard French.

In the 1970s and 1980s, spurred by the ethnic-pride movement, came several attempts to provide a framework for learning French, aimed at a generation that was Cajun by culture but not by language. James Faulk's *Cajun French I* was criticized for its nonstandard orthography based on a phonetic system devised by the author. Randy Whatley's *Conversational Cajun French I* avoided that problem but was limited in scope. And unfortunately, as with Faulk's book, volume two never appeared. (Both books were accompanied by audio tapes.)

The effort to transcribe a teachable Cajun French continued with David Marcantel's noteworthy efforts in *Notre Langue Louisianaise*. This text combines standard French expressions with Cajun expressions to create a solid, standard-language basis for elementary students while enabling them also to communicate with their strictly Cajun-speaking relatives.

Richard Guidry has compiled several works relating to language, including *C'est p'us pareil*, *La famille Richard*, *Les jeunes Louisianais*, and *Lexique cadien-français*. Becky Brown delves more specifically into sociolinguistic patterns in her articles on Cajun French and Cajun orthography. In Quebec, the Université Laval's ongoing *Projet Louisiane*, begun as a consortium with McGill and York universities, and headed by Dean Louder and Eric Waddell, documented many important aspects of Cajun language.

Jules O. Daigle's *Dictionary of the Cajun Language* is the first attempt at a systematic description of Cajun vocabulary. Daigle's comments, which precede the lexicon, offer an interesting outlook on the relationship between Cajun French and standard French. Cajun scholars have been inspired by Daigle's work and are beginning to add to and improve this pioneering effort.

More has been written *about* Cajun and Creole language than written *in* it—although several authors are remedying that situation. Breaking the barrier in recent times was Revon Reed's *Lache pas la patate*, which was unique not only for being a book about Cajuns by a Cajun but also because it was written unabashedly in Cajun French. *Cris sur le bayou: Naissance d'une poésie acadienne en Louisiane* (Barry Ancelet, ed.) is a compilation of some of the first texts to be expressed in a Cajun voice. Another anthology, *Acadie tropicale*, presents fourteen additional authors and has helped to launch a new literary series, les Editions de la Nouvelle Acadie. Zachary Richard's recent *Voyage de nuit* records his observations of life in south Louisiana in poetic form. Antoine Bourque's *Trois saisons* is the first collection of contemporary Louisiana French prose. Cajun and Creole authors, such as Ancelet, Richard, Bourque, Debbie Clifton, Richard Guidry, and others, validate Louisiana's languages and ethnicity in their writings. Finally, Allain and Ancelet's *Anthologie: Littérature Française de Louisiane* is a vital source of information regarding Louisiana literature.

Oral Tradition

Many scholars have found Louisiana's fertile and diverse oral history worthy of study. Brandon and Claudel, in dissertations from, respectively, Université Laval and University of North Carolina, insist on explaining Louisiana's folktale heritage in connection with France, the "mother" country. Corinne Saucier's study of Avoyelles Parish's oral tradition develops the same connection. Ironically, Saucier, in *Folk Tales from French Louisiana*, presents her collection in English translation only. Côte Blanche Productions' thirty-two-part radio series of Cajun and Creole storytelling reflects a desire to record Louisiana's linguistic raconteur heritage in its own terms and language. The same company has produced several dramatic films, some in Cajun French, and set in historical Cajun contexts.

Aarne, Antti, and Stith Thompson. *The Types of the Folk-Tale; A Classification and Bibliography*. 2nd rev. ed. *Folklore Fellows Communications*, 184. Helsinki, 1961.

Allain, Mathé, and Barry Ancelet, eds. *Anthologie: Littérature française de Louisiane*. Bedford, N.H.: National Materials Development Center for French, 1981.

Allan, Johnnie. *Memories*. Lafayette, La.: Jadfel, 1988.

Ancelet, Barry. *Cajun Music: Its Origins and Development*. Lafayette, La.: Center for Louisiana Studies, 1989.

———. *Travailler, c'est trop dur: The Tools of Cajun Music*. Lafayette, La.: Lafayette Natural History Museum Publications, 1985.

———. La truie dans la beronette: Etude comparée de la tradition orale en Louisiane francophone." Dissertation, Université Aix-Marseille I, 1984.

———, ed. *Acadie tropicale*. Lafayette, La.: Editions de la Nouvelle Acadie, 1981.

———, ed. *Cris sur le bayou: Naissance d'une poésie acadienne en Louisiane*. Montreal: Editions Intermède, 1980.

Ancelet, Barry, and Elemore Morgan, Jr. *The Makers of Cajun Music*. Austin: University of Texas Press, 1984.

Arceneaux, Maureen G. *Acadian to Cajun: Population, Family and Wealth in Southwest Louisiana, 1765–1854*. Ph.D. diss., Brigham Young University, 1982.

Arsenault, Bona. *Histoire et généalogie des acadiens*. 6 vols. Québec: Conseil de la Vie française en Amérique, 1978.

Baker, Vaughn. "The Acadians in Antebellum Louisiana: A Study of Acculturation." In *The Cajuns: Essays on their History and Culture*, ed. Glenn R. Conrad, 115–29. Lafayette, La.: Center for Louisiana Studies, University of Southwestern Louisiana, 1978.

Barde, Alexandre. *Histoire des comités de vigilance aux Attakapas*. Edgard, La.: Le Meschacebe, 1861.

Bergeron, Maida Owens. "Cajun Curing Practices." Undergraduate research paper in folklore submitted to Professor Jay Edwards, Louisiana State University. Approx. 50 pp. Copy on file, Fred B. Kniffen Cultural Resources Lab, Dept. Geography & Anthropology, 1975.

Blank, Les, and Chris Strachwitz. *J'ai été au bal*. Videocassette. San Francisco: Flower Films, 1989.

Bourque, Antoine. *Trois saisons*. Lafayette, La.: Editions de la Nouvelle Acadie, 1988.

Brandon, Elizabeth. "Studies of Vermilion Parish folklore and folklife," M.A. thesis, Université Laval, 1955.

Brasseaux, Carl A. *The Founding of New Acadia: The Beginnings of Acadian Life in Louisiana*. 1765–1893. Baton Rouge: Louisiana State University Press, 1987.

———. *In Search of Evangeline: Birth and Evolution of the Evangeline Myth*. Thibodaux, La.: Blue Heron Press, 1989.

———, ed. *A Comparative View of French Louisiana, 1699 and 1762: The Journals of Iberville and Jean-Jacques Blaise D'Abbadie*. Lafayette, La.: Center for Louisiana Studies, University of Southwestern Louisiana, 1979.

Brassieur, C. Ray. "The Louisiana Sailing Lugger: Survival of Traditional Form and Method." *Pioneer America Society Transactions*, Vol. XIII (1990): 23-34.

Broven, John. *South to Louisiana: The Music of the Cajun Bayous*. New Orleans: Pelican, 1983. Vols. 1–9. Quebec: Les Presses de l'Université Laval, 1966–72.

Brown, Becky. "Cajun/English Code-Switching." *Current Issues in Linguistic Theory* 53(1986): 399–406.

———. "Cajun French and the Dynamics of Pronominal Equivalence." In *Linguistic Change and Contact*, ed. K. Ferrara, B. Brown, K. Walters and J. Baugh, 56–64. Austin: University of Texas Press, 1988.

———. "Naissance d'une littérature, naissance d'une orthographe." In *Revue Francophone de Louisiane* 4(1989): 45-54.

Brown, Louise. "Louisiana Costume from 1700–1900." M.A. thesis, Louisiana State University, 1939.

Cable, George Washington. *Creoles and Cajuns: Stories of Old Louisiana*. Ed. Arlin Turner. Garden City, N.Y.: Doubleday, 1959.

————. *The Creoles of Louisiana*. New York: Charles Scribner's Sons, 1910.

————. "Notes on Acadians in Louisiana." Ms. in Tulane University Library, Historic Collection. (1880.)

————. *Old Creole Days*. New York: Charles Scribner's Sons, 1978.

Chandler, R.E. "End of an Odyssey: Acadians Arrive in St. Gabriel, La." *Louisiana History* 14(1974): 69–87.

Charlevoix, P.F.X. de S.J. *Journal of a Voyage to North America*. 2 vols. London: R and J. Dodsley, 1761.

Chopin, Kate. *The Awakening*. New York: Rinehart, 1981.

Clark, Andrew Hill. *Acadia: The Geography of Early Nova Scotia to 1670*. Madison: University of Wisconsin Press, 1968.

Claudel, Calvin A. "A Study of Louisiana French Folktales in Avoyelles Parish." Dissertation, University of North Carolina, 1948.

Comeaux, Malcolm. *Atchafalaya Swamp Life: Settlement and Folk Occupations*. Baton Rouge: Louisiana State University Geoscience Publications 2, 111 pp., 1972.

Conrad, Glenn R., ed. *The Cajuns: Essays on their History and Culture*. Lafayette, La.: Center for Louisiana Studies, University of Southwestern Louisiana, 1978.

Côte Blanche Productions, Inc. "Cajun and Creole Stories, 32 half hour programs on cassette." Cut Off, La. 1983.

————. "En bas du bayou" Collection. Videocassette. Cut Off, La. 1976.

————. "Memories of Terrebone" Collection. Audiotape. Houma, La. 1982.

Daigle, Jules O. *A Dictionary of the Cajun Language*. Ann Arbor, Mich.: Edwards Brothers, 1984.

DeLapouyade, Robert. *The Robert DeLapouyade Collection, 1848–1936*. Louisiana State University Archives, Baton Rouge.

Del Sesto, Steven, and John L. Gibson, eds. *The Culture of Acadiana: Tradition and Change in South Louisiana*. Lafayette, La.: University of Southwestern Louisiana, 1975.

Duffy, John, ed. *History of Medicine in Louisiana*. Vol. 1. Baton Rouge: Louisiana State University Press, 1958.

Duplantier, Stephen. *An Essay on Lower Louisiana: An Ethnohistory of 12,000 Years of Life on the Brink*. New Orleans: A Report to the Jean Lafitte National Historical Park of Louisiana, 1981.

East, Lorraine Daigle. *My Acadians: A Grand Lady's Love Affair with Her French-Acadian Heritage*. Burnet, Tex.: Eakin, 1980.

Edwards, Jay D. *An Architectural History of the Property at 417–419 Decatur St., New Orleans*. A Report to the Jean Lafitte National Historical Park of Louisiana, 1989.

———. "The Complex Origins of the American Domestic Piazza-Veranda-Gallery." *Material Culture* 21(2)(1989): 2-58.

———. *Louisiana's French Vernacular Architecture: A Historical and Social Bibliography*. Monticello, Ill.: Vance Bibliographies (A-1603), 1986.

———. *Louisiana's Remarkable French Vernacular Architecture*. Monograph No. 1, Fred B. Kniffen Cultural Resources Laboratory. Baton Rouge: Geoscience Publications, Louisiana State University, 1988.

———. "The Origins of the Louisiana Creole Cottage." In *French and Germans in the Mississippi Valley: Landscape and Cultural Traditions*, ed. Michael Roark, Cape Girardeau, Mo.: Center for Regional History and Cultural Heritage, Southeast Missouri State University, 1988: 9-60.

———. *A Survey of Louisiana French Vernacular Architecture*. A report to the Jean Lafitte National Historical Park of Louisiana and the Division of the Arts of Louisiana. 2 vols. Baton Rouge, La., 1982/1985.

Esman, Marjorie R. *Henderson, Louisiana: Cultural Adaptation in a Cajun Community*. New York: Holt, Rinehart and Winston, 1985.

Estaville, Lawrence E. "Mapping the Cajuns." *Southern Studies* 25(2) (1986): 163–71.

Faulk, James Donald. *Cajun French I*. Crowley, La.: Cajun Press, 1977.

Fortier, Alcée. "The Acadians of Louisiana and Their Dialect." Baltimore, Md.: Reprinted from the Publications of the Modern Language Association of America, v.6, no. 1, 1891.

———. *A History of Louisiana*. 4 vols. New York: Goupil & Co. of Paris, 1904.

———. *Louisiana Folk-Tales in French Dialect and English Translation*. Memoirs of the American Folklore Society, 2. Boston and New York: Houghton Mifflin, 1895.

————. *Louisiana: comprising sketches of counties, towns, events, institutions, and persons, arranged in cyclopedic form.* 2 vols. Atlanta: Southern Historical Association, 1909.

Gagnon, Camille. *Le folklore bourbonnais.* Moulins: Crepin-Leond, 1947.

Gayarré, Charles. *History of Louisiana.* Vols. 1 and 2. New York: Harper, 1851–52.

Gilmore, Jeanne, and Robert Gilmore. *Chantez Encore, Folksongs of French South Louisiana.* Gretna, La.: Pelican, 1984.

Giraud, Marcel. *Histoire de la Louisiane Française.* 4 vols. Paris: Presses universitaires de France, 1953–.

Gould, Philip. *Les Cadiens d'asteur: Today's Cajuns.* Lafayette, La.: Acadiana Press, 1980.

————. *Louisiana: A Land Apart.* Lafayette, La.: Galerie Press, 1985.

Griffiths, Naomi. *The Acadian Deportation: Deliberate Perfidity or Cruel Necessity?* Toronto: Copp-Clark, 1969.

Guidry, Richard. *C'est p'us pareil.* Lafayette, La.: Center for Louisiana Studies, University of Southwestern Louisiana, 1982.

————. *La famille Richard.* Baton Rouge: Louisiana State Department of Education, 1983.

————. *Les jeunes Louisianais.* Baton Rouge: Louisiana State Department of Education, 1981.

————. *Lexique cadien-français.* Baton Rouge: Louisiana State Department of Education, 1981.

Hale, Robert. "Journal of a Voyage to Nova Scotia Made in 1731 by Robert Hale of Beverly." *Historical Collection of the Essex Institute* 42(1906): 217–44.

Hall, John W. "Louisiana Survey Systems." Dissertation, Louisiana State University, 1970.

Hallowell, Christopher. *People of the Bayous: Cajun Life in Lost America.* New York: E.P. Dutton, 1979.

Hamilton, Sam, ed. *The Cajuns: Their History and Culture.* 5 Vol. A Report to the Jean Lafitte National Historical Park of Louisiana. Opelousas, La.: 1987.

Hearn, Lafcadio. *Gumbo Zhèbes: Little Dictionary of Creole Proverbs Selected from Six Creole Dialects.* New York: Will A. Coleman, 1885; rpt., New Orleans: Aurian Society Publications, 1977.

————. *Louisiana cuisine créole.* New Orleans: Pelican, 1967 (rpt. of 1885 ed.).

Hebert, Donald. *South Louisiana Records* and *Southwest Louisiana Records*. Cecilia/Eunice, La.: 1976–present.

Heinrich, Pierre. *La Louisiane sus la Compagnie des Indies*, 1747

Huber, Leonard. *L'Amour de maman: Louisiana tradition acadienne de tissage en Louisiane*. La Rochelle: Musée du Nouveau Monde, 1983.

Hyde, Roy E. "Rural Family Organization on Bayou Plaquemine." M.A. thesis, Louisiana State University, 1932.

Jehn, Jeanne, comp. *Acadian Exiles in the Colonies*. Covington, Ky.: privately published, 1977.

Kammer, Edward Joseph. *Four Southwestern Louisiana Parishes*. Washington, D.C.: The Catholic University of America Press, 1941.

Klapper, Carla S. *Acadiana, A Classified and Annotated Bibliography, 1955–73*. M.A. Thesis, San Jose State University, 1974.

Kniffen, Fred. "Louisiana House Types." *Annals of the Association of American Geographers* 26 (1936): 179–93.

———. *Louisiana: Its Land and People*. Baton Rouge: Louisiana State University Press, 1968.

———. "Material Culture in the Geographic Interpretation of the Landscape." In *The Human Mirror*, ed. Miles Richardson, 252–67. Baton Rouge: Louisiana State University Press, 1974.

———. "A Spanish (?) Spinner in Louisiana." *Southern Folklore Quarterly* 13(1949): 192–99.

Kniffen, Fred B., and Malcolm L. Comeaux. *The Spanish Moss Folk Industry of Louisiana*. Mélanges Series, 12. Baton Rouge: Louisiana State University Geoscience Publications, 1979.

Lançon, John. "Des remèdes aux traiteurs: An Introduction to Folk Medicine in French Louisiana." Honors thesis, University of Southwestern Louisiana, 1986.

Laussat, Pierre-Clément de. *Memoirs of My Life to My Son During the Years 1803 and After*. Trans. Agnes-Josephine Pastiva., ed. Robert D. Bush. Baton Rouge, La.: Published for the Historic New Orleans Collection by Louisiana State University Press, 1978.

LeBlanc, Dudley J. *The Acadian Miracle*. Lafayette, La.: Evangeline, 1966.

———. *The True Story of the Acadians*. Lafayette, La.: Tribune, 1937.

Lebreton, Clarence. *Hier l'acadie: Scènes du Village Historique Acadien*. Montreal: Iris Diffusion Enrg., 1981.

Le Page du Pratz, Antoine Simon. *The History of Louisiana* trans. of French ed. of 1774. Baton Rouge: Louisiana State University Press, 1975.

Lomax. *Our Singing Country*. New York: Macmillan, 1941.

Longfellow, Henry Wadsworth. *Evangeline*. Boston: J.R. Osgood, 1875.

Marchand, Sidney A. *Acadian Exiles in the Golden Coast of Louisiana*. Donaldsonville, La.: Published by author, 1943.

———. *An Attempt to Reassemble the Old Settlers in Family Groups*. Baton Rouge, La.: Claitor's, 1965.

Martin, François Xavier. *The History of Louisiana from the Earliest Period* (1827). 2 vols. Gretna, La.: Pelican, 1975.

McCloskey, Kathleen. "Archaeological Manifestations of Acadian Settlement in St. James Parish, Louisiana," M.A. thesis, Louisiana State University, 1981.

McWilliams, Richebourg G., trans. and ed. *Fleur de Lys and Calumet*. Tuscaloosa: University of Alabama Press, 1953.

Mercier, Alfred. *L'Habitation St. Ybars*. New Orleans: Imprimerie franco-américaine (E. Antoine), 1881.

Mugnier, George François. *Louisiana Images*. New Orleans: Louisiana State Museum, 1975.

Newton, Milton. *Atlas of Louisiana*. Baton Rouge: Louisiana State University School of Geoscience, 1972.

———. *Louisiana House Types: A Field Guide*. Mélanges 2. Geoscience Publications, Louisiana State University, 1971.

Olmsted, Frederick Law. *A Journey in the Seaboard Slave States*. New York: n.p., 1856.

———. *A Journey Through Texas; or, a Saddle Trip on the Southwestern Frontier*. New York: n.p., 1857.

Parenton, Vernon J. "The Rural French-Speaking People of Quebec and South Louisiana, A Comparative Study of Social Structure and Organization with Emphasis on the Role of the Catholic Church." Ph.D. diss., Harvard University, 1948.

Phillips, Yvonne. "The Bousillage House." *Louisiana Studies* 3(1) (1964): 155–58.

Pitre, Loulan, Jr. *Chenière Caminada avant l'ouragan*. Cut Off, La.: Côte Blanche Productions, 1983.

Post, Lauren. *Cajun Sketches: From the Prairies of Southwest Louisiana*. Baton Rouge: Louisiana State University Press, 1962.

Ramsey, Carol. *Cajuns on the Bayous.* New York: Hastings House, 1957.

Reed, Revon. *Lache pas la patate.* Montreal: Parti Pris, 1976.

Reinecke, George F. "Early French Louisiana Life and Folklore." *Louisiana Folklore Miscellany* 2(3) (1966): 24–26.

Richard, Zachary. *Voyage de nuit.* Lafayette, La.: Editions de la Nouvelle Acadie, 1987.

Rickels, Pat, ed. *1776–1976: 200 Years of Life and Change in Louisiana.* Lafayette, La.: Lafayette Natural History Museum, 1977.

Robin, C.C. *Voyages dans l'intérieure de la Louisiane, de la Floride occidentale et dans les isles de la Martinique et de Saint-Domingue pendant les années 1802, 1804, 1805 et 1806 . . . En outre, contenant ce qui s'est passé de plus intéressant, relativement à l'établissement des Anglo-Américains à la Louisiane.* 3 vols. Paris: F. Buisson, 1807. *Voyage to Louisiana.* Trans. Stuart O. Landry. Gretna, La.: Pelican, 1966.

Robison, Warren. "Louisiana Acadian Domestic Architecture." In *The Culture of Acadiana: Tradition and Change in South Louisiana,* ed. Stephen Del Sesto and Jon Gibson, 63–77. Lafayette, La.: University of Southwestern Louisiana, 1975.

Rushton, William Faulkner. *The Cajuns: From Acadia to Louisiana.* New York: Farrar, Straus, Giroux, 1979.

Saucier, Corinne. *Folk Tales from French Louisiana.* Baton Rouge: Louisiana State University Press, 1962.

———. "Histoire et traditions de la paroisse des Avoyelles en Louisiane." Dissertation, Université Laval, 1949.

Savoy, Ann Allen. *Cajun Music: A Reflection of a People,* Vol. 1. Eunice, La.: Bluebird Press, 1984.

Saxon, Lyle. *Gumbo Ya Ya.* New York: Bonanza, 1945.

———. *Old Louisiana.* New York: Century, 1929.

Smith, T. Lynn. "An Analysis of Rural Social Organization Among the French-Speaking People of Southern Louisiana." *Journal of Farm Economics* 16(4): 17(4): 1934.

Spitzer, Nicholas, ed. *Louisiana Folklife.* Baton Rouge, La.: Moran, 1985.

Taylor, James William. "The Agricultural Settlement Succession on the Prairies of Southwest Louisiana." Ph.D. diss., Louisiana State University, 1956.

Taylor, Joe Gray. *Louisiana, A History*. New York: W.W. Norton, 1984.

West, Robert C. *An Atlas of Louisiana Surnames of French and Spanish Origin*. Baton Rouge: Geoscience Publications, Louisiana State University, 1986.

Whatley, Randall. *Conversational Cajun French I*. Baton Rouge: Louisiana State University Press, 1978.

Whitfield, Irene. *Louisiana French Folk Songs*. New York: Dover, 1939.

Winzerling, Oscar W. *The Acadian Odyssey*. Baton Rouge: Louisiana State University Press, 1955.